MEMORY EFFECTS

D0165065

MEMORY EFFECTS

THE HOLOCAUST AND THE ART OF SECONDARY WITNESSING

DORA APEL

RUTGERS UNIVERSITY PRESS *New Brunswick, New Jersey, and London*

N
7417.6
.A64
2002

Library of Congress Cataloging-in-Publication Data
Apel, Dora, 1952–
Memory effects : the holocaust and the art of secondary witnessing / Dora Apel.
p.cm.
Includes bibliographical references and index.
ISBN 0–8135–3048–2 (alk. paper)—ISBN 0–8135–3049–0 (pbk. : alk. paper)
1. Art, Jewish. 2. Holocaust, Jewish (1939–1945), in art. I. Title.
N7417.6 .A64 2002
704.9'499405318—dc21 2001048793

British Cataloging-in-Publication information is available from the British Library.

Permission has been generously granted for use of the following copyrighted works.

Paul Celan, "(I know you)," from Breathturn, *trans. by Pierre Joris (Los Angeles: Sun and Moon Press, 1995), 93. Copyright © 1995 by Pierre Joris. Reprinted with the permission of the publisher.*

Edmond Jabes, first poem in the second part of The Book of Yukel in the chapter "In Touch with the Book," from The Book of Questions *reprinted by permission of Wesleyan University Press. Charles Reznikoff, section 5 of the poem "Massacres," from* Holocaust *reprinted by permission of Black Sparrow Press, 24 Tenth Street, Santa Rosa, California 95401.*

Chris Tysh, "Tombeau II for Paul Celan (1920–1970)" © Chris Tysh from Continuity Girl, *United Artists Books, 2000.*

Copyright © 2002 by Dora Apel
All rights reserved
No part of this book may be reproduced or utilized in any form or by any means, electronic or mechanical, or by any information storage and retrieval system, without written permission from the publisher. Please contact Rutgers University Press, 100 Joyce Kilmer Avenue, Piscataway, NJ 08854–8099. The only exception to this prohibition is "fair use" as defined by U.S. copyright law.

BOOK DESIGN AND TYPOGRAPHY BY JENNY DOSSIN

Manufactured in the United States of America

LONGWOOD UNIVERSITY LIBRARY
REDFORD AND RACE STREET
FARMVILLE, VA 23909

For Rachel Apel Wittkopp

with love

■

LONGWOOD LIBRARY
1000368471

CONTENTS

ILLUSTRATIONS

COLOR PLATES (between pages 146 and 147)

FIGURES

PREFACE AND ACKNOWLEDGMENTS

MY MOTHER, Ethel Apel, who survived the disaster though seventy members of her family perished, is the primary witness most responsible for transmitting her traumatic experience to me, insuring my obsession with this subject. She is, therefore, the catalyst for this book. She also inspired me with her resilience, vivaciousness, radiance, and tenacity. My father, now long deceased, said little about the war years, but when he finally spoke, it was devastating. To him I owe a heightened love of reading, intellectual pursuits, and engagement with politics. I am grateful to both my parents for never losing their sense of humor.

I thank my cousin, Jean Pelz, who died recently, for consenting to have her testimony videotaped at the Yale Fortunoff Video Archives for Holocaust Testimony, for spending hours beyond that recounting her Holocaust experiences to me, and for the gorgeous red satin dress she wore to my brother's Bar Mitzvah. I thank her deceased husband Leo, also a survivor, for his great kindness and good humor, and Jean's sister, Eve Silver, for making the long trek to visit my mother some sixty years after they had last seen each other in Poland.

For thinking about the Holocaust, I have relied on the work of many scholars from a variety of fields, but particularly wish to acknowledge the important work of Saul Friedländer, James Young, Sander Gilman, Ernst van Alphen, Jon Stratton, Barbie Zelizer, Marianne Hirsch, Jonathan Boyarin, Michael Rothberg, and Peter Novick, as well as Charlotte Delbo and Primo Levi.

Among my colleagues and friends, I thank Joan Weinstein for her unfailing support, for sending me the article on Marina Vainshtein that got me started, and for always understanding the relationship between scholarship and life. To Nancy Jones I owe a debt of deep gratitude for our discussions on antisemitism, for opportunities to present my research in lectures and classes at the Detroit Institute of Arts, and for her friendship and support. I thank Chris Tysh for keeping me vigilant with her literary perspicacity, poetic sensitivity, and critical suggestions. Both Chris Tysh and Nancy Jones were impassioned participants, along with Terry Lewis, in a Holocaust reading group with me. I thank Buzz Spector for pointing artists working on Holocaust representations my way and for his astute insights and thoughtful suggestions, advice, and support. I thank Andrea Mensch for her sensitive perceptions and enthusiasm. For reading all or parts of the manuscript, I thank Joan Weinstein, Buzz Spector, Gregory Witthopp, Andrea Mensch, and Chris Tysh, as well as Ernst van Alphen. I also thank my editor, Leslie Mitchner, whose advice was inspirational, for her intelligence and warmth.

I thank all of the artists in the book who have generously shared their work, views, and images with me, as well as the art dealers, curators, and directors who have provided images, press reviews, and other materials. I also thank Jeanne Moore for her assistance in tracking down images, and the students in my seminars, *The Postwar Generations: Representing the Holocaust,* cosponsored by the Detroit Institute of Arts and the American Studies Program at Wayne State University, and *Imagery of War from the Goya to the Present,* as well as audiences at the Detroit Institute of Arts, State University of New York at New Paltz, Wayne State University, the Midwest Art History Society Conference in Detroit, and the College Art Association Annual Conference in Chicago at my session, "The Holocaust and the Art of Secondary Witnessing."

I am grateful to the National Endowment for the Humanities for a summer stipend and to Wayne State University for large and small research grants that helped support this book, as well the College of Fine, Performing and Communication Arts and the Wayne State University Office of Research and Sponsored Programs for subsidies to support publication. I also thank the Holocaust Educational Foundation for a grant to develop the seminar on *Representing the Holocaust.*

My thanks go to my husband Gregory Wittkopp, always my first reader, most honest critic, and sincerest enthusiast, who has done more than anyone to help me realize this project, offering boundless support in ways as countless as they are deeply generous, humorous, caring, perceptive, endearing, and enduring. My daughter Rachel Apel Wittkopp has also played a crucial role, inspiring me with her impossible-to-answer questions, her wit and intelligence, and her willingness to confront the legacy of the past in contemplation of her own future. I dedicate this book to her.

A condensed version of "The Tattooed Jew" was published in *New Art Examiner* (June 1997) and in an expanded version in *Visual Culture and the Holocaust,* edited by Barbie Zelizer (New Brunswick, N. J.: Rutgers University Press, 2001). Portions of the text from the section "Blacks, Jews and the Two 'Holocausts'" in chapter 1 appeared in the essay, "Images of Black History: The Charles H. Wright Museum of African American History," published in *Dissent* (summer 2001).

MEMORY EFFECTS

INTRODUCTION

THE ARTIST AS SECONDARY WITNESS

■

(I know you, you are the deeply bowed,
I, the transpierced, am subject to you.
Where flames a word, would testify for us both?
You—all, all real. I—all delusion.)

PAUL CELAN
from *Breathturn,* translated by Pierre Joris, 1995

■

ART ILLUMINATES traumatic experience through the sideways glance, allowing the viewer to apprehend what can only be shown indirectly, allusively and in sometimes surprising ways. Perhaps even more than literature, film or theater, visual art affects viewers in ways that are nonnarrative and noncognitive, in other words, in affective and emotional ways that are unsuspected, sometimes uncomfortable, raising contradictory or unresolved feelings. This is not to suggest that meaning itself is suspended, but that it operates in less than obvious ways, is multivalent and open-ended. This is especially true with representations of the continuing trauma of the Holocaust, which refuses to be historicized as an event safely ensconced in the past, and continues to drive a compulsion toward forms of reenactment by those who did not experience the original events, in response to the trauma experienced through intergenerational transmission. These reenactments are both similar to and different from the events or conditions to which they refer, expressing affinity and distance, embrace and resistance. Despite continuing theorization by historians about the causes of the genocide, such interpretations often seemingly have little influence on the affective consequences of the historical trauma of the Shoah, even evoking a refusal of comprehension, most trenchantly expressed by filmmaker Claude Lanzmann:

> All these fields of explanation (referring to the unemployment in Germany, and so on) are all true and all false. They're all true together and all false in the same way. And it is a very flat truth, because you cannot proceed in that way—you cannot precisely engender the Holocaust. It is impossible. Between all these conditions—which were necessary conditions maybe, but they were not sufficient—between all these conditions and the gassing of three thousand persons, men, women, children, in a gas chamber, all together, there is an unbreachable discrepancy. It is simply not possible to engender one out of the other. There is no solution of continuity between the two; there is rather a gap, an abyss, and this *abyss* will never be bridged.[1]

If the abyss can never be bridged, then what is the point of the reenactments and reconfigurations by those born later? Are they simple repetition compulsions in an endless and unproductive identification with the victims? Commenting on such a practice, Ernst van Alphen suggests, "Victimhood cannot control the future."[2] But for others, the issue is not one of identification with victimhood; rather, it is a question of the continuity of a community of memory, the delay or absence of closure, the questioning of received assumptions, a working through of trauma that leads, if not to a totalized understanding, to a greater incorporation of the holes in understanding, and, to varying degrees, an assertion of resistance, that is, a recognition of and refusal to be subsumed by the abyss.

Postwar artists who address the effects of the Holocaust often turn to an interdisciplinary art practice that is nonnarrative, polyvalent, metaphorical, enigmatic and ambiguous. This is not surprising, given the difficult, elusive, enormous, and even ungraspable nature of the subject. "It is perhaps not so strange that this task of protecting the thread of continuity in a culture falls to the art practice most attuned to its gaps, silences, and absences," observes artist Vera Frenkel.[3] Artists of the postwar generations are ultimately in the position of unwilling post facto bystanders. Thus they may, theoretically at least, choose their forms of identification—bystander, perpetrator or victim. Anselm Kiefer's *Occupations* series, in which he assumed the pose of the Heil-Hitler salute in various sites throughout Europe, paved the way for a number of other European and American artists to imagine themselves in the position of the perpetrators or to gaze, however ironically or satirically, at the unscrupulous face of power, as demonstrated in the exhibition *Mirroring Evil: Nazi Imagery/Recent Art* at the Jewish Museum in New York (2002), which included the work of thirteen such artists. In the catalog for the exhibition, van Alphen further argues, "Soliciting partial and temporary identification with the perpetrators makes one aware of the ease with which one can slide into a measure of complicity. To raise the possibility of such identification with the fundamental, cultural other is appealing to heteropathic identification."[4] This is an important insight about an approach that may produce a useful form of knowledge and serve as an unexpected figure of Holocaust pedagogy. From another perspective, James Young has produced several well-known explorations of the role of the Holocaust memorial in public memory, particularly in terms of how nations memorialize the Holocaust according to their own ideals, experience and ideologies and how those meanings evolve.[5] As the debate in Germany over a national memorial in Berlin to the European Jews killed in World War II demonstrated, a central question was: How should the perpetrators remember their victims?

But these are not the questions that concern us here. In this book, we will look at the choices made by those who attempt to work through and beyond victimhood to other ways of interrogating, encompassing, and living with the Holocaust, including the construction of memory through representation as another form of knowledge that serves, in unexpected ways, to interpellate the blind spots of comprehension and to perform as a site of resistance.

REPRESENTATION AS A SITE OF RESISTANCE

THE DEBATE over the limits and possibilities of Holocaust representation has extended across several disciplines. A brief examination of the theories of two contributors to this ongoing discussion within Holocaust studies in the fields of pedagogy and English literature will help illuminate the approach I take to visual art.

Discussing traumatic remembrance in relation to pedagogy, Roger Simon formulates what he regards as the two primary strategies or pedagogies for preserving traumatic history: "In the first, remembrance is constituted as a *strategic practice* in which memorial pedagogies are deployed for their sociopolitical value and promise." This includes the hope that by telling these horrible stories, the moral lessons will be learned to create a better tomorrow: "The hope enacted in and through such remembrance is dependent on a moralizing pedagogy: the provision of images and narratives against which the future is defined as different, a time in which the past 'must never happen again.'" As Simon notes, continuing genocidal violence around the world attests to the failure of this redemptive promise of a greater moral vigilance. In the second strategy, "remembrance is enacted as a *difficult return,* a psychic and social responsibility to bring the dead into presence, a responsibility that concurrently involves learning to live with, and in relation to, loss." This form of remembrance "inevitably instantiates loss and thus bears no ultimate consolation." There is no redemptive promise, but rather, an unsettling of the present, which, in its refusal to offer a better future, defies the very terms of remembrance as strategic practice.[6] Simon critiques strategic remembrance on the grounds that it collapses the historical specificities of Holocaust events with contemporary "political and social use-value" while also warning that remembrance as a difficult return risks an overidentification with the past that could "threaten to collapse differences across space/time and through performances of surrogacy that may leave the living in the breach of melancholia."[7] Thus these strategies risk either a falsely manipulative and moralizing political instrumentalization or a depressing sense of obsession and despair. Simon gestures toward a third form of remembrance that recognizes the mutability of meaning over time and acknowledges both continuity and discontinuity through "a repetition (a retelling) of the story of another but also the *story of the telling of the story*."[8] This is the strategy Art Spiegelman adopted for the *Maus* books, and, in so doing, paved the way for others.

Michael Rothberg formulates the two main strategies for traumatic remembrance in formalist terms, as realist and antirealist. Rothberg defines the realist position as "an epistemological claim that the Holocaust is knowable and a representational claim that this knowledge can be translated into a familiar mimetic universe." The antirealist position is defined as "a claim that the Holocaust is not knowable or would be knowable only under radically new regimes of knowledge and that it cannot be captured in traditional representational schemata."[9] The latter is the position articulated by Claude Lanzmann. As with Simon's categories of remembrance as strategic practice or difficult return, the realist and antirealist positions would appear to be mutually exclusive, yet they coexist within the field of Holocaust studies and Holocaust representation just as the categories defined by Simon do. Although Rothberg applies this framework to literature, it can also be applied usefully to visual art. Indeed, the contemporary art examined here evidences a distinct disillusionment with the certainties of a realist approach, even while retaining realist armatures for its content. How then are these two opposing modes reconciled? Rothberg posits a third strategy of *traumatic* realism, in which the traumatic is defined as "the peculiar combination of ordinary and extreme elements that seems to characterize the Nazi genocide."[10] Traumatic realism thus "mediates between the realist and antirealist positions in Holocaust studies and marks the necessity of considering how the ordinary and the extraordinary aspects of genocide intersect and coexist."[11] Traumatic realism as a representational strategy bridges two seemingly incompatible modes of representation and perhaps most nearly describes the strategies embraced by the artists discussed here. Responding to the cultural and political conditions of the present, these artists, in a variety of ways, commingle or juxtapose the ordinary and the extreme, but not as dialogic events in the past. Their representations are chronologic, traversing time from then to now, retelling the story while telling the contemporary conditions of the telling of the story and bringing the recognitions of the present to bear not only on our understanding of the past, but also on the effects of the past in the present.

Another way to map the binary strategies of Holocaust representation is through the categories of the sacralized and the desacralized, the former corresponding to a modernist aesthetic and the latter to a postmodernist one. The discourse of sacralization finds its best-known exponent in Elie Wiesel, the most influential American interpreter of the Holocaust. Wiesel assigns a religious significance to the events of the Holocaust, seeing it as "equal to the revelation at Sinai"; he suggests that attempts to desanctify or demystify the Holocaust are subtle forms of antisemitism.[12] Sacralization of the Holocaust corresponds to Simon's definition of remembrance as strategic practice or a moralizing pedagogy and Rothberg's definition of antirealism, which claims that the Holocaust is unknowable, thereby placing it outside the bounds of history. These definitions, in turn, correspond to a kind of transcendental modernism. A postmodernist approach is defined here as a self-consciousness that always places the Holocaust in relation to the circumstances of its representation in the present, eschewing the stance of objective observer who registers timeless truths. The approach instead recognizes the altered ideological contexts of the present, the fragmented and conflicted nature of experience and subjectivity, and the difficulty of retrieving knowledge from the past, while using the events of the past to produce new knowledge and greater awareness in the present, that is, as sites of resistance.

The address to traumatic memory serves as a site of resistance to both the loss of the historical specificity of the Holocaust and to the historical homogenization of Jewish identity, in particular, and difference in general, within the dominant culture. In response to the resurgence of ethnic identity among younger Jews, the rejection of decades of assimilationist trends, the rise of antisemitism, a growing willingness to explore once taboo territory, and continuing ambivalence about being marked as Jewish, both contemporary art and heated debates about the Holocaust have flourished. To a great extent, these are attempts to interrogate history now a half-century-old, in order, more urgently, to examine the problems of constructing contemporary ethnic identity in a world of continuing, unabated genocides. Identity here is understood as something that is not merely a fixed entity to be located in the past, but an evolving phenomenon, a matter of becoming as well as being, subject to constant transformation. This is a concept articulated by Stuart Hall: "Far from being grounded in a mere 'recovery' of the past, which is waiting to be found, and which, when found, will secure our sense of ourselves into eternity, identities are the names we give to the different ways we are positioned by, and position ourselves within, the narratives of the past."[13] Secondary witnesses, or those born later, often view themselves as links to an obliterated past, yet Jewish identity is an evolving phenomenon that depends not only on a contemporary positioning in relation to the Judeocide, but to its continuing impact on the political landscape of the twenty-first century.

I have selected a number of artists and issues that provide telling perspectives on the subject position of secondary witnesses who relate to the victims of the Holocaust, and the way the dilemmas they face raise important questions about our understanding of the effects of the Holocaust regardless of our ethnic identification.[14] The book begins with a short history of Holocaust reception in America, both politically and culturally. This includes the public debate over the legitimacy of Holocaust studies in the university, and the competing claims between blacks and Jews over whose victimhood is greater. This is followed by an exploration of the work of projection artist and photographer Shimon Attie and his revisioning of the vanished Jew in Germany, in which the role of the archive and the lost history of unassimilated East European Jews, the German stereotypes of pariah and parvenu, and continuities between past and present are interrogated in the context of contemporary attacks against Turks and other foreigners. The fate of Nazi-looted art is examined in a chapter on Vera Frenkel's video installation and website project *Body Missing,* which inquires into the art theft policies of the Third Reich while opening a space for the intervention of the contemporary witness/art restorer/provocateur against the cultural despoliation of the Third Reich. Turning to the form of the testimonial, photographer Jeffrey Wolin's efforts to meld text and image into testimonial documents that implicate the hand of the secondary witness are investigated, along with a video work by Pier Marton in which the form of the oral testimonial is directly appropriated by secondary witnesses to reveal their deep ambivalence toward Jewish identity and their simultaneous resistance to ethnic stereotyping. Other chapters explore the camps as memory sites, the body and Nazi-fetish-based desire. James Friedman's photographs of the camps, which drop the pretense of going back in time, frustrate the mythology of the camps and turn a blinding light on the present. Susan Silas, following the original time-line, rewalks a forced march from Germany to Czechoslovakia, documenting it through video and photographs, while Mikael Levin retraces the journey of his father, writer and journalist Meyer Levin, who traveled to the battlefields and concentration camps of Europe as a war correspondent in 1945, each exploring the ways in which landscape reveals and conceals memory. Matthew Girson attempts to find a new visual language for painting akin to Paul Celan's search for a new language for poetry after the Holocaust. At the site of the body, the effects of traumatic historical memory on contemporary erotic desire in the form of Nazi fetish-based sadomasochistic practices are probed as a site for the intersection of desire and terror, while "The Tattooed Jew" examines the most radical expression of contemporary Jewish ethnicity in the form of full-body tattoos of graphic Holocaust imagery as a talisman against the horror it represents. This daring public declaration of Jewish identity marks the emergence of a newly conscious postmodern Jew who has replaced the pre-Holocaust Jew associated with the orthodox Yiddishkeit (Jewish way of life) reimagined by Shimon Attie.

CHAPTER ONE

A SHORT HISTORY OF HOLOCAUST RECEPTION

■

AS THE ACTUAL EVENTS of the Holocaust recede in time, interest in the Holocaust continues to grow. Yet historian Omer Bartov finds "most Americans have only the vaguest possible notion of what the Holocaust was about."[1] This seems borne out by a 1998 opinion poll conducted by the U.S. Holocaust Memorial Museum in Washington, D. C., which found that 19 percent of Americans answered "false" when asked whether the Holocaust took place during World War II; another 19 percent weren't sure; 21 percent did not know or were not sure whether Jews were murdered in gas chambers, although they knew that Nazis murdered six million. The gap of knowledge is wide. What, for instance, is the significance of not knowing the primary method of death? One of the singular features of the Judeocide is the modern, industrial nature of the mass slaughter. Another is that it served no politically expedient or economic purpose in the course of prosecuting the war; on the contrary, as a number of historians have pointed out, it has long been understood that desperately needed labor power, in the form of Jewish slave labor, and the needed war matériel they produced, was sacrificed when it was most needed by the German army, out of the blind drive to kill the Jews at all costs.[2] The extremeness of the Nazi genocide has led many historians to speak of it as a defining event of the twentieth century, unprecedented in comparison to other genocides historically. Yehuda Bauer cogently summarizes the key arguments for its unprecedented nature: that pragmatic considerations, such as economic, territorial, or political motives that were central to all other genocides were not the cause of the Judeocide; that other genocides were limited geographically, whereas the intended murder of Jews was global in character, meant to extend from Europe to the whole world; that the Nazis were not looking merely to eliminate Jews as a distinct national or ethnic group, but established a governmental plan for the extermination of each and every actual Jew; that the Nazi regime itself was unprecedented, attacking "everything that had been defined as humane and moral before it."[3]

Despite the degree of popular ignorance about the specific nature of the Holocaust, at the turn of the millennium, the Holocaust has moved from the margins to center stage, leading Bauer to observe, "the impact of the Holocaust is growing, not diminishing."[4] Greater awareness of the Holocaust has produced a veritable explosion of representation in the form of museums, films, college and university study programs, literature and memoirs, art exhibitions, and the surge to record survivor testimonies. All of this testifies to the drive to confront anew the events of the Nazi genocide and its implications for our present and future. With the additional attention given to public debates and lawsuits over Nazi gold, dormant Swiss accounts, insurance claims by survivors and heirs, controversies over Nazi-looted art, recompense for slave labor and drug experiments, and debates about commemorative public monuments from Albuquerque to Berlin, the Holocaust has become nearly ubiquitous.

A 1994 exhibition organized by the Washington Project for the Arts in Washington, D. C., *Burnt Whole: Contemporary Artists Reflect on the Holocaust*, proclaimed itself the first U.S. exhibition of contemporary art devoted to the Holocaust. It included thirty-one postwar artists from six countries: the United States, Israel, Germany, France, England, and Argentina.[5] Critic Donald Kuspit considered the exhibition's conceptual strategies inadequate for failing to address "what has become the major significance of the Holocaust." This Kuspit judged to be "its function as a leading symbol of the perversity of modernity" and, bizarrely, "a demonstration of the power of instrumental reason over our lives."[6] While condensing the enormity of the Holocaust into a symbol of perversity, in the same breath Kuspit fails to understand the most profound aspect of that perversity, which was precisely its irrationality or lack of instrumental reason. Perhaps with greater justice, Kuspit suggests that some of the artists demonstrate a "naive," if heartfelt, identification with the victims.

In an enthusiastic review for *New Art Examiner*, Martha McWilliams, approaching the issue of identification with the victims from the opposite perspective, judged the exhibition to be such a success that it warranted a radical alteration of the prevailing view that the Holocaust was fundamentally unintelligible and unrepresentable. McWilliams asserted that because the postwar generations have grown up in a world "saturated with cruelty and suffering," they have developed an ability to understand, though she qualified this sweeping statement with the proviso that "this is not necessarily an intellectual understanding, but rather an experiential and emotional one."[7] But, we must ask, what is the nature of such an "experiential and emotional" understanding—and is it enough?

As the survey statistics indicate, there is a great deal of confusion about the historical facts and their interpretations. The general postwar understanding of the Holocaust comes through transmission of the stories of survivors, whether in person, through films, photographs, videotape, or through the burgeoning publication of memoirs. The experiential and emotional understanding produced through intergenerational transmission and representation is, for the most part, partial, subjective, and not generally based on broad historical knowledge of the catastrophe. Hence, Auschwitz survivor Primo Levi's lament that there is a fatal slide "toward simplification and stereotype" of the Holocaust experience as time passes. He writes in *The Drowned and the Saved:*

> This is a trend against which I would like here to erect a dike. At the same time however, I would like to point out that this phenomenon is not confined to the perception of the near past and historical tragedies; it is much more general, it is part of our difficulty or inability to perceive the experience of others, which is all the more pronounced the more distant these experiences are from ours in time, space, or quality. We are prone to assimilate them to "related" ones, as if the hunger in Auschwitz were the same as that of someone who has skipped a meal, or as if escape from Treblinka were similar to an escape from any ordinary jail.[8]

The children of survivors, now grown up, have played a key role in reviving interest in the Holocaust. As one child of survivors declares, "The most important event in my life occurred before I was born."[9] Another notes, "I was told by my father that it was a moral imperative that I stay Jewish, that I was not to assimilate because six million Jews had been murdered and countless generations before that had been persecuted simply because they were born Jewish. By the age of four I recognized myself as living on top of a pile of corpses."[10] From Helen Epstein's search for distinctive characteristics and common patterns among the children of survivors in *Children of the Holocaust* to the success of Art Spiegelman's *Maus* comic books, those born later have engendered a self-consciousness among the second generation that has led to organizations and support groups among children of survivors.[11] Unfortunately, this has not necessarily led to greater historical understanding. Clinical psychologist Aaron Hass, investigating the effects of a legacy of suffering on the second generation, asserts that most of those born later have wide gaps in their knowledge of their parents' experiences. They often create myths both about the Holocaust and about their parents' Holocaust experiences based on their own fantasies, especially where parents have been silent about their experiences. Hass observes that many children of survivors feel they know a lot about the Holocaust because of its aftereffects on their parents, but when questioned, reveal that they know little of the Third Reich or the genocidal program against the Jews and others.[12] Thus the experiential and emotional understanding of the postwar generations must be approached cautiously.

Nevertheless, there is a widespread compulsion among the postwar generations to come to terms with the Nazi genocide, in part out of a desire to continue to bear witness to the suffering of Nazi victims and to safeguard the memory of those events. As the stewardship of memory passes into the hands of those born later, there is a desire to uncover what has been repressed, hidden, and denied, to establish a greater accounting that may possibly be verified by the last living witnesses, and to vindicate the victims, paying a debt to those who did not survive. The massive efforts at recording survivor testimony signifies not only the desire to preserve memory, but to codify durable evidence against the forgetfulness of history and the resistance to accountability, despite the tricks of memory that call into question the absolute verity of testimony. Postwar artists as secondary witnesses have other reasons as well for confronting the Holocaust. They deal with the memory effects of the Holocaust and the consequences of those effects on contemporary understanding of ethnic identity and ethical agency. The art of secondary witnessing examines the transmission of Holocaust experience as a form of secondary trauma and deals with the tensions and discontinuities between the past and the present. Recognizing the ways in which collective memory has been shaped by the visual record, their work refers, directly or allusively, to the public archive of the Holocaust; at the same time, documentary is subverted, as the difficulties of recuperating the past are made apparent.

THE AFTERMATH OF THE HOLOCAUST

IMMEDIATELY AFTER THE WAR, the act of bearing witness took place through the publication of photographs of Holocaust atrocities in the daily and weekly press, magazines, on radio broadcasts, and newsreels shown in movie theaters. Once the world was informed, a long period of amnesia followed, beginning in the 1950s, in which there was little public mention of the Holocaust for two decades. The reasons most commonly advanced to explain this vary, but tend to converge on the belief that an emotional numbing took place, causing a repression which later returned. This repression, it is said, was compounded by government guilt over the abandonment of the Jews and American Jewish guilt over passivity during the war. In *The Holocaust in American Life,* historian Peter Novick challenges these notions with a carefully constructed historical and political account of the years during and following World War II in America that offers a set of more convincing and complex causes.[13] In 1945, few could comprehend the unprecedented scale and nature of systematic genocide. The concept of "Holocaust" as a war against the Jews did not exist in public discourse and was a retrospective construction that came years later, in the 1960s, as an English translation of the Hebrew word *Shoah.* Thus the Holocaust as a separate and significant event was not a part of public perception. Although it was understood that the Nazis hated the

Jews and atrocities against the Jews were known by the end of 1942, Nazi atrocities were, nonetheless, framed as more generally targeting political opponents of the Third Reich in order to promote support for the war in a climate rife with antisemitism. There was scant reference to the Jews in news reports. This was not only a calculated strategy, but a spontaneous perception, as Jews comprised only about a fifth of those left alive in camps such as Buchenwald that were liberated by the Americans at the end of the war. After the war, the horror of the death camps was historicized as a phenomenon that ended with the defeat of Germany, while the horror of Hiroshima and Nagasaki had a more immediate and resonating impact on Americans. Novick observes of the bombing of Hiroshima and Nagasaki: "Unlike the Holocaust, Americans were involved both as perpetrators and as potential victims; unlike the Holocaust, there were practical reasons for undergoing the ordeal of facing the horror."[14] Another factor in the silence on the Holocaust was the repudiation of the status of victim by American Jews, out of the conviction that the victim image exacerbated rather than alleviated antisemitism. To be avoided was "the common negative stereotype of the whining, complaining, or self-pitying Jew—the stigmata of the Jew as victim."[15]

In addition to the powerful assimilationist impulse among Jews, the demands of cold war ideology had a major impact on the effacement of the Holocaust. After the war the "evil" empire of Germany suddenly became an American ally, while the former ally of the U.S., the Soviet Union, became its archenemy. The emphasis shifted from hating the Nazis to hating the communists. Totalitarianism was invoked as a category that was shared by Nazis and communists, making them "essentially alike" and justifying what was in essence, "a continuation of World War II, a struggle against the transcendent enemy, totalitarianism, first in its Nazi, then its Soviet version."[16] The genocide of the Jews now became the "wrong atrocity," because any insistence that it was a central and defining feature of the Nazi regime undermined the purported essential identity between the Nazis and the Soviets. Novick notes that a search through the literature on totalitarianism provides only the "most glancing and casual" mention of the Holocaust.[17]

To make matters worse, Jews, who in disproportionate numbers were associated with the Bolshevik Revolution, became identified with communism in the interwar years in both Europe and America, culminating in what Novick aptly calls "the ultimate public relations disaster for Jews," the case of Julius and Ethel Rosenberg, who were convicted and executed as Soviet spies in the early 1950s. Because only the American communists opposed accepting Germany as a cold war ally, Jewish organizations were acutely uncomfortable in placing themselves in the same camp as the communists and accommodated the rehabilitation of Germany. Eager to prove that they were patriotic Americans, especially in the shadow of McCarthyism and the cold war, most American Jews resisted drawing attention to the plight of the Jews in Europe, universalized the meaning of the atrocities of the Holocaust, and downplayed the ethnic specificity of its primary victims. Such were the pressures against those survivors who *wanted* to tell their stories but were told to forget, to shun the image of the Jew as victim, to look to the future, to minimize difference and to assimilate.

On the other hand, the Holocaust was not entirely swept away. Jeffrey Shandler argues that television has played a strategic role in shaping how we feel and think about the Holocaust and in establishing it as "a master moral paradigm" against which all other atrocities are measured.[18] The broadcast of the war crimes trial of Adolf Eichmann in Jerusalem in the spring and summer of 1961 was the first major landmark in Holocaust television, in which the Holocaust not only received extended coverage and made information about it widely available, but established the word "Holocaust" as meaning the murder of European Jews. The antisemitic backlash against Jews as pathetic victims anticipated by American Jews did not occur, and was counterbalanced by the image of activist Israeli Jews who captured and tried Eichmann.

The 1967 Arab-Israeli Six Day War was another major turning point in the public discourse of the Holocaust, renewing fears among American Jews of another Jewish annihilation. The swift Israeli victory in that war had a profound impact on American Jewish consciousness, promoting a more assertive and openly Jewish identity. The triumphalist mood engendered by the war finally superseded the guilt and embarrassment of victimization, allowing a public acknowledgment of the memory of catastrophe, "as if miraculously," notes Michael Morgan, "the American Jewish community was unburdened of its commitment to subordinate, even to repress the death camps, to set them aside as a deeply distressing wound, a painful memory that would not go away but also could not be assimilated."[19] The disintegration of the liberal consensus in America in the late 1960s, the rise of identity politics, and the Six Day War led to an effort to reconstitute Jewish identity through a more open confrontation with Auschwitz and a heightened identification with Israel.

The Yom Kippur War of October 1973 was perhaps even more decisive in positioning the Holocaust in the center of American Jewish consciousness. In this conflict the Israelis nearly lost; they suffered heavy casualties, triumphing only after the airlifting of American supplies. Novick observes: "Illusions of Israeli invincibility and self-sufficiency were among the casualties of this war. A related casualty was the contrast, traditionally drawn by Zionists, between the vulnerability of Jews in the Diaspora, culminating in the Holocaust, and the security that Jews could find in a Jewish homeland. Clearly there was no place in the world less secure for Jews than in Israel."[20]

The Vietnam War also boosted "a sympathetic attention to the condition of victimhood," which allowed Jews to embrace a victim identity based on the Holocaust.[21] From the late 1960s onward, American Jews came to see themselves as an endangered species, reversing their earlier push for integration to an inward regrouping that would promote Jewish identity and stem the tide of intermarriage and a too-successful assimilation. The Holocaust served as a unifying theme, becoming emblematic of "an eternal Jewish condition."[22]

As a master moral paradigm, the Holocaust entered the general American mainstream in April 1978 with the second major landmark in Holocaust television, the mini-series *Holocaust: The Story of the Family Weiss,* written by Gerald Green. It was rebroadcast in 1979, by which time some 220 million people had seen *Holocaust,* and in West Germany, fifteen million.[23] At the same time President Carter nationalized the Holocaust by an executive order establishing a President's Commission on the Holocaust charged with recommending an appropriate national Holocaust memorial; this eventually led to the founding of the U.S. Holocaust Memorial Museum. At the same time, an Office of Special Investigations was established to look for perpetrators in the United States. It was also at this time that books, courses, and conferences on the Holocaust began to proliferate, and picture magazines such as *Time-Life* began issuing a series of retrospectives on World War II that included the concentration camps in text and photos. The Holocaust continued to be presented on television with films such as *Playing for Time, Escape from Sobibor, Triumph of the Spirit, War and Remembrance,* and many others.[24]

By the 1980s antisemitism was linked to hostile political reactions to Israel, which was regarded as both owing its existence to the Holocaust and as a historical alternative to it—a tragic vindication of Zionism. Support for Israel led sculptor George Segal, for example, to create his 1983 Holocaust monument at the Legion of Honor in San Francisco, after initially declining the invitation to do so. Responding to what he perceived to be the antisemitic tone and language of American newscasters in describing Israel's invasion of Lebanon in June 1982, Segal felt he could not "abandon my support for the state of Israel and my fellow Jews, despite my objections to Begin and Sharon" by refusing to conceive a Holocaust monument.[25] After examining all the United Nations proceedings that established the state of Israel, Israeli historian Evyatar Friesel, however, asserts that Israel was neither brought into existence by the Holocaust nor offered a clear alternative to it. Friesel found "little indication in the opinions expressed by the different nations to show that the Holocaust had influenced their position . . . The Zionist representatives who appeared . . . barely alluded to the subject."[26] In the Displaced Persons camps in Germany after the war, Israeli Zionists engaged in a public relations battle for Israeli statehood, pressuring survivors to choose Palestine/Israel over the United States.[27]

In April 1985, the Holocaust erupted at the center of a national controversy when the prominent survivor and writer Elie Wiesel, after being presented with the Congressional Gold Medal of Achievement by then-president Ronald Reagan, opposed Reagan's impending visit to the World War II military cemetery in Bitburg,

West Germany, as part of ceremonies commemorating the fortieth anniversary of V-E Day on 5 May. Bitburg held the graves of German soldiers, including a number of men who had served in the SS. The controversy and Reagan's eventual visit to Bitburg received wide media coverage.[28] By the mid-1990s, hundreds of books existed about the Holocaust—in 1995 alone more than one hundred books were published in the United States and in 1995 and 1996 more than one hundred dissertations focused on it; the scholarly journals *Holocaust and Genocide Studies* from Oxford University Press and *History and Memory* from Indiana University Press are devoted to its study.[29]

With the opening of the U.S. Holocaust Memorial Museum in Washington, D. C. in 1993, the primary perspective of either perpetrator or victim in the Holocaust narrative was replaced by one with which Americans could more readily identify—that of observer. As a result, the story is universalized and the focus is shifted from the crimes of the perpetrators to the moral complicity of the bystanders.[30] Since, however, the pragmatic approach of Americans to history is a fundamentally optimistic one, Americans, suggests Alvin Rosenfeld, are eager to draw lessons from the past in order to emphasize "the saving power of individual moral conduct and collective deeds of redemption." As a result, the Holocaust "has had to enter American consciousness, therefore, in ways that Americans could readily understand on their own terms. These are terms that promote a tendency to individualize, heroize, moralize, idealize, and universalize."[31] Despite the graphic power of the story told in the Holocaust Museum, many Americans are able to see themselves as inheritors of a different tradition, marking the Holocaust as "an alien experience," while perceiving an American continuity with traditions of "fair play, decency, and justice for all."[32] These democratic and egalitarian notions are a comforting mythology belied by the history of slavery and black oppression, Native American genocide and oppression, McCarthyism, blacklisting, and concentration camps for Japanese Americans during World War II, to name a few examples. Thus, Peter Novick suggests that "the pretense that the Holocaust is an American memory," even as complicit bystanders who share responsibility for the Holocaust, "works to devalue the notion of historical responsibility" by allowing Americans to shirk the responsibilities that do belong to them.[33]

New generations not tied directly to the war have evinced a heightened willingness to confront the catastrophe in the 1990s. In Europe, the pressure to remember before perpetrators and victims are gone from the scene has evoked a series of unprecedented apologies, from the International Committee of the Red Cross to the Vatican. The Vatican, after mulling over the issue of apology for eleven years, released a general statement in 1998 chastising the sons and daughters of the Church for not doing more to help the Jews (though the statement was criticized by many for laying blame on the laity while remaining silent on the responsibility of the Church leadership). In France, apologies were produced by Catholic bishops and the national French police organization for their failure to do more against the persecution and murder of the Jews, while Maurice Papon, only the second and probably the last Vichy official to come to trial, was convicted, at the age of eighty-seven, for his role in deporting Jews during the war. First charged in 1981, Papon represents the administrative elite of the Vichy regime that largely escaped scrutiny for its actions during the war. It took a new generation of French leaders who were not complicit with Vichy, as former President François Mitterand was, to even let the trial proceed. In Germany, the phenomena of students searching through archives, digging through local histories, and questioning their parents and grandparents is captured in director Michael Verhoeven's 1990 film *The Nasty Girl.* Based on an actual story of a German historian from the small Bavarian town of Passau, Verhoeven's comic satire of German attitudes reveals a sordid history of collaboration and the discomfort of the townspeople with the protagonist's probing of the past. The rise of neo-Nazi ideology and the recrudescence of antisemitism in Europe has led many young people to reconstruct the events of the Holocaust era anew with a large dose of skepticism and mistrust toward official state histories.

In America, the discussion also "gets louder and more heated," as Hilene Flanzbaum notes, "rather than more muted and moderate as time passes." Flanzbaum points to the myriad stage and literary versions of and forty-year debate over the "real" Anne Frank.[34] In addition to this history and reception, the huge success and passionate debate over Steven Spielberg's *Schindler's List* and Daniel Jonah Goldhagen's *Hitler's Willing Executioners* are other examples of the escalating interest in and response to the Holocaust that have taken place in the nineties.[35] Significantly, the increased interest in the Holocaust by the American Jewish community comes at a time when that community feels besieged by a too-successful integration into American society. A 1990 National Jewish Population Survey that suggested the rate of intermarriage was over 50 percent and would reduce the American Jewish community to a remnant within a hundred years officially triggered this fear.[36] The evocation of the Holocaust serves as a kind of unifying historical reminder of the inescapability of Jewishness, even if only distant relatives were Jews. The most recent codification of the centrality of the Holocaust for American Jews is the American Jewish Committee's "1998 Annual Survey of American Jewish Opinion," which asked respondents to rate the importance of various listed activities to their Jewish identity. "Remembrance of the Holocaust" was listed for the first time. Peter Novick describes the results: "It won hands down—chosen as 'extremely important' or 'very important' by many more than those who chose synagogue attendance, Jewish study, working with Jewish organizations, traveling to Israel, or observing Jewish holidays."[37]

REPRESENTATION AND RECEPTION

American artists in the immediate postwar period felt compelled to confront the grim facts as directly as they could, but, corresponding to the political pressures of the period, this impulse subsided in the late 1940s and throughout the 1950s. Visual imagery of the war became generalized and its connection with the Holocaust was subsumed by the trend toward liberal democracy that encouraged universalization of traumatic experience and a downplaying of ethnic specificity that might invite further isolation or discrimination.[38] The approaches to representation by contemporary artists, however, vary profoundly in conception and methodology from the visual strategies of the war generation. As James Young observes, debates and crises of representation have followed all of this century's major wars and catastrophes, such as World War I, the Spanish Civil War, the bombing of Hiroshima and Nagasaki, and the murder of European Jewry.[39] This has resulted, since the caesura of the Holocaust, in some of the most indirect and irresolute forms of representation, which Young characterizes as "often ironic and self-effacing conceptual installations that mark the national ambivalence and uncertainty of late-twentieth-century postmodernism."[40] The heroically monumental figurative forms of the late nineteenth century have slowly given way to a loss of faith in redemptive meanings and triumphant certainties. Young comments:

> Much post-Holocaust literature and art is pointedly antiredemptory. The post-Holocaust memory artist, in particular, would say that not only is art not the answer, but after the Holocaust there can be no more "final solutions." Some of this skepticism has been a direct response to the enormity of the Holocaust, which seemed to exhaust not only the forms of modernist experimentation and innovation but also the traditional meanings still reified in such innovations. Most of this skepticism, however, has stemmed from these artists' contempt for the religious, political, or aesthetic linking of redemption and destruction that seemed to justify such terror in the first place.[41]

For contemporary artists who address the difficulties of representation, the figurative forms of realism are often regarded as a debilitating imaginative limitation on what must remain partial and unimaginable. Realist work, as opposed to the "traumatic realism" defined by Michael Rothberg, can easily become unbearable to look at, driving viewers away instead of drawing them in, or worse, becoming grotesque and maudlin. Perhaps worst of all, such work can become fetishistic, attempting to fix historical meaning with an aura of sacralized permanence.

A monument to the Holocaust erected in Albuquerque, New Mexico, in 1997 is an example of such a work, illustrating the romantic ideology of representation.

Against the wishes of a group of Albuquerque-based Holocaust survivors and relatives, the city, supported by the Jewish Federation, constructed in its Civic Plaza a 15-foot-tall figurative steel sculpture shaped like a smokestack containing twisted, emaciated human figures floating upward. Preferring the modest plaque commemorating the Holocaust already in place, Albuquerque survivors found this new monument "garish" and in bad taste. They suggested that people at the plaza didn't want to see "bodies sucked up smokestacks." But with support for the project from the mayor, the executive director of the Jewish Federation, Andrew Lipman, coldly responded, "I'm sorry this has brought painful memories for them [the survivors], but they're not going to get their way and put sugarcoating and rainbows on our project. Albuquerque needs this metaphor for man's inhumanity to man."[42] Does opposition to such graphic imagery constitute a desire to sugarcoat the truth, as Lipman suggests, or does it seek to convey a more difficult truth?

Lipman makes the assumption that the genocide of European Jews will be universalized as "man's inhumanity to man," while the Jewish survivors fear that no such universalization will occur. Instead, they anticipate that the monument will become a target for the wrath of Albuquerque's skinheads, making these "universal" victims once again specifically Jewish objects of antisemitic attack. "Some of us are already nervous that skinheads will take aim at this," proclaimed Andy Holten, a fifty-nine-year-old engineer who spent the war years in hiding in Holland and whose parents died at Auschwitz. "No doubt they already have the spray paint out."[43] The goals and aims of this particular memorialization point to a redemptive idealism that has been seriously undermined. It is therefore in danger of reducing the horror of mass murder to an over-literalized and fetishized image that can only be regarded as kitsch. Kitsch has been defined by Saul Friedländer as a return to a debased romantic inspiration both pre-and anti-modern that is founded on a concept of a hero who is identified as the one who must die, but whose death is transformed into a sentimental idyll that creates a harmony of kitsch and death. At the level of individual experience, Friedländer observes, kitsch and death are utterly incompatible.[44]

Four days after the installation and dedication of George Segal's realist depiction of a splayed group of corpses in San Francisco, vandals spray-painted the faces of the cast white figures black and added their own counter inscription to the wall behind which said, "Is this necessary?" The monument has since been sprayed with Nazi swastikas and cleaned a number of times, while an anonymous donor has sent flowers to be laid weekly at the site, as if this were a real graveyard. The experience of the Segal monument and the hundreds of examples of cemetery and synagogue desecrations counted annually by the Jewish Anti-Defamation League have no doubt contributed to Albuquerque survivors' fears of skinheads with spray cans at the ready. The concerns of the Albuquerque survivors, however, are perhaps not only a desire to refrain from provocations that might invite an antisemitic response but also a revulsion to the vulgarization of the events the monument seeks to represent. Bodies, after all, were not sucked up chimneys but burned in ovens, leaving only smoke to float up chimneys. Something so ephemeral, approaching emptiness, cannot fulfill the agenda of heroic monuments. Thus, we see that the monument is, after all, despite its truth-telling agenda, fantastically antirealist. This antirealism corresponds to the moralistic pedagogy (in Roger Simon's terms) of its promoters, and supports the notion of unknowability (in Rothberg's terms) through a sacralizing form of representation. This sentimentalized abstraction, however, encourages distance from the Shoah, promoting a kind of voyeurism remote from responsibility, rather than more sensitive to it.

Ultimately, the desire to memorialize may represent a paradoxical desire to forget, to psychically rid ourselves of an overly burdensome memory by depositing it in a huge public object. Young suggests, "It is as if assigning monumental form to memory divests us to some degree of the obligation to remember."[45] The grandiose pretensions of the Albuquerque monument appear to be an attempt to permanently fix the solemn status of the Jewish victims as martyrs in a redemptive myth that endows their deaths with meaning, an illusion called into question most vigorously by the survivors themselves.[46]

Many contemporary artists engaged by the memory effects of the Holocaust have made clear their rejection of redemptive myths and archaic forms of commemoration rooted in nineteenth-century heroic figuration. They have largely rejected the iconic forms of barbed wire, corpses, guard towers, train tracks, and smokestacks as clichéd images whose power has been vitiated through overuse. The memory work of artists as secondary witnesses is founded on an understanding of the complication of meaning and its mutability over time. Postmodern thought has established a recognition that the past is continually recreated according to the needs of the present—a rather "frightening notion," as Jonathan Boyarin points out (referring to George Orwell's parable of where this might lead in *1984*).[47]

The sense of the present as permeated by the past, but without moralizing pedagogy or redemptive sacralization, is nowhere more consciously addressed than in Art Spiegelman's two-volume comic book series, *Maus.* Dominick LaCapra, employing a psychoanalytic approach, observes that in *Maus,* the source of traumatic disorientation for the parent is transfigured into a founding trauma for the son and holds the "elusive (perhaps illusory) promise of meaning and identity . . . in the present."[48] This transfiguration of the victim's trauma may be regarded as a form of secondary trauma, a sense of unresolved shock and injury that the secondary witness shares with the victim. Its elusive promise of meaning and identity is hard to overestimate. Spiegelman was the first to bring to the popular imagination a story about the relationship of the secondary witness to the memory of the Holocaust. This sense of vicariousness in the postwar generation has been described by Marianne Hirsch as "postmemory" and by James Young as "afterimages," in which secondary witnesses, since they cannot recall events themselves, recall their relationship to the memory of the events.[49] But in recalling his relationship to the memory of the events, Spiegelman also seeks to do something else, to draw a line of resistance, to the loss of historical specificity, to a historicizing closure, and to the sentimentalization of the survivor.

Spiegelman's *Maus* books are really two stories: the war experiences of the father, Vladek, and the experiences of the son, Artie, in learning the father's stories, that is, the conditions of the storytelling sessions themselves. We discover the way Artie's relationship to Vladek is mediated by his having survived Auschwitz, and the way Vladek's telling of the story is constructed by Artie's relentless intervention. Young's analysis of *Maus* is useful: "As a process, it makes visible the space between what gets told and what gets heard, what gets heard and what gets seen. The father says one thing as we see him doing something else. Artie promises not to betray certain details only to show us both the promise and betrayal together."[50] Spiegelman tells the story in the present, with all its interruptions, ruptures, lacunas and emotional repercussions. The difficulty of discovering the story and telling the story addresses the problems of the generation gap between a cantankerous foreign-born father and a thoroughly Americanized, assimilated son. Spiegelman faithfully depicts Vladek's suffering but refuses to sacralize the survivor, presenting the present day tensions between father and son and their clashes in values, particularly the father's racism, thereby raising difficult questions about the Holocaust experience both for survivors and their children. As Young points out, *Maus* refuses the paradigm of objective history telling by refusing to obscure the role of Artie, who both elicits the story and through whom the story is told. The past historical events necessarily include the contemporary conditions in which the events are revealed to the extent that past and present are entangled and conflated. In this sense, Spiegelman both paves the way and is the preeminent visual practitioner of representation conveying the memory effects of Holocaust experience on secondary witnesses. *Maus* may be read as meditating as much on questions of postwar values and identity as on the Nazi genocide.

Artists as secondary witnesses, then, are those who confront the horror of the Nazi genocide and the suffering of its victims, and who continue to bear witness through reconfigured forms of contemporary testimony to events they have never seen or experienced. Because of their distance from the events, however, secondary witnesses do not deal with the Holocaust directly but in ways that bring to the surface the tensions and discontinuities between the past and the present, ambiguities, impasses and lacunas that are part of the "memory effects" of the Shoah. Investigating the way these memory effects inflect representational strategies in Holocaust imagery in turn sheds light on the continued construction of Jewish identity. It is still very difficult to be a public Jew. While traditional definitions of Jewish identity have largely lost their validity, precisely because of their destruction in the Holocaust, no single coherent replacement for an identity based on the memory of genocide has emerged. Thus, the unresolved trauma of the Holocaust and the attempt to come to terms with it continues to function within culture, politics, and aesthetics.

IS HOLOCAUST STUDIES LEGITIMATE? THE HARVARD CONTROVERSY

"Postmodern thought doesn't subscribe to the idea of continuity. It insists, rather, that 'tradition' is never whole, that it's never a perfect transfer from generation to generation, that we annihilate memory or renew it at every moment in time."

DANIEL BOYARIN
from "Yiddish Science and the Postmodern" in *Thinking in Jewish,* 1996

At the seeming height of an expansive interest in the Holocaust and with the success of high-profile enterprises such as Steven Spielberg's Survivors of the Shoah Project, which collected tens of thousands of survivor testimonies on videotape following the acclaim of *Schindler's List,* Ken Lipper, a wealthy Jewish philanthropist, businessman, and former New York deputy mayor, in 1994 pledged a gift of $3.2 million to Harvard to endow the Helen Zelaznik Chair in Holocaust and Cognate Studies, in honor of a family member who was killed in the Holocaust. Lipper's only condition was that the professor be hired with tenure. A committee of Harvard professors began interviewing scholars in 1995.

A number of other colleges and universities around the nation have established Holocaust studies programs; one of the most recent is the Center for Holocaust Studies founded at Clark University in Worcester, Massachusetts, in 1996, and headed by Debórah Dwork. The Clark program is the first to grant a Ph.D. degree. The proposed chair at Harvard, however, unleashed a heated debate that started out with concerns over the qualifications candidates should possess—whether their skills and training would focus on perpetrator history or Jewish history—and the department to which the chair might belong, but quickly escalated to whether such a chair should exist at all. In decided opposition to the heightened wave of attention to the Holocaust, it was argued by a number of scholars and others, mainly Jews, that a new chair should focus on the larger achievements of Jewish history rather than on the events of Jewish destruction. In one letter to the editor of the *New York Times* it was suggested that the life of the Jews, rather than their death, was a more appropriate focus: "There is something unsettling about a chair at Harvard devoted exclusively to the Holocaust. Jewish culture has always been centered on life. Even our prayer for the dead, the Kaddish, avoids any mention of death, emphasizing life instead. A thousand years of civilization should not be commemorated or examined with exclusive emphasis on twelve years of humiliation and slaughter. Let us, and Harvard, focus on the rich lives of the Jews of Europe—not on the malignancy that killed them."[51] This view echoed an earlier editorial in which it was argued that a chair in Holocaust studies "risks allowing the Holocaust to overshadow other defining events in the Jewish people's long, rich history."[52] To this, a letter writer replied, "The Holocaust, with no help from Harvard, has already overshadowed the history of the Jewish people, of all European peoples, of the world. It is the most horrific genocide in what will probably be remembered as the century of genocides."[53]

The debate as played out in the public press focused on the Holocaust as an exclusively Jewish event. But the split over the Holocaust as a study of Jewish victims and Judaic culture, or as a historical analysis of the Nazi perpetrators is a false dichotomy. The integration of both perspectives has been effectively realized in works such as Saul Friedländer's *Nazi Germany and the Jews.*[54] The argument that the Holocaust has swallowed up the Jewish past, overshadowing a more important Jewish history, may be seen as engendering a desire to forget the Holocaust. Omer Bartov (one of the proposed candidates for the Harvard chair) has discerned two contemporary trends of thought aimed at removing the Holocaust from view. One regards the Holocaust as an inevitable development, "a core event of Western Civilization . . . with the tragic Jewish fate as its centerpiece, a culmination of (anti-Jewish) persecution throughout the ages and of the unfolding of divine will." The other trend sees the Holocaust as "a block that distorts and obscures our view of the past and our hopes, plans, and dreams of the future, that relegates all other barbarities and achievements to a secondary place." The former view regards the Holocaust as a "vast sacrificial act," while the latter suggests that it must be put into objective, unemotional, perspective.[55] Although Bartov refers specifically to debates in the late 1980s and early 1990s among the community of historians in Israel, Germany, and the United States, the latter argument, that the Holocaust blocks our view of the past, has come to characterize much of the opposition to the Harvard chair. The desire to remove the Holocaust from view as an obstacle to seeing a greater Jewish past may also be understood, in part, as a conservative backlash to the resurgence of interest in the Holocaust that began after the Arab-Israeli Six-Day War in 1967 and attained a broad scope by the mid-1980s.

When Jimmy Carter created the President's Commission on the Holocaust on November 1, 1978, and charged its thirty-four members with exploring how the nation should commemorate the Holocaust, a debate over the envisioned U.S. Holocaust Memorial Museum ensued and a number of prominent Jews opposed it. Holocaust scholar Deborah Lipstadt, for example, suggested that the Washington museum would create an image of Jews as "perpetual victims." "I think there has been too much emphasis among Jews on the Holocaust," she argued. "If you only look at the Holocaust, you develop what Salo Baron called the 'lachrymose theory of Jewish history.' The tearful becomes the prototype. Jews come to see themselves and gentiles come to see them as perennial sufferers. In other words, it risks letting the enemy define us. Yes, we should try to understand and remember the Holocaust, but within the context of what we are trying to preserve—a special heritage and tradition. If our image is only of suffering, we will have robbed ourselves of the joy and replenishment that Jewish tradition has always fostered."[56] Leon Wieseltier of *The New Republic* agreed: "The centrality of the Holocaust for American Jews amounts virtually to a cult of death. How many American Jews know anything about the Jewish medieval poets, the wealth of culture, the Jewish philosophers? To American Jews, the six million who died were born a few minutes, at best a few years before they were killed."[57]

This perspective was taken around the bend in the arguments against Holocaust studies at Harvard, however, which suggested that the Holocaust need *not* be studied. The irony is that Americans are the least well-informed people in the West on the Nazi genocide, which has not yet been sufficiently erected as an area of study to block the view of anything preceding it. In Bartov's words, "I would argue that it is wholly gratuitous to call for a new campaign of forgetting as regards a community notorious for the weakness of its historical memory."[58] This is not to say, however, that Holocaust history should be substituted for Jewish history, or European history; on the contrary, these separations can be seen as entirely artificial. Both Jewish history and Holocaust history are part of the European experience and should not be kept in tight compartments. Bartov observes: "The way we study history now tends to separate the two, so that the Jews are kept out of the general stream of history, and the general stream of history is seen as having had nothing to do with the Jews. So, too, with the Holocaust. Just as Auschwitz was part of a general European scene, so, too, Jewish history does not simply lead to Auschwitz and therefore consist mainly of it . . . Auschwitz must not be made into the focus of Jewish existence, for it is a black hole that sucks everything beautiful and hopeful into its void. By the same token, however, no member of Western civilization may study his or her history without knowing that one of its potentials was, indeed, Auschwitz."[59]

Other arguments opposing the Harvard chair suggest that the Holocaust should only be studied in the context of other genocides, or in terms of the abstract relationship between state power and violence. But as one of the major events of the twentieth century, its proper context is not simply a transhistorical category of genocide but twentieth-century European history with all the social, political, economic and psychological specificities that have been produced by fifty years of historical study. Otherwise, the Nazi genocide stands in danger of being dehistoricized in a search for general similarities with other genocides; it is rather the historical distinctions that most need to be studied and elaborated.

Opposition to the Harvard chair and, indeed, to the entire field of Holocaust studies, has also come from an anti-Zionist perspective, exemplified in its most extreme form by the political theorist Norman G. Finkelstein. In addition to suggesting that the Holocaust has become ideologically linked to U.S. support for Israeli policy in the Middle East, Finkelstein argues that Holocaust studies is merely part of a "Holocaust industry," producing a book by that title and arguing in various forums that the "Holocaust industry" is not only entirely politicized but unethical.[60]

The political instrumentalization of the Holocaust is indeed beyond question: in the decades following the Arab-Israeli war, the Holocaust increasingly became an issue that was linked to fund-raising campaigns and support for this or that Israeli policy. It has also been used to place a chill on criticism of Israeli policy toward the Palestinians, implying that criticism of Israel is not only antisemitic but risking another Holocaust.

Invocation of the Holocaust as a defense for Israeli policy reached a peak during the 1982 Lebanon War, when Menachem Begin justified massive attacks on a civilian population because, in his view, "1982 was just like 1945: Arafat in Beirut was Hitler in his bunker under the Reichschancellery."[61] Menachem Begin's likening of Yassir Arafat to Hitler was echoed by Prime Minister Yitzhak Shamir in 1989. In an interview with Arnaud de Borchgrave, editor of the *Washington Times,* Shamir likened Arafat to Hitler, because "they belong to the same family of demagogues and totalitarians, enemies of the Jewish people, men who think nothing of killing millions to achieve their objectives." One aspect of the demagoguery here lies in the merging of Arafat, who has not killed millions, with someone who has, making the former responsible for the crimes of the latter.[62]

No political persuasion has a monopoly on using the Holocaust for emotional effect, however, so that the Holocaust has also been used against Israel, particularly after the massacre of Palestinians by Christian Phalangists, dispatched by Israeli forces, at the Sabra and Shatila refugee camps during the Lebanon War. As Israel became the dominant military power in the region during the 1980s, sparking a Palestinian uprising (*intifada*) in 1987, Zionists were increasingly less able to plausibly invoke the Holocaust as a framework for Israeli circumstances and were charged with being just like the Nazis. But arguments against the nationalist agenda of Zionism are no more justified in producing the historical distortion that equates Zionism with Nazism than the Zionist equation of other nationalist leaders with Nazis. Neither are American leaders exempt from the emotional abuse of the Holocaust, as evidenced by George Bush's identification of Saddam Hussein with Hitler in the 1991 Gulf War.

Spielberg's award-winning film *Schindler's List,* just one of many cultural expressions dealing with the Holocaust in the last decade, illustrates the pro-Zionist misuse of the Holocaust. Many observers have noted that the nostalgia for an idealized shtetl that dominated American Jewish memories in the 1960s and found cultural expression in works such as *Fiddler on the Roof,* gave way after the 1967 Arab-Israeli Six-Day War to triumphalist military support to the state of Israel and a revival of interest in works about the Holocaust. There have been Zionist implications to a number of such works, including *Schindler's List.* During the course of the film, the melancholy strains of a Yiddish song—*Oif'n Pripichik*—are heard as the audience follows the fate of the Jews to the camps. At the film's conclusion, however, switching from black and white to color in present-day Jerusalem, the narrative switches from the past to the present and the music heard is *Yerushalayim shel sahav,* a Hebrew hit song from the Six-Day War. The ending is thus implicitly redemptive. Critics such as Claude Lanzmann, whose 1985 film *Shoah* avoided any kind of realist narrative, criticized Spielberg's film, among other reasons, because the ending suggests that the horror of the Holocaust was meaningful since it led to the creation of the state of Israel.

The Holocaust has been used to justify and defend the Zionist enterprise in ways that lead to a peculiar kind of historical revisionism. During Israeli President Ezer Weizman's address to the German Parliament on January 16, 1996, meant to improve Israeli-German relations, the Israeli leader, in an emotional speech thanking Germany for its support of Israel over the last forty years, commented on the fact that he felt obliged to speak in Hebrew because it was "the language that was screamed in the gas chambers."[63] At one blow, Weizman effaced all the languages spoken in the Babel of the concentration camps, but most importantly Yiddish, the language predominantly spoken among Jews from Poland and Eastern Europe who constituted the majority of murdered Jews.[64] Just as Yiddish was rejected in Israel as a diasporic language, Weizman effectively effaced the Yiddish-speaking eastern Jew in favor of the tiny minority of Hebrew-speaking Zionist Jews. (Theodor Herzl, the Austrian founder of Zionism, attempted to normalize the Jewish condition and eliminate Jewish otherness by arguing that only German could be the official language of the Zionist state. Herzl characterized Yiddish dialects as "those miserable, stunted jargons, those Ghetto languages which we still employ."[65])

Norman Finkelstein, however, sees politicization of the Holocaust in every arena where it may come into view, leading to his assertion, in response to the Harvard controversy: "Holocaust studies are a nonsense. It has nothing to do with scholarship and everything to do with politics."[66] This blithe dismissal of Holocaust scholars and scholarship is indefensibly extreme and unjustly rejects the enormous contribution produced by serious scholars through decades of work. We must reject the appropriation of the Holocaust by Zionist or other political agendas, and study the Holocaust as a crucial part of European history that demands further investigation from a variety of disciplinary perspectives, no less than other profound events in history such as the American Civil War or the Russian Revolution.

Finkelstein has further suggested that the study of the Nazi genocide without equal status for all other genocides is somehow unethical: "It was to be called the

Chair in Holocaust and Cognate Studies . . . . In other words, the rest of humanity and its sufferings got dumped in the residual generic title of 'cognate.' I find this morally repellent."[67] Others "feared that exclusive concentration on the murder of 6 million Jews would overlook the genocide of other communities—the Cambodian massacres by Pol Pot, the Rwandan slaughter and the wholesale murder of 1.5 million Armenians by Turks and their allies in 1915."[68] Various historians have noted that the Holocaust is the only field of study that scholars are continually required to justify, a measure of the discomfort it arouses in so many quarters. For any depth and specificity to be achieved in the study of other genocides, they must be studied individually as well, with knowledge of the necessary languages. Historian Steve Paulsson argues the case succinctly but comprehensively: "If the Holocaust is to be put in a context, it is not the abstract context of 'genocide,' but the concrete context of European history, where it becomes clear that the Holocaust is one of the major events of the 20th century. This has nothing to do with the number of victims or even the intentions of the killers. Rather, the Holocaust is a major event because it challenges Christian and European claims to moral and intellectual superiority, is entwined with European and Christian traditions of antisemitism, religious and ethnic intolerance, nationalism, militarism, imperialism, and with various scientific and pseudo-scientific ideologies, some of which still have a following; because it demonstrates that there are no moral limits to bureaucracy, and that murder can be organized industrially just like the production of cars or university degrees; because, in fact, it challenges European civilization on all fronts, in a way that has not happened since the Enlightenment or perhaps even the Reformation. No other genocide has had that kind of impact."[69]

The candidates for the Harvard position included distinguished historians Christopher Browning, Dan Diner, Samuel Kassow, Omer Bartov, and Saul Friedländer. Friedländer, near retirement, was proposed on a temporary basis while the search continued. He was rejected by the donor, Ken Lipper, who favored hiring Daniel Jonah Goldhagen, an untenured professor already teaching at Harvard when his controversial book *Hitler's Willing Executioners* was published. (Numerous historians have critiqued Goldhagen's simplistic theory of "eliminationist antisemitism" and other shortcomings of his methodology.) After all proposed candidates for a chair in Holocaust Studies were disputed and rejected, in April 1998, three years after the Lippers offered millions to one of America's leading universities, the plan was abandoned. The initial one million dollar donation was diverted to a program for genetic research at Harvard Medical School.

Following the Harvard controversy, the debate over the legitimacy of Holocaust studies has continued. In an article for America's best-known neoconservative magazine *Commentary,* published by the American Jewish Committee, senior editor Gabriel Schoenfeld argued that the institutionalization of the Holocaust in the academy has produced a "sense-deadening phenomenon of 'naturalization.'"[70] Bashing the academicism of the university, Schoenfeld asserted, "Today, not only are academic careers built on the Holocaust, but research into it has also been thoroughly academicized. The very language in which the murder of six million Jews is discussed has become in no way distinguishable from the language of agricultural macroeconomics or the sociology of chimpanzees—which is to say that even at its best, it is often full of the most egregious professional jargon."[71] Schoenfeld suggests that Holocaust studies have been turned into careerist "Holocaustology," a term first coined in 1977 by Yehuda Bauer (but since abandoned by him). Referring to Saul Friedländer's assertion that endowed chairs and concomitant study centers are needed to study the Holocaust in "a significant way," Schoenfeld counters that Holocaust study centers may be "simply spreading jargon, ideology, and distortions both monstrous and trivial."[72] Schoenfeld goes on to cite gender studies as "a voguish hybrid" responsible for "the worst excesses" in recent Holocaust research. Writes Schoenfeld: "That feminist scholarship on the Holocaust is intended explicitly to serve the purposes of consciousness raising—i.e., propaganda—is, as it happens, something its practitioners proudly admit, just as they are proud of their use of the Holocaust as a means of validating feminist theory itself. Unfortunately, in order to find these statements of intent one has to be willing to subject oneself to their prose—the general execrableness of which, let it be said, easily surpasses that of their male colleagues, while adding its own special notes of querulousness and righteous self-regard."[73] Schoenfeld concedes that, "in itself, such an undertaking is hardly without merit," but objects to what he asserts is the "naked ideological 'agenda'" of such research.

Schoenfeld's thesis evoked a barrage of responses. Historian Sid Bolkosky agreed that concern over the "naturalizing" of the Holocaust is a valid worry, but argued, "What Mr. Schoenfeld fails to do is cite the best of the Holocaust scholars and writers, including Debórah Dwork, whose work is meticulously documented and carefully sensitive to the issues of popularization and clichés. Where are Lawrence Langer, Geoffrey Hartman, and Raul Hilberg in this article? Where are Christopher Browning (he manages to include Daniel Jonah Goldhagen) and Martin Gilbert? Does Schoenfeld mean to suggest that Saul Friedländer, among the most respected and thorough scholars in the field, is 'simply spreading jargon, ideology, and distortions both monstrous and trivial'? Where, too, are the works and words of Primo Levi, and even Yehuda Bauer, who obviously does not now cling to his earlier warnings against 'Holocaustology'?"[74] Railing against "separate centers" for Holocaust study, Schoenfeld, however, failed to discuss an alternative, prompting historian Aharon Meytahl to comment that it was "possible to conclude that although [the] university is improper for discussing the Holocaust, *Commentary* is [proper]." Meytahl countered, "Because it [the Holocaust] is important, it fits every medium of expression: university studies, literature, poetry, painting and sculpture, Hollywood, popular fiction, even *Commentary.* What matters is not the medium of expression but the content and manner of exposition."[75]

On the feminist front, Joan Ringelheim argued, "for Jewish women, the Holocaust produced a set of experiences, responses, and memories that do not always parallel those of men." To attack the legitimacy of the field, suggested Ringelheim, "trivializes the human experience of victims in the Holocaust."[76] Indeed, it has been widely accepted that male experience cannot stand in for universal experience, as Schoenfeld himself seems to recognize; therefore research into gender-differentiated behavior under Nazi persecution may yield important insights into the different ways women experienced the ghettos and the camps, including, as Ringelheim notes, an examination of such issues as "sexual victimization, pregnancy, abortion, childbirth, killing of newborn babies in the camps to save the mothers, care for children, and many decisions about separation from children."[77] Lenore Weitzman points out the four "systematic sources of gender differences during the Holocaust" explored in her book *Women in the Holocaust* as related to economic status, strategies of hiding or remaining, work regulations, and the different responses to progressive victimization, concluding that "for Gabriel Schoenfeld to characterize this serious scholarship as 'feminist consciousness-raising' is both false and misleading."[78] An open letter signed by twenty-nine scholars and writers, including Barbara Kellerman (Center for the Advanced Study of Leadership, University of Maryland), Hank Greenspan (University of Michigan), Stephen Feinstein (Center for Holocaust and Genocide Studies, University of Minnesota), and Myrna Goldenberg (Montgomery College, Maryland), asserted, in full:

> We, as teachers, scholars, and researchers, reject Gabriel Schoenfeld's thesis in his article, "Auschwitz and the Professors," and affirm that serious scholarship on the Holocaust within the university is both appropriate and necessary. Indeed, the vast body of knowledge that is the result of scholarship on the Holocaust has increased national and international awareness and understanding of this seminal event in the history of the world. Study of the Holocaust, especially in institutions of higher learning, is characterized much more by responsible scholarship than by ideological or self-serving approaches.
>
> Like other moral persons, we do not accept the exploitation and trivialization of the Holocaust in any sense. We, therefore, deplore Mr. Schoenfeld's malicious and unfounded attack on the academic pursuit of the Holocaust.[79]

Schoenfeld, in a reply to his critics, rather disingenuously announced that he opposes only "the establishment of separate academic centers on Holocaust study," but favors "serious research and teaching about the Holocaust in a university setting," implying, ipso facto, that serious research and teaching about the Holocaust cannot take place in separate academic centers on the Holocaust, despite the fact that they do, in fact, exist primarily "within the university setting."

What, then, is the real source of Schoenfeld's waspish arguments? The answer may turn on the issue of sacralization of the Holocaust. In a discussion of Claude

Lanzmann's film *Shoah,* Dominick LaCapra analyzes Lanzmann's internalization, in his own voice, of an SS guard's response to Primo Levi, *"Hier gibt's kein Warum"* (there is no why here). This became the title of a one-page manifesto by Lanzmann on his film. The manifesto begins, "All one has to do is perhaps formulate the question in the simplest form, to ask: 'Why were the Jews killed?' The question immediately reveals its obscenity. There is indeed an absolute obscenity in the project of understanding."[80] The emphatic use of such a phrase as "absolute obscenity" raises for LaCapra a question of secular religiosity in Lanzmann's approach. "I would suggest," says LaCapra, "that Lanzmann returns to what he explicitly denies, represses, or suppresses: a tendency to sacralize the Holocaust and to surround it with taboos. He especially affirms a *Bilderverbot,* or prohibition on images, with respect to representation, notably representation relying on archival documentation or footage, and he also insists on what might be called a *Warumverbot,* or prohibition on the question *why.*"[81] Schoenfeld similarly expresses a tendency to sacralize the Holocaust as he rails against the possibility of academic "naturalization" and feminist distortion. *Commentary*'s self-description as "the home of the most honest and sustained defense of Israel" ironically places Schoenfeld, and his arguments opposing Holocaust studies, in the same camp as Norman Finkelstein, who argues that the sole purpose of Holocaust studies is to cultivate ideological support for Israel. How did the staunch Zionist and the zealous anti-Zionist end up on the same side? Finkelstein fears that Holocaust studies, focusing on the uniquely Jewish aspect of the events, will sacralize the Holocaust and make criticism of Israel coequal with anti-semitism. Schoenfeld, proceeding from a neoconservative standpoint, is suspicious of university liberalism and his perception of the relativing agenda of postmodernist methodologies such as feminism, which threaten to destabilize a sense of the Holocaust's uniqueness. Thus his underlying objection must be read as a fear of the desacralization of the Holocaust, which, by extension, makes criticism of Israel more acceptable. From opposite perspectives, both Finkelstein and Schoenfeld worry about the instrumentalization of Holocaust studies vis-à-vis the Jewish state.

Schoenfeld has defined one of his critics, Stephen Feinstein, as "Israel-bashing," but his attack on critic John K. Roth has been most telling in this regard. Roth, both a Christian theologian at Claremont McKenna College in California and coeditor of the feminist collection *Different Voices,* became a subject of controversy when he was slated to become director of research at the Holocaust Memorial Museum in Washington, D.C., in 1998. A number of conservative Jewish organizations opposed Roth on the basis of a comment he had made in 1988 comparing Israeli policy toward the Palestinians with the Nazi pogrom of *Kristallnacht.* In an op-ed piece in the *Los Angeles Times,* Roth wrote, "*Kristallnacht* happened because a political state decided to be rid of people unwanted within its borders. It seems increasingly clear that Israel would prefer to rid itself of Palestinians if it could do so . . . . As much as any other people today, they are being forced into a tragic part too much like the one played by the European Jews 50 years ago."[82] Joining Roth's conservative critics, Schoenfeld rehashes this controversy, calling Roth's comparison "outrageous." While Roth may be invoking the Holocaust to serve contemporary political purposes, Schoenfeld's dismissal of Roth as a serious Holocaust scholar is founded on using the Holocaust to serve his own political objectives, in which criticism of Israel is not tolerated. For Schoenfeld, the link between understanding the Holocaust and unmitigated support for the state of Israel is indissoluble and self-evident.

Other scholars joined the public debate over Holocaust studies in the pages of the *New York Times* when the newspaper invited commentary from Steven T. Katz, director of the Center for Judaic Studies at Boston University, and Ruth R. Wisse, professor of Yiddish literature and comparative literature at Harvard University. Katz, who has argued for the singularity of the Shoah, supports teaching the Holocaust as a specialized program not only because of its significance for Jewish history but for the modern era as a whole. The very importance of the Holocaust, he argues, is what accounts for the "massive effort to relativize and de-Judaize it." Its distinctive features include not only "nationalism, the decline of religious authority, an innovative political ideology, bureaucracy, technology, the secular state, racial theory, and intentional state-sponsored genocide," but "the inversion of all moral and metaphysical values . . . all the classical Western doctrines of ethics, philosophy and theology."[83] Katz cautions, however, that the Holocaust must be contextualized within the stream of history to be taught properly: "Of course, to teach this pivotal subject without either a sufficient knowledge of its larger historical circumstance, including the makeup and character of the Nazi state, or of Jewish history is to tell less than the whole story and thus, by design or ignorance, to distort it. One must know, among other things, the remarkable character of that Jewish civilization that was destroyed, the nature of the cultural, social, political, and religious life that was carried on in the Polish and Lithuanian ghettos, the details of the impossible and unprecedented position of the Jewish Councils, and the story of Jewish resistance."[84] Katz concludes that the large scholarly demands that are made on those who would teach the Holocaust are the circumstances of any academic field and provide all the more reason for setting up first-rate training programs.

For Ruth Wisse, the issues are entirely different and focus on a belief that the contemporary construction of Jewish identity should be grounded in the teachings of Judaism and a history of militancy rather than victimization. She approvingly quotes a Jewish college sophomore as saying, "The Jews of Europe may have been killed for what they believed in, but I was never told what they believed in."[85] The Jews, however, were *not* killed for what they believed in, but on the basis of a racialist ideology, regardless of belief. Wisse asserts that teaching the Holocaust runs the risk of reducing the Jews to an abstraction, reinscribing the ideology of the Nazis, and constructing Jewish identity as always already dead victims. Her objection to teaching the Holocaust, then, is her fear that it will overshadow the past with a gloomy history of death and loss. In contrast to Katz's argument that the Holocaust and its context must be studied as part of any attempt to understand the modern era, Wisse's perspective is that of the nationalist Jew whose allegiance is both to Israel and to a "positive" construction of Jewish history. Hence her view that "those who exploit the Holocaust as a moral fable make no connection between it and the political predicament of the Jewish people: being perceived and used as a target. In fact, Hitler's victorious war against the Jews inspires as much imitation as regret."[86] Tying study of the Holocaust to a passive reverence for the dead that fails to promulgate an activist program of Jewish national defense, Wisse thus concludes that the Holocaust should not be taught as a separate study.

The very fact of the existence of undergraduate and graduate courses in the Holocaust at many universities reflects a need by scholars and students to examine this defining event of the century. A positivist focus on Jewish history and belief without an understanding of Jewish history in the modern era is a distortion of history and a grave disservice to the next generation.

BLACKS, JEWS, AND THE TWO "HOLOCAUSTS"

"The Holocaust is the same; it cannot change. But the world in which we live, whether we welcome or do not welcome the development that is before us, changes the meaning of the Holocaust as time passes before our eyes."

RAUL HILBERG
"Opening Remarks: The Discovery of the Holocaust," in *Lessons and Legacies: The Meaning of the Holocaust in a Changing World,* 1991

THE IDEA THAT there were two holocausts, the Jewish Holocaust and the African or Black Holocaust, has gained wide currency among African Americans, who retroactively apply the term of the mid-twentieth-century disaster to events that, in their origins, preceded it by several hundred years and terminated in the previous century.[87] Similarly, the attempts at Armenian genocide by the Turks in 1915 and 1923 are retroactively figured as the Armenian Holocaust, "in terms of another people's catastrophe" so that the events become part of a "larger continuum of destruction created *in* the naming of the catastrophes, one in light of the other."[88] The similarities and differences between the Armenian genocide and the Judeocide have, to a great extent, become subsumed by the historical continuum created through naming. What about the similarities and differences between American slavery and the murder of European Jews?

On Martin Luther King Day in 1994, a group of more than sixty students from

Castlemont High School in Oakland, California, a mostly black and Hispanic school, went on a field trip to see a showing of *Schindler's List* at a local movie theater. After the first hour, agitated movie patrons complained to the management that the students were disruptive, especially when they laughed at a scene of the killing of a Jewish prisoner by a Nazi guard, and the students were expelled before the film was over. Given the explosive underlying conflict that has developed between blacks and Jews in this country, the episode received national attention and became a subject of heated controversy in the local media and at Castlemont High School. Student leaders made speeches to the Oakland School Board to apologize and explained, "a majority of us didn't know about the Holocaust."[89] Others explained that it is not unusual for them to laugh at screen violence because they know it's not real, and that this should not be confused in this case with laughing at the Holocaust itself; still others insisted that "we should understand our own pain before we can understand someone else's pain."[90] The school responded by organizing a full day of teaching on the African Holocaust, in which students learned about the history of the slave trade, U.S. slavery, lynching, and Reconstruction. A group of speakers was brought in for the special program, including two speakers who presented questionable information, including the false assertion that Jews had owned the majority of slave ships.[91] This fed a growing antisemitic sentiment among some students that had been fueled by the public reaction to the original incident. Thus the paradoxical situation developed in which an attempt to place the long history of enslavement and atrocities in a historical continuum with the Judeocide produced an oppositional rivalry and hostility that continues to reinforce some of the very stereotypes that underlay the antisemitic terror, and exacerbates the decades-long tension between American blacks and Jews.[92]

Two weeks after the Academy Awards, when *Schindler's List* won for best picture, Steven Spielberg went to visit Castlemont High School and was joined by California Governor Pete Wilson. Some students organized a protest demonstration, carrying signs such as "Zionism=Racism"; others supported Spielberg's visit but regarded Wilson's presence as a cynical ploy in which he was using the school as a staging area for political gains in the next election. In his speech to the students, Spielberg observed sympathetically that he himself had once been kicked out of a theater for talking and he enthusiastically endorsed the new program instituted at the school as a result of the initial controversy, a course that was to be called "The Human Holocaust: The African-American Experience."

These events raise a number of disturbing questions: Why was it deemed appropriate that a group of largely black and Hispanic students be required to see a film about the Nazi destruction of European Jews on Martin Luther King Day? Why had they previously been taught nothing about either the Holocaust or slavery? How did a story about the Holocaust become equated with Zionism? And what is the significance of universalizing the term so that it becomes not just the Black Holocaust, but loses all boundaries as the human Holocaust?

In a scathing attack on *Schindler's List* and its effects, Michael André Bernstein observed that there appeared to be "widespread official support for the assumption that screening a film about the horrors inflicted on European Jews [would] improve relations between African-Americans and Jews in this country, especially in urban high schools and universities." Bernstein noted that the failure of this assumption occurred at more schools than just Castlemont, which received the most coverage and triggered the bitterest controversy over "whose history had been more traumatic." "The whole notion," observes Bernstein, "that whatever hostility and misunderstanding exists between two ethnic groups living in the United States today could be diffused by showing that one of them had, in another time and country, suffered catastrophic persecution, appears both psychologically and historically naive, willfully so. In spite of such pious wishes, there is no reason whatsoever to assume that the sight of Jews being brutalized by the Nazis will do anything to change the ways in which American Jews are viewed today."[93] The choice of Martin Luther King Day for the film viewing was obviously related to the idea that the movie's educational value would somehow provide a message of tolerance and compassion that crossed boundaries between blacks and Jews. Supported by both Democratic and Republican political leaders, as well as high school teachers, Spielberg had encouraged free, even mandatory showings of his movie for ethnically mixed high school districts throughout the country because, in Spielberg's words, "this is a story about tolerance and remembrance, and it is for everyone . . . [It] represents racial hatred everywhere in the world."[94] But the Holocaust is not a parable of universal suffering; it cannot stand in for events in Bosnia, Rwanda, the Middle East, Northern Ireland, Africa, and the American South or any place else. Specific historical conditions must be evaluated on their own terms. A focus on these issues sets aside questions about the nature of Spielberg's film itself, which has been amply discussed elsewhere.[95]

The equation of the Holocaust with Zionism by some of the students may be seen as a result of American Jewry's linkage of the Jewish genocide with the establishment of the state of Israel, particularly since the 1967 Six-Day War, and the resulting equation by much of mainstream American Jewry of anti-Zionism with antisemitism. Faced with accusations of antisemitism, Castlemont students simply reversed the equation and claimed a position of anti-Zionism. In the conflict between Zionists and Palestinians, and the absence of a class analysis to cut through the irresolvable nationalist antagonisms, many American blacks have sided with the perceived underdogs, the Palestinians.

At the core of these debates, however, is the issue of competing victimhoods between blacks and Jews. Unlike Armenians and Jews, between African Americans and Jews there seems to be a developing struggle for ownership of the name *Holocaust* itself. Bernstein has suggested that this is based on the idea that "the sentimentalization of victimhood [is] a guarantor of inner nobility," a notion with which

Schindler's List is deeply complicit.[96] The destructive struggle over a fixed status of noble victimhood stems in part from the incredible lack of education and resulting ignorance about either slavery or the Holocaust, in which the real histories and complexities, the moral "gray areas" which Primo Levi has explored so profoundly in *The Drowned and the Saved,* the contradictions and implications of the specific conditions, times, and places in which events took place are not understood, and cannot be understood without ongoing study. Not only should studies about slavery and the events of World War II become part of standard American education but much sooner than is currently available to a majority of students. Many educators suggest it should begin in elementary school. This makes the debate over the Harvard chair in Holocaust studies, or rather, the opposition to the establishment of the chair, at the college level, all the more disturbing.

WHAT'S IN A NAME?

An example of the widening of the term holocaust can be found at the Charles H. Wright Museum of African American History in Detroit, which opened in June 1997, and has been acclaimed as the largest African American history museum in the world. The permanent exhibition is organized around eight historical stations, with the first half focusing on the history of Africa and the African slave trade. The exhibition subtly intimates that slavery was a holocaust where a model of the slave ship *Sunny South* is displayed in a Plexiglas case with a label that reads: "The model was made by Dr. Robert Bland, of Detroit, with wood from a mahogany chest that had been passed on by generations of his family for over 100 years. Mr. and Mrs. Michael Bennett, sailmakers of Jewish descent, contributed sail canvas, as old as the wood, that had been kept over the years in their own family. The model, made from heirlooms of two families, each with the memory of a holocaust of its people, exemplifies the possibilities of healing." The fact of two holocausts is taken for granted. Fath Davis Ruffins notes, "This interpretation of Africans' history in America as a genocide has become a key aspect of the internal cultural symbolism of most African-American institutions in the 1990s."[97]

There is no date given for the building of this model slaver, nor are the healing possibilities of the text spelled out. We assume that the mere fact of collaboration is the basis for this hopeful assessment, in which case we might expect the far more politically potent collaboration of blacks and Jews during the Civil Rights movement to be mentioned, but it never is. The history of the civil rights movement itself is generalized (film clips of civil rights leaders lack specific historical context, providing no dates or places), and the one photograph that directly alludes to interracial collaboration is placed high on a vertical shelf. This four-by-six-inch photograph of men in a field has a caption explaining that three civil rights workers, James Chaney, Andrew Goodman, and Michael Schwerner, were murdered by racist whites in Mississippi, but not that two of them, Goodman and Schwerner were Jewish (or white).

The final panels of the museum exhibition begin with the phrase, "Becoming the Future Means" and are followed by such prescriptions as, "exerting power as consumers . . . being in business, small, medium, or large, corner stores or multimillion-dollar corporations . . . investing in stocks and bonds, in money markets and mutual funds . . . welcoming immigrants . . . from the South, Canada, the Caribbean and Africa . . . putting more African nutrition in our diets and African flavors in our recipes . . . learning African languages and dialects . . . traveling to Africa . . . " With this emphasis on black entrepreneurial enterprise, the exhibition seems to ignore the poor and working-class layers of black American society while addressing itself to middle-class and affluent blacks. The museum narrative elides the focus on race with an emphasis on class as it promotes individual achievement based on a sense of black pride that links American blacks to a motherland, the continent of Africa. The "nobility of past victimhood" is transformed into an Africa-based construction of middle-class identity, an Afrocentrist response to centuries of oppression in which blacks were officially excluded from American national culture. This also means, however, that the Museum of African American History implicitly relegates the Jewish genocide to the sphere of white history, just as it consigns the history and struggles of poor and working-class black Americans, their militant organizations, and their allies, both white and Jewish, to a murky obscurity. But both American slavery and the Jewish genocide must be understood in historical terms for their impact on the subsequent development of American and European civilization, not simply as black or Jewish histories.[98]

"HOLOCAUST ENVY"

THE MOST POPULAR contemporary exponent of the Nation of Islam is Louis Farrakhan, who promotes distrust of both Jews and whites. Not surprisingly, the rivalry over the right to the name holocaust led a participant in Farrakhan's Million Man March in October 1995 to confront the Jewish sociologist Jonathan Rieder with the question: "Which is worse, what happened to six million Jews or what happened during slavery? Six million or 600 million?" When Rieder declined to make such a comparison of suffering, the man cried: "You got your recognition! You got your movie!"[99] When Spielberg created a pendant to *Schindler's List* in the form of *Amistad,* based on the mutiny of African captives aboard a slave ship in 1839, renewed attention was focused on the history of slavery and the concept of "the black holocaust" has been brought into heightened prominence and has increasingly cropped up in academic venues and publications.[100] In 1988, James Cameron of Milwaukee established a museum documenting more than three centuries of African American oppression and resistance and named it America's Black Holocaust Museum.[101]

Taking the antisemitic rhetoric of Louis Farrakhan to an extreme and linking it to the rhetoric of white Holocaust deniers, another African American leader, Khalid Abdul Muhammad (who died in February 2001) repudiated the Judeocide altogether. In a speech at San Francisco State University on 21 May 1997, Muhammad declared: "The so-called Jew claims that there were six million in Nazi Germany. I am here today to tell you that there is absolutely no evidence, no proof. There is absolutely no evidence to substantiate, to prove that six-million so-called Jews lost their lives in Nazi Germany."[102] In the same speech, Muhammad referred to the "hook-nosed, bagel-eating, lox-eating, perpetrating-a-fraud so-called Jew who just crawled out of the ghettoes of Europe just a few days ago," and queried: "Who's pimping the world? The hairy hands of the Zionist in the world." On the one hand implicitly questioning the legitimacy of the Jew as a category of identity, Muhammad at the same time rereads Jewish identity as Zionist.

Muhammad was a protégé of Louis Farrakhan and a former official of the Nation of Islam. Both Farrakhan and Muhammad have accused the Jews of playing a disproportionate role in the slave trade, a theory that has been broadly debunked, and oppressing blacks ever since through control of what they call the banking, publishing, and entertainment industries. In a search for bourgeois respectability and a desire to forge an alliance with the head of the NAACP, Farrakhan began to soften his rhetoric, while Muhammad forged ahead with hate-filled tirades at college campuses. A speech in 1993 at Kean College in Union, New Jersey, caused an avalanche of criticism that forced Farrakhan to suspend Muhammad from his position as national spokesman for the Nation of Islam (though many suspect this was a mere public relations ploy). Muhammad continued on the lecture circuit, surrounding himself with acolytes and continuing to reach out to young Nation of Islam members across the country. On September 5, 1998, he presided over a rally in Harlem, the "Million Youth March," in which several thousand people gathered to hear speeches that included anti-white and antisemitic repugnancies. The rally became highly controversial, first in Mayor Rudolph Giuliani's opposition to it on the basis of Muhammad's hate mongering, then in his handling of it. When a court ruling allowed it, Giuliani turned the six blocks in Harlem where the rally was held into an armed police encampment. As the peaceful rally was about to end, police, claiming that Muhammad was inciting the crowd to riot and murder, stormed the speakers' stage and shut down the rally, further inflaming black distrust of the white city government. Muhammad, for his part, fled from the rally, leaving his listeners as potential targets for the wrath he incited.

Gerald Early, author and the director of African and African American Studies at

Washington University in St. Louis, attempts to look beyond the obvious differences between American slavery and the Jewish genocide in explaining the claim to the name Holocaust: "The use of the word 'Holocaust' brings the dimension of atrocity to slavery that black people feel is necessary for whites—and for themselves—to understand what slavery was, and what it means. We lost who we were as a people. If people can see behind even some of the crude antisemitism, they'll see a profound sense of not having your tragedy understood."[103] Early thus suggests that the retroactive appropriation of the term is motivated by a desire to raise the visibility of the tragedy of slavery by positioning it within what Young called, "the larger continuum of destruction created in the naming of the catastrophes, one in light of the other."[104] Jonathan Rieder, co-editor of *Common Quest: The Magazine of Black-Jewish Relations,* further points to "a pattern of black appropriation of Jewish terms—black Holocaust, black Diaspora, Day of Atonement."[105] The appropriation of the term Holocaust for the experience of slavery is regarded by many Jews as threatening to obscure the very referent that endows it with the desired historical weight, creating a rivalry that feeds on the impulse to privilege one form of experience over the other in an impossible comparison of suffering. Since Jews *have* been successful in positioning their tragedy at the center of American consciousness, as a yardstick by which other atrocities are judged, a fair amount of resentment has been understandably produced—what Peter Novick calls "Holocaust envy."[106]

Daniel Boyarin and Jonathan Boyarin, in *Jews and Other Differences,* have tried to address this issue as part of their argument for Jewish cultural studies, suggesting that the politics of difference for different groups can be read in light of one another. "To a profound extent, a retrospective devaluation of Jewish difference in exile has been a key component of the dominant historiography of Jews since World War II," such that "Jews and Jewish culture both are obviously in their own state of crisis." The Boyarins suggest that "the rubric of Jewish cultural studies is to move toward the recognition of Jewish culture as part of the world of differences to be valued and enhanced by research in the university, together with the differences of other groups hanging onto cultural resources similarly at risk of being consumed by a liberal universalist ethos."[107] The crystallization of the Holocaust as a major public component of Jewish identity requires its inclusion in such an ambitious project, one which aspires to "shape a space of common discourse between Jews and others who share a critical approach to the politics of culture . . . an understanding of history and identity that fully respects the powerful ways that they inform each other, yet also understands that in exploring and articulating our various identities we are simultaneously remaking history." With the strain between African Americans and Jews in mind, the Boyarins argue that such an approach "is vital to our contention that difference can be enriching and nonexclusive rather than constraining and competitive."[108]

In a move that recognizes the larger historical implications of both slavery and the Jewish genocide, the *Mississippi Quarterly: The Journal of Southern Culture* released a "call for papers" for a special cluster for its January 2000 issue on the subject of Holocaust studies and the American South. Simultaneously, it called for abstracts on the same subject for a panel at the American Studies Association meeting in Montreal in October 1999.[109] Questions to focus entries/abstracts were given as follows: "How can problems of representation raised by European Holocaust studies be applied to the Black Holocaust? What lessons about literary, artistic, and cultural representations of the Black Holocaust teach us about the European Holocaust? How do swastikas and confederate flags resonate with each other? What cultural factors decide what is and is not a permissible representation of the past? Is the South Europe's Other? How do the cultures' different processes of denial, acting out, and working through illuminate each other?" Here, in a scholarly arena, the emphasis is placed on how the cultural representations of the destruction of European Jewry and slavery in the American South might resonate with or illuminate each other, although the existence of an undefined "Black Holocaust" is already taken for granted as an established frame of reference. And, while some of these questions may be stretching the point too far, there is an interesting relationship between black and Jewish racial oppression. It is well known that the Jim Crow segregation laws of the United States (1877–1954) served as a model for Hitler's racial purity citizenship laws in 1935 and after; Hitler even praised the United States in *Mein Kampf* for this rational policy toward citizenship. The effects of the Nuremberg trials in the wake of Germany's defeat, conversely, must have affected American consciousness of Jim Crow segregation, an embarrassing situation in light of U.S. condemnation of similar laws in Germany, and have acted as a spur to the civil rights movement.

When it comes to the term holocaust, there has been as much constraint and competitiveness as inclusiveness. Vivian Patraka addresses the issue in an essay in *Jews and Other Differences:* "Even if some contemporary groups do deliberately use the term *Holocaust* in a way designed to compete with or even erase the original referent, if we assert an exclusive, proprietary claim over the term in response, we run the risk of magnifying one current perception: that the discourse of Jewish Holocaust functions as a kind of controlling or hegemonic discourse of suffering that operates at the expense of the sufferings of other groups." Nonetheless, Patraka recognizes that meaning is found precisely within the master-narrative of the Jewish Holocaust: "I wonder whether so much of the history of the Jewish genocide, the meanings attached to it, even the ethical, cultural, and linguistic protocols of where to look for meaning about such events, is so deeply embedded in the word Holocaust as to make the Jewish genocide a paradigmatic frame for other genocides located within the term."[110] The sense of the enormity of history with which the Jewish genocide has endowed the term Holocaust brings with it, in Patraka's words, "all the protocols of the unspeakable, the incommensurate, and a sense of unlimited scope to the pain and injustice."[111] The appropriation of Holocaust for the experience of American slavery is perhaps best understood in this sense. Patraka is willing to go further and accept slavery as a form of genocide, confining her argument for this to a parenthetical question: "The call for African American civil rights is the call for removing the last vestiges of genocidal slavery (when is massive slavery not genocidal?)," yet she concedes that "the elimination of civil rights for Jews in Germany is the beginning of the escalation toward genocide (a teleological narrative that would not suit the African American example)."[112] This is not a minor difference. If we understand genocide to mean an attempt at the extermination of a people, we cannot speak of "genocidal" slavery. While grotesquely and brutally denying all civil rights to slaves, and despite the many deaths, slavery was nonetheless driven by economic reasons to keep slaves alive for their labor power. The Judeocide, by contrast, meant to eradicate all Jews (both as a people and as individuals), and was not driven by economic motives. Historian Charles Pete Banner-Haley observes, "Afrocentrists have taken to proclaiming the Atlantic slave trade as a horrific Holocaust perpetuated by Western Europe. The use of the term and the none too subtle insistence on its gravity regarding the enslavement of Africans are obviously aimed at overshadowing the twentieth century's most glaring historical incidence of humanity's inhumanity." Banner-Haley notes that slavery was "not intentionally genocidal" and "resulted in the creation of a New World Afro-American."[113]

Holocaust historian Yehuda Bauer has attempted to untangle this knot by distinguishing between the terms holocaust and genocide. The term *genocide* was coined by Raphael Lemkin, a Polish-Jewish lawyer, in late 1942 or early 1943, as a form of "denationalization accompanied by selective mass murder" and was later codified with modifications at the Genocide Convention on 9 December 1948, as "any of the following acts committed with the intent to destroy, in whole or in part, a national, ethnical or religious group, as such."[114] Such acts included deliberate physical destruction through mass murder, living conditions calculated to bring about physical destruction in whole or in part, and the prevention of births within the group. If, however, genocide is used to mean the gross denationalization of African blacks in America—that is, the mass destruction of an originating national or ethnic identity, carried out through enslavement, torture, conditions leading to death (during the Middle Passage), and murder—then genocide, in this context, may be understood as signifying this wholesale transformation of African peoples into "New World Afro-Americans," in which the partial destruction of a group (separated from the originating group), as such, has taken place. Holocaust, then, may be regarded as an extreme form of genocide, as Bauer argues, which signifies the intent to physically annihilate every person of the targeted group. Though not a holocaust, recognizing slavery as a form of genocide promotes further recognition of the historical magnitude of the atrocity of slavery, the suffering and injustice it engendered.

THE "HOLOCAUST" BANDWAGON

THE TERM holocaust itself is undergoing a conceptual and ideological transformation in which it refers not only to the Nazi genocide of the Jews, but also, with increasing frequency, to diverse kinds of human suffering. In particular, it enters discussions of moral dimensions and becomes the yardstick by which all evil is measured. There are a number of trends aiming to appropriate the term holocaust for a variety of increasingly disparate causes. Two examples of the most egregious misuses will suffice here. In the first case, there is the attempt by right-wing anti-abortionists to instrumentalize the historical dimensions of both slavery and the Judeocide by equating holocaust with voluntary abortion. In anti-abortion posters displayed all over the campus of the University of Kansas in September 1998, during the week of the Jewish new year, Rosh Hashanah, these banners offered three images: a swastika and a photograph of Holocaust victims headlined "Religious Choice"; abortion photographs headlined "Reproductive Choice"; a photograph of a civil rights-era lynching over the words "Racial Choice." "Abortion is genocide. That's the whole point," said Gregg Cunningham, director of the Los-Angeles-based Center for Bio-Ethical Reform, when campus students were outraged. "Frankly, I'm weary of genocide snobs who focus solely on their causes," he added.[115] The group took the posters to the University of Pennsylvania and had fifteen or twenty additional campus campaigns planned. Cunningham defended the posters' appropriate use of "shock" techniques, while students rightly considered the images a trivialization of history.

In another example, the Christian persecution movement, a new kind of solidarity movement, has sprung up among Christians across the United States who assert that Christians throughout the world have been targets of abuse solely because of their faith. International scholars and some foreign aid groups have said that what is labeled Christian persecution is often far more complex, and where Christian persecution does occurs, it happens in societies where many other religions and ethnicities are also persecuted. The nationwide lobbying of the Persecuted Church, as its followers call it, is exerting an influence on American foreign policy and has succeeded in getting the Senate to pass legislation requiring sanctions against foreign countries that violate the religious rights of its citizens. But an extraordinary aspect of the persecuted church movement is the comparison made between Christian persecution and the Holocaust. The *New York Times* noted in a front-page article, "In church services, in literature and in videos put out by the persecuted church movement, they are likening Christian persecution to the Holocaust. They quote from Anne Frank and Elie Wiesel . . . 'The same thing that happened to the Jews—to the people of the book—is now happening to Christians,' said John Noska, the concrete salesman whose prayer group in Pennsylvania has produced a video on Christian persecution for cable television."[116]

Setting aside the indifference and complicity of the church in the events of the Holocaust, the persecuted Christian movement now exploits the moral authority of the historical disaster in order to position itself as history's latest victims and thus links itself to Christianity's legacy of martyrdom. A crucial difference between persecuted Christians and victimized European Jews, however, is that Christian missionaries have a choice—Jews didn't; martyrs die for their beliefs—Jews died for being born, regardless of any religious or political beliefs they may have held. Even those who were Christian converts were persecuted. As István Deák notes: "Whether religious or irreligious, baptized or unbaptized, submissive or defiant, the Jews were under irrevocable sentence of death; they were victims. To call them martyrs, that is, people who were given a chance to choose between life and death, is to deny the absolute evil of the Nazi system."[117] Thus, what happened to the Jews was neither religious persecution nor martyrdom, but genocide based on a racialist ideology.

CHAPTER TWO

PICTURING THE VANISHED/ TRANSGRESSING THE PRESENT

■

They gathered some twenty *Hasidic* Jews from their homes,
in the robes these wear,
wearing their prayer shawls, too,
and holding prayer books in their hands.
They were led up a hill.
Here they were told to chant their prayers
and raise their hands for help to God
and, as they did so,
the officers poured kerosene under them
and set it on fire.

CHARLES REZNIKOFF
from *Holocaust,* 1975

■

SHIMON ATTIE: *THE WRITING ON THE WALL*

LONG AFTER THE destruction of the Yiddish world in the catastrophe of the Shoah, in an era of widespread assimilation, the question "What is a Jew?" is more difficult than ever to answer. Since World War II, Jewish self-understanding has rested largely upon the memory of genocide and identification with a long history, but it is always subject to external definition. In the words of critical theorist and Jewish ethnographer Jonathan Boyarin, Jewish identity is "marked by a constant tension between self-identification, and identification by and as the Other."[1] Investigating the relationship between the Jews and the ideological construction of Europe, Boyarin observes that the story of Europe has historically excluded the voice of the Jewish collectivity. He notes the continuation of this condition in "the historical European Christian tendency to see living Jews as fossils," and asks, "Is there a Jewish place in Europe, beyond Otherness?"[2] Addressing the question of the place of the Jews in Europe, photographer and installation artist Shimon Attie has attempted to illuminate the problem of Otherness through a series of provocative European installations. His European public projects and their documentation are founded on a post-Shoah examination of national mythologies in relation to the memory of the Jews, and the role of this memory, or its lack, in the construction of national identity.

Attie's best-known installation and photography project, *The Writing on the Wall: Projections in Berlin's Jewish Quarter* (1992–1993), unexpectedly brought the memory of the forgotten Jews of Berlin back into the midst of German daily public life. In *The Writing on the Wall,* Attie projected black and white slides onto architectural locations in former East Berlin, vividly rematerializing the former world of unassimilated East European Jews in the 1920s and 1930s who had lived in the old Jewish quarter known as the *Scheunenviertel.* The project began when Attie, a Jewish American whose grandfather had lived in Berlin, walked the streets of Berlin in 1991 and became alarmed at finding no traces of former Jewish life. "I felt the presence of this lost community very strongly, even though so few visible traces of it remained."[3] "Strangely enough," comments James Young, "it was not the absence of Berlin's lost Jews that Attie felt so strongly, but their presence."[4] By making the presence of the murdered Jews visible to contemporary Germans, Attie stirred a political pot already boiling over with near daily debates and violent incidents on the issue of foreigners in Germany. Following the year-long series of installations, *The Writing on the Wall* was shown through photographs at a number of international museums and galleries, including the Museum of Modern Art in "New Photography 10" (1994–1995) and the Jewish Museum in New York in "The Art of Memory" (1994), and published as a book the same year.

In seeking to revive the presence of the Jews of the Scheunenviertel, Attie took his search for evidence of the Jews of Berlin to a score of archives where he discovered remnants of their lost Yiddish world, and learned that the Scheunenviertel was not only a refuge for *Ostjuden* (Jews from the east) from the former eastern *shtetlach* or villages, but also "a neighborhood of ill repute, where prostitutes and black marketeers plied their trades openly," known to the Yiddish-speaking Jews of Berlin as the *finstere medine* (dark district).[5] It was not this aspect of the quarter that most interested Attie, however, but the Jews themselves, who "continued to dress as they had in the *shtetl,* keeping their beards, forelocks, long coats and fur-trimmed hats" while their storefronts carried signs in Hebrew and Yiddish.[6]

The Scheunenviertel (Barn Quarter) was a Jewish working class district and refuge for Jews who had fled persecution in Poland and Russia. It was located near Alexanderplatz, which once had lain outside the city gates, dominated by barns and cattle sheds. Russian Jews began to arrive in small groups in 1868 to escape the desolation wrought by cholera and famine, but the emigration grew rapidly after the pogroms of 1881. During the depression that followed the economic boom after German unification in 1871, Jews were increasingly identified with the evils of capitalism and blamed for the collapse of the German stock market in 1879. A racist furor ensued in which Jews were beaten in the streets, and the slogan "Do not buy from Jews!" was scrawled on Jewish businesses. Racists demanded harsh measures against the Jews. Heinrich von Treitschke, author of the popular historical work, *History of Germany in the Nineteenth Century* (1879), wrote of the danger represented by the eastern Jews, noting that although their number was small, "over our eastern borders lies an inexhaustible Polish cradle, from it streams year after year a host of hustling second-hand pants peddlers whose children and grandchildren will one day rule Germany's stock market and newspapers."[7] Treitschke and many educated Germans hoped to end the influx of Polish Jews and limit the civil rights of German Jews. Extremists wanted them thrown out altogether. Treitschke asserted that, "The Jews are our misfortune!" a phrase that in 1923 ended up on the masthead of Julius Streicher's racist journal *Der Stürmer.* Tens of thousands of Jewish immigrants from the Russian provinces of Poland arrived in the last decades of the nineteenth century and first decade of the twentieth century (while tens of thousands of others went to London's East End and New York's Lower East Side). As the number of eastern Jews began to rise, some 50 percent were identified as *Schnorrers,* or panhandlers, forced to live on the margins and sell cheap goods. Another 35 percent worked as industrial laborers and were not visible. The remaining fifteen percent became beggars and were most visible, becoming, for Germans, the stereotypical Ostjuden—the lazy unemployed who deserved to be deported.[8] Other stereotypes included *Luftmenschen,* defined as students, artists, and writers who appeared to live by their wits alone and who threatened to "Jewify" German culture while raising the specter of political radicalism. This fear was intensified by the immigration of Russian Jews after the failed revolution of 1905. Thus, "the *Ostjude* became a contradictory figure in the public mind: a corrupt, calculating, and opportunistic trader, a destitute, diseased, and backwards *Schnorrer,* and a radical revolutionary fighting for a Communist utopia."[9] The unifying symbol for these contradictory characteristics was the parasite, or pariah.

The definition of Jews as a pariah people was a Christian legacy. Traditional Christian myths held that Jews were deicides who murdered Christ, and parasites who lived off the misery of others through their commercial activities, even living off the literal blood of Christian children. The hostility of Christians in the early centuries that restricted Jews to the lowest, least profitable, and most despised branches of commerce until the late eighteenth century was reinforced in Germany in particular by the virulent racism of Martin Luther and the Protestant Reformation. Jewish pariahs were traditional Jews, unemancipated and living in their ghettos, subjected to a host of discriminatory laws, forced off the land, barred from guilds, and despised in their roles as moneylenders and peddlers to which they had been consigned. Pious antisemitism, moreover, was dominated by a dislike of the city and a fear of commercial capitalism, both of which were identified with the Jews. In the exemplary setting of the bourgeois revolution, emancipation of the Jews from their ghettos became a benefit of the Enlightenment.

Enlightenment thinkers of the eighteenth century generally believed that no people had fixed or innate traits and that ethnic character was the result of social and historical experience. In Germany the Jews were emancipated in 1871, when the country was unified; in France, Jews were liberated during the Revolution. Known as Les Lumières in France, the Aufklärung in Germany, the Haskala in the Jewish world, and the Enlightenment in English-speaking countries, this emancipation permitted Jews not only to leave the ghettoes but also to become citizens of the nations in which they resided, with concomitant civil rights. As historian Pierre Vidal-Naquet reminds us, however, this ideology is not to be confused with reality: "The reformers did not seek to emancipate the Jews, they were seeking to emancipate *their* Jews, and not everyone, even in their own country, had the right to be treated as such. Thus, the entire question in effect centers on the extent to which the Jews were recognized as having as their vocation no longer to be a nation, in the almost medieval sense of the term—there was a (Jewish) Portuguese nation at Bordeaux and another one at Bayonne—but to be part of the nation, which would soon come to be called the 'Grande Nation,' entering therein under the same heading (in France, for example) as the Protestants."[10] With emancipation, there was an expectation that Jews would become normalized. This meant either abandoning their religion or converting to Christianity. When normalization largely failed, the main threat became the unity of the Jewish people in its dispersed state. Modern antisemitism can be said to have begun with this understanding of the Jew as a citizen of some abstract and independent Jewish nation rather than as the citizen of a single country. The extension of this thinking is the elaboration of a biologic theory that separates the Jews as a people in physiologic terms from the rest of French or German citizenry. It must be remembered that even among Enlightenment philosophers, a case for antisemitism can be made, based on the innumerable texts that call for Jews to be held in contempt, particularly among the writings of Voltaire.

By 1923 there were thousands of people in Germany armed and mobilized under antisemitic slogans. Jews were blamed for the German defeat in 1918, Bolshevism, the Versailles treaty, the Weimar Republic, the black market and inflation. The Weimar Republic was often called the "Jews' Republic."[11] A pogrom took place in 1923 against the eastern Jews in the Scheunenviertel, which was, nonetheless, an unusual event for the time. Looting and rioting occurred over the course of two days during which thousands of young men attacked, robbed, and beat people in the streets, a majority of them Jews. On November 5, four days before Hitler's attempted putsch in Munich, unemployed workers outside an employment office on Alexanderstrasse were told they would receive no relief money that day. They were provoked into riotous action by a rumor that eastern Jews from the neighboring Scheunenviertel had bought up all the relief money in order to lend it at high rates later on. Such rumors were spread, according to the Berlin police, by professional agitators from the Deutsche Herold, a völkisch organization. Within an hour, thousands of unemployed workers descended on the Scheunenviertel and began to loot shops and even private homes, attacking anyone who "looked Jewish." The police looked the other way, arriving late and arresting Jews for their "own protection." By evening the rioting had spread to other parts of the city and did not abate until the next day. The most extensive damage, however, was concentrated in the Scheunenviertel and the majority of assaults were directed against Jews.[12] The social democrats characterized the riots in *Vorwärts* as the culmination of "a calculated agitation by Deutschvölkisch elements against the Ostjuden,"[13] having the character of "an orchestrated pogrom." The liberal *Vossische Zeitung* placed the blame on the nationalist right, noting that the *National Zeitung,* a mouthpiece of heavy industry, had for years counseled violence against the Ostjuden in the Scheunenviertel. The newspaper pointed out that the barons of heavy industry profited the most from the collapse of the mark while fanning the flames of antisemitism to scapegoat the Jews. The *National Zeitung* disputed the charges that its articles about the "Jewish menace" had provoked the pogrom in the Scheunenviertel, and suggested instead that the attacks were the spontaneous eruption of rage over the "unscrupulous profiteering of the Jews in a time of widespread misery."[14] Thus the right simply reiterated its charges against the Jews, exploiting the crisis.

The large Jewish population in Berlin was split over the meaning and implications of the Scheunenviertel riot. Most Jewish commentators saw it as "a confirmation of warnings they had been making since the war about the likely outcome of unrelenting agitation against the Jews" and they were "unanimous in condemning the political factions that channeled people's economic misery into racist attacks."[15] But they differed on the lessons to be drawn. The Zionists asserted that the attacks proved that Jews were no longer safe in Germany and that the politics of assimilation and accommodation were bankrupt. They argued that the cultural line dividing Ostjuden and native Jews and the desire to see the Scheunenviertel pogrom as a local event directed only at eastern Jews should be rejected. "This was not an Ostjudenpogrom," said their organ, the *Jüdische Rundschau,* "it was a Judenpogrom."[16] They warned assimilated Jews that turning their backs on the Ostjuden would not avoid the hatred extended to all Jews in Germany. The most extreme right wing of assimilationists in Berlin, the nationalist-German-Jewish faction, argued in their organ, *Der nationaldeutsche Jude,* that the Ostjuden had partly brought the trouble on themselves by pursuing unethical currency transactions and suggested the need for native Jews to proclaim their Germanness and loyalty to the Fatherland more passionately. Orthodox German Jewry criticized the Zionist and nationalist extremes of the Jewish community in their organ, the *Israelit,* calling on Jews to turn inward and rekindle their religious faith rather than enter the political fray. The main organization of the assimilationists, the Central Association of German Citizens of the Jewish Faith (Zentralverein deutscher Staatsbürger jüdischen Glaubens), counseled patience and forbearance: "If we exercise self-control, do not come across as too ostentatious but nonetheless bear our Jewishness with pride, we have no reason to fear the future."[17] Historian David Clay Large notes that these responses from the Jewish community were "writ large" in the catastrophe to come, with native Jews making distinctions between Ostjuden and themselves, hoping that as native citizens, their record of patriotism and loyalty would save them in the end.[18]

The high visibility of the Jews in the Scheunenviertel is important to Attie's project as the only means we have for identifying them in a country where assimilated Jews were effectively invisible. The atypical Orthodox Jew thus becomes the paradigmatic German Jew and a stand-in for all Jews.[19] The Weimar archive itself is seen to construct the German Jew as an Ostjude, and Attie's photographs both double this effect and call attention to it.

Focusing on street life, Attie slide-projected portions of the old photographs onto the original or nearby architectural locations and left them on view for one or two evenings where they were visible to neighborhood residents, passers-by, and traffic, briefly bringing the eastern Jews of Berlin to life again. Using prewar Berlin city maps, Attie found nearly one-quarter of the original locations in the current neighborhood just east of Berlin's Alexanderplatz; others had been destroyed. Attie photographed the installations of the nighttime projection so that the project continues to exist as a body of color photographs, created through time exposures lasting from three to four minutes. For Attie, however, the acts of remembrance initiated by the project were the installations themselves, which included a performative and interactive quality that the photographs only document. "The point was to intervene in a public space and project right onto those spaces," Attie has remarked. "By attempting to renegotiate the relationship between past and present events, the aim of the project was to interrupt the collective processes of denial and forgetting."[20]

The contrast between the darkroom-enhanced color saturation of the modern city in Attie's photographs and the black and white archival fragments inserted into this cityscape produce jarring juxtapositions of past and present that induce the specter of the intervening sixty years. Signs of the contemporary metropolis appear more incongruous than ever in relation to the Jewishness of the Ostjuden in the Scheunenviertel. Their visibility as different in appearance, dress, language, and custom, in short, their seeming unassimilability is emphasized by the black and white of the photographs set against the color background of the city, highlighting the old-fashioned obsolescence of the former against the sleek and glittering modernity of the latter. The Jews peer out as from a lost, irretrievable past, their otherness irredeemable and exotic. In *The Imaginary Jew,* Alain Finkielkraut observes, "And so the Jewish people have been made to suffer a double death: death by murder, and death by oblivion," pointing in particular to our continued inability to accept the traditional observant Jew as one of "us": "Collective memory reserves space only for those who look like we do, or for museum artifacts or circus freaks . . . portraying the actions and gestures of the ancient Hasidim, pathos is de rigueur . . . . By reducing Jewish life to something archaic, the Holocaust is implicitly defined as a rapid historical advance. Haste may be cruel and inhuman, but weren't they victims—those anemic scholars who studied, interpreted and chanted nothing but the sacred word—of progress itself?"[21] Indeed, the strangeness of the traditional Jews in the Scheunenviertel is heightened by Attie's formal distancing techniques. The culture of before is doubly displaced, both by its destruction in the Holocaust and its obliteration through forgetfulness. The Jews of the Scheunenviertel appear as relics from a past so antiquated and outmoded that their disappearance may be read as a historical inevitability. The idea that the failure of the eastern Jews to thrive was ultimately a result of their inability to adapt to the modern world was integral to the view of the Jew as a pariah. Even among assimilated German Jews, the Ostjuden were regarded as anachronistic. In the 1920s, the writer Joseph Roth described a "strange sad ghetto world" without the cars and lights of western Berlin; he saw "grotesque eastern figures" wearing long black caftans who seemed like "an avalanche of disaster and dirt, growing in volume and rolling irresistibly from the east over Germany."[22]

And yet—what have been the fruits of progress? Progress itself is ironized in Attie's photograph *Wilhelm-Pieck-Strasse 40,* which slide-projects a sign of a Jewish hospital, the *Israelitisches Krankenheim,* onto a wall above a contemporary outdoor cigarette machine. Critic Kenneth Baker describes the "special horror" of the transformation in German society between the wars evoked by this juxtaposition: "It is clear enough that both the Jewish hospital and the cigarette machine connote mortality. But where one is a symbol of charity and segregated community, the other evokes a society made safe for exploitation, unified by susceptibility to addictions."[23] Another example is *Mulackstrasse 37, Former Jewish Residents (ca. 1932),* which depicts two Jewish boys sitting on the curb (Plate 1). The top edge has been painted out on the slide, but the crumbled corners at the bottom are left visible, allowing the legs and feet of the boys to spill onto the street in a milkflow of projected light. The archival photo is projected onto architecture on which a contemporary graffiti worker has scrawled the words, "Was der Krieg verschonte" (What the war has spared). The image presents the spectral depiction of the boys against the building they might once have inhabited, conjuring a sense of the easy destructibility of flesh compared to brick and stone, and with it, the easy destructibility of memory. Scaffolding indicates the renovation of the building, while the eerie Alexanderplatz television tower needle in the background alludes to the dawn of the cold war era and the technological competition between the Soviet Union and the United States. Still missing is the history of the boys and the events that occurred on Mulackstrasse that led to their disappearance. While brick and stone are reconstructed, the photo seems to suggest, the archives of memory locked within them are left to crumble away. Progress means a loss of history and memory; the scaffold and the mound of fresh earth near the building provide "an intimation that excavation and rebuilding will further bury Berlin's past."[24] Attie's reconstruction rescues the boys from oblivion but not anonymity.

The half sentence of graffiti evokes an irony that is radically altered in another image, a slide projection of a former kosher butcher's shop and laundry (1930) in which the rest of the words are visible, forming the complete sentence, "Was der Krieg verschonte, überlebt im Sozialismus nicht!" (What the war has spared does not survive in socialism!) Written after the fall of the Berlin wall in 1989, the graffiti

Fig. 1. Shimon Attie, *Mulackstrasse 37, Former Kosher Butcher Shop and Laundry (1930)*, from *The Writing on the Wall*, Berlin, 1992. Courtesy Jack Shainman Gallery, New York.

adds yet another layer of history onto the image (fig. 1). Further along on another wall, and visible in another picture, someone has written, "Der Kampf geht weiter" (The struggle continues). Attie's project, produced in the immediate period after the fall of the Berlin Wall, reminds us of the renewed focus on Berlin as the emblematic capital of Germany and the debate over how to memorialize the murder of European Jews that had just begun.

Mulackstrasse 32, Former Jewish Residents and Hebrew Reading Room (1931), projects an image of a young mother and her two children on the street as indigent paupers next to a former Hebrew reading room, an emblem of intellectual labor and scholarship (fig. 2). Here, Sander Gilman's work on the myth of Jewish superior intelligence, a myth that first became popular in the nineteenth century (and continues to this day), also has a bearing on the stereotypes of difference.[25] In Gilman's analysis, Jewish superior intelligence, considered strongest among Ashkenazi Jews from Eastern Europe, is seen either as false intelligence that is really a form of economic craftiness, or else a hidden form of compensation for physical weakness and, perhaps

Fig. 2. Shimon Attie, *Mulackstrasse 32, Former Jewish Residents and Hebrew Reading Room (1931)*, from *The Writing on the Wall*, Berlin, 1992. Courtesy Jack Shainman Gallery, New York.

most significantly, a lack of virtue. The lack of virtue may be read as an inability to accomplish worldly success. Thus, the destitute on the street and the absent scholars for whom the Hebrew reading room exists, present both sides of the coin: the apparent absence on the part of the Jewish mother and her sons of any superior intelligence with which to prevent their economic victimization, and the failure of virtue on the part of the intellectuals to save the Jews from poverty. Like the boys of Mulackstrasse 37, whose existence appears incongruous with the space-age of the television tower needle, this failure may be read as an absence of both modernity and true "masculinity" among the Jews, for demasculinization, as Gilman shows, became a constituent part of the image of Jewish intelligence, signaling the feminization of eastern Jews, in particular, and thus their weakness and victimization. Finkielkraut captures both aspects of the demasculinized Jewish stereotype in his reference to "anemic scholars" who were victims of "progress itself."[26]

Revealing class differences in the Jewish community, *Linienstrasse 137, Police Raid on Former Jewish Residents (1920)* reproduces the archival image of a police raid on Jewish residents, in which everyone stands around calmly, posing for the camera, waiting for something (Plate 2). A group of working-class Jews peers at the photographer with varying degrees of concern and apprehension; a man at the far right wears the apron of a butcher. At the center, however, and standing apart from the group at the right, is what appears to be a well-dressed bourgeois Jew, wearing a hat and holding a cigarette—the landlord of the building, perhaps, where the others live as tenants or work in the shops. He betrays no apprehension at all; on the contrary, he seems fairly secure that it will all blow over soon enough, a view shared by many even after the Nazis came to power.

The continuities and ruptures of time are also evident in *Almstadtstrasse (formerly Grenadierstrasse)/Corner Schendelgasse, Religious Book Salesman (1930)* (Plate 3). The archival image of the bookseller is made to fit inside the space of a doorway, presenting a picture reminiscent of fifteenth- or sixteenth-century Northern paintings. The iconography of the hand-carved desk and books with a figure hunched over it recalls Jan van Eyck's *St. Jerome in His Study,* while the bookseller's beard brings to mind the lovingly detailed beard of Joseph in Robert Campin's *Merode Altarpiece.* The crumbling building surrounding the bookseller appears continuous with the archival image of sixty years earlier, but the building next door is of another era, constructed with the typically inexpensive materials and esthetics of the Stalinist period, with an unexpected display of two simple modernist compositions in the upper story windows. Between the buildings, a steep recession leads to a single Greek column, framed by strips of deep blue sky, conjuring a Mannerist sense of perspectival distortion and displacement. Attie's work produces a progressive displacement of time, of the past surging forward to the present in a compression of successive eras. One critic felt "as if myriad and often morbid layers of German history were suddenly clearly visible"; another noted "the sense that the surfaces of the scenes themselves are being peeled back like old wallpaper to reveal the history buried beneath them."[27] The notion that histories have been papered over continues with the gentrification and renovation of these former East Berlin neighborhoods. As time passes, the traditional Jew in Germany becomes increasingly buried and forgotten, a phantasm of German memory.

But in the photos they are very much alive. The fulfillment of the emancipation process that had begun during the Enlightenment occurred during the Weimar era, and included the liberatory effects of the Russian Revolution. The majority of Attie's images evoke the fugitive nature of this "golden age" for Jews in Germany in the form of briefly illuminated historical phantoms who seem to be "stepping out of a third dimension."[28] In some photographs the fragile archival images, already indistinct, are projected onto textured architectural backgrounds that render them even more difficult to read, while the people pictured are engaged in ordinary, banal actions. In *Steinstrasse 22, Former Jewish Residents (1932),* for example, two men lean their heads together in a discussion on the street while a third looks on (fig. 3).

Fig. 3. Shimon Attie, *Steinstrasse 22, Former Jewish Residents (1932)*, from *The Writing on the Wall*, Berlin, 1992. Courtesy Jack Shainman Gallery, New York.

The figures are blurred, vague, ambiguous—impossible to identify. They are present in an ephemeral haze of white light with jagged edges. Attie actually painted out the edges of the archival image right on his slides, projecting and repainting again and again until he got the shape and effect he wanted, of the past "burning through the facade."[29] Illegibility itself becomes a metaphor for the Ostjuden—foreign, exotic, unassimilable, anonymous—both then and now. In *Joachimstrasse/Corner Auguststrasse, Former Jewish Resident (1931),* Attie makes the dichotomy between observant Jews and gentiles of Weimar-era Berlin more explicit, showing an Orthodox Jew in phylacteries sitting in a window in prayer beneath a white Star of David. Across the street, three rows of illuminated window mullions in the form of crucifixes seem to march up the street like a crusading army surrounding the lone star in a dawn raid (fig. 4).

A Jewish record shop appears as an eerily abandoned storefront in *Alte Schönhauser Strasse, Former Jewish Record Shop (ca. 1930)* (fig. 5). Though a menorah stands at the bottom of the window, signifying observant practice, it is overshad-

Fig. 4. Shimon Attie, *Joachimstrasse/Corner Auguststrasse, Former Jewish Resident (1931)*, from *The Writing on the Wall*, Berlin, 1992. Courtesy Jack Shainman Gallery, New York.

owed by the large sign "Jüd Schallplatten" (Jewish records), flanked by two record albums on white squares mounted in the window. Any thoughts of musical liveliness this image might conjure up are immediately dampened by the heavy gloom of the dark, foreboding atmosphere, the peeling posters on the wall, the rapidly receding street around the building, and the virtual absence of life. The forlorn urban landscape only heightens the sense of an expunged Jewish presence.

Following the March Reichstag elections after Hitler came to power, the Nazis organized a boycott of Jewish businesses and the vandalization of Jewish shops on 1 April 1933 in Berlin and throughout Germany. On 9 April, the Storm Troopers (*Sturmabteilungen,* or SA) raided the Scheunenviertel and arrested many Jews. Eastern Jews were the first objects of German Jew-hatred, and were also the first to be sent off to concentration camps. Exclusionary laws reintroduced discrimination against the Jews throughout Germany for the first time since their emancipation in 1871. The closing of Jewish shops and the dismissal of Jewish lawyers, judges, university professors, and doctors began.[30] Attie's photographs evoke the

Fig. 5. Shimon Attie, *Alte Schoenhauser Strasse, Former Jewish Record Shop (ca. 1930)*, from *The Writing on the Wall*, Berlin, 1992. Courtesy Jack Shainman Gallery, New York.

sordid history to come through an imaginative reconstruction of the historical archive.

THE ARTIST AND THE ARCHIVE

Ernst van Alphen has challenged the strict dichotomy between historical and imaginative discourse in Holocaust representation.[31] Though long discredited theoretically, documentary realism, with its old associations with guarantees of objectivity and transparency, has been reactivated in the field of Holocaust representation and associated with historical accuracy. This has led to a hierarchy of genres, in which historical discourse—in the form, primarily, of testimony—is regarded as more objective, while imaginative discourse is seen as more subjective, and therefore intrinsically less trustworthy. But documentary realism, including testimony, cannot be separated from the interpretation of events; on the contrary, the experience of history depends on cultural and narrative frames in order for it to be processed and narrated. Memory itself is produced by these narrative frames into which experience is ordered. Experience that has not been processed cannot be narrated, constituting trauma, not memory. Thus, documentary is a form of subjective truth. On this basis, van Alphen observes that the hierarchical opposition between history and imagination may be seen as structuring another opposition between forms of representations, that of "objective cognitive remembrance versus aesthetic pleasure and distraction."[32] The rhetorical use of documentary realism within the realm of the imaginative, however, produces an "undermining or hollowing out" of this opposition.[33] Attie's work produces just such a challenge to the hierarchy of Holocaust genres through his use of the archive, as a form of documentary realism, within the realm of the imaginative. His manipulation of the archive demonstrates once again the constructedness of realism, in which the original context cannot be recaptured and new meanings or possibilities are made available to the viewer. The act of referring to a factual reality through the use of the archive, while allowing the artist to qualify himself as a historian, nonetheless leaves room for the imaginative evocation of the Holocaust in ways that are unavailable to the historian, but which are just as powerful in the truth they convey. In Michael Rothberg's terms, a form of traumatic realism is produced, evoking the ordinary and the extraordinary simultaneously.

The same can be said for Christian Boltanski's work, which shares concerns with that of Attie, though the latter at times has been promoted as closer to the documentary tradition of realism, avoiding the sentimentality sometimes ascribed to Boltanski's work. But Attie's pictures are no more realist than Boltanski's; they both employ, in different ways, the trappings of realism and the archive to achieve historical effects in imaginative ways. Yet neither can actually reproduce the past. As van Alphen suggests, Boltanski's works appear to "embody the promise of the presence of the past" without ever fulfilling that promise, just as the historian cannot fulfill this promise; instead Boltanski's works serve as a critique of the historical method and of "the domestication of the past."[34] Boltanski himself was also drawn to the old Jewish quarter of Berlin, where he created *Missing House* in 1990, a project in a conspicuously empty lot in the middle of a narrow street. On the walls of the buildings that flank the missing house, Boltanski installed plaques with the names, dates of residence (ending during the war), and professions of the last inhabitants of the destroyed house. The nameplates remain today.[35]

Similarly, Attie's examination of prewar Jewish life proceeds from the perspective of the postwar observer, aware of the stereotype of the Jew as pariah, the long history of German antisemitism, the limits of assimilation, and the German inability to remember the Jews. The reminder of thriving prewar Jewish forms of life, salvaged from the archives, is a kind of instrumental realism that brings historical awareness to contemporary consciousness, while the reminder that this is a long-vanished culture or component of German culture may be seen as a form of sentimental realism. The combined effects of instrumental and sentimental realism, however, provide Attie's photographs with their intellectual and emotional power, rescuing them from an aestheticization of history that merely reinforces the otherness of the Jew. Read in light of photographer and theorist Allan Sekula's partisan contention that "the archive has to be read from below, from a position of solidarity with those displaced, deformed, silenced, or made invisible,"[36] Attie, like Boltanski, succeeds in reading the archive from below, in solidarity with those who have been made invisible and "interrupts the collective processes of denial and forgetting" by constructing a living archive that implicates those of us in the present as agents for the future.[37]

Attie used ten different archives for his Berlin project: press archives, government archives of the city of Berlin and state archives, Jewish Community archives, the private archive of Eike Geisel, a now-deceased political scientist, and the private photo albums of Jewish families in Berlin. Most of the photographs he employs, however, are anonymous press photos.[38] Sekula has suggested that the photographic archive constitutes a "territory of images" whose "meanings are up for grabs."[39] While new meanings are made available, the original context and use of the photograph are always lost and can even be made invisible. The photo agency files for newspapers, no longer useful for topical journalism and turned into archives, give us no insight into their original uses. Were the photographs of Ostjuden on the street in the Scheunenviertel a form of contemporary visual ethnography? Police surveillance? The use of old file photos makes us aware that there is no easy and unproblematic retrieval of the past from the superior vantage point of the present.

Though these photographs may reveal many things, we cannot suddenly comprehend the complexity and reality of prewar Jewish life simply by looking at these photographs. Yet Attie's images are not designed to be read as rendering history through representation; rather, they must be read as reversing the documentary claim to pictorial history by showing us its erosion, its faded trace, its futureless future. Even as Attie's project addresses itself to the origins of the photographs, attempting to recontextualize them by projecting them on or near their original sites, at the same time his photographs make apparent the impossibility of recontextualization. The real impact of these photographs lies elsewhere. By inserting the past into the visual field of the present, the temporary installations and resulting color photographs present jarring juxtapositions of past and present that powerfully raise the specter of the intervening sixty years and the resulting contemporary attitudes toward foreigners. The unpictured antisemitic terror that occurred between then and now is all the more ominously present, producing not a documentary claim to the representation of history, but photographs that derive their effect from what is omitted. By indirection, allusiveness, and paradox, *The Writing on the Wall* presents the loss of history and the irremediable damage to identity. At the same time, the project of reconstructed memory becomes a site of resistance. For whom, after all, does the writing on the wall signify and act as a warning? For us, in the present, as much as for those in the past.

By picturing the most visible Jews in Germany, and having them stand in for all Jews, the Eastern European Jew becomes the universal Jew; yet by using the less representative image of the orthodox Jew, Attie also presents the ambiguous otherness of the Jew, reproducing the illegibility of the forgotten Ostjuden, erasing individual identity, and reinscribing the foreignness of the collectivity. In this way the photographs allude to the preconditions for annihilating anonymous masses of people. The project stops short, however, of reenacting the ideology of the perpetrators in which objectification of the subject is followed by their disappearance. Instead, Attie frames the period leading up to the antisemitic terror with the contemporary aftermath of that history, which keeps the loss and its implications present.

The images heighten our awareness of distance and loss by providing two simultaneous points of view. As viewers, we identify with the experience of photographic authority and the viewpoint of the camera. Here, the authority of the camera in the archival image is in dialogue with the greater authority of Attie's camera. Allan Sekula has observed, in looking at historical pictures, that the authority of the camera "characteristically veers between nostalgia, horror, and an overriding sense of the exoticism of the past, its irretrievable otherness for the viewer in the present."[40] Attie's images exaggerate the experience of nostalgia and horror as well as exoticism and irretrievable otherness by embedding the archival images in contemporary landscapes. The meaning of the photographs then depends on understanding the historical relationship between the present and the past. The body of the archive, which carries within it an "unknowable weight," to borrow from a phrase from Derrida, is transformed in a new relation to the contemporary observer. Attie, therefore, may be seen as continuing the Holocaust archive into the present in an act of "archivization" that Derrida describes as "a movement of the promise and of the future no less than of recording the past."[41]

"Memory," writes Pierre Nora, "is in a permanent state of evolution, open to the dialectic of recollection and of amnesia, unaware of its successive deformation, vulnerable to all the ways in which it is used and manipulated, susceptible to long periods of latency and of revitalization."[42] In the context of the rise of a neo-Nazi movement, especially in former East Germany, and continued acts of racist terror against foreigners, the covert fear and continued antipathy toward Jews is dramatized by the reception of Attie's work. Attie reports that at first most people responded positively with curiosity or outright fascination. One man emotionally recounted to Attie how his Jewish grandfather, whom he'd never known, was deported to Auschwitz. On another occasion, a teenage boy offered to help and kept Attie company for a few evenings. But as the year progressed and economic conditions in East Berlin deteriorated, reactions grew aggressive and hostile. One resident, seeing the projection on his apartment of a Jew praying under a Star of David, called the police and protested that his neighbors would think he was Jewish. Another shouted down from his fifth-floor apartment, ordering Attie to stop his projections of the Jewish record store on a building across the street. He threatened to douse Attie and his equipment with water, which he then did. Another incident occurred while a German state television news team was filming a report on Attie's project for a nightly news program. As Attie projected an image of a former Hebrew bookstore onto its original site, a middle-aged man rushed out of the building toward Attie and the film crew, shouting, "My father purchased this building fair and square from Mr. Jacob in 1938." When Attie asked the man whether he knew what had happened to this Mr. Jacob after 1938, the man shot back, "Mr. Jacob was a multimillionaire and moved to New York." And then he added, "One of my best friends is Nina Rosenblatt." The threatened resident responded in a literal way to Attie's symbolic reclaiming of the bookstore. In the final three months of the project, Attie was harassed and threatened in some way almost every evening.[43] Thus, the present is not merely a frame for the past; the intricate relationship between the two, with its painful traces and belated recognitions, reveals the past to be continually riven by the concerns of the present, which constitutes a site of resistance to contemporary rationalizations for the past.[44]

The Berlin press also commented on the impact of the project on residents of the former Scheunenviertel. One reviewer noted the "mixed feelings" evoked by seeing the layers of German history exposed on the building facades; another remarked on the fact that former residents of the Scheunenviertel who might have managed to survive the concentration camps did not return to the quarter after 1945, leaving no one to tell its stories. He noted that most current residents of the area had no idea of the quarter's history or knew what it had looked like before the war and were provoked to consider it for the first time as a result of Attie's project.

THE PARIAH AND THE PARVENU

After *The Writing on the Wall* in Berlin was completed, Attie produced another series of installations that explored the image of the most representative German Jew, the parvenu. If the pariah in prewar Germany was generally an Eastern Jew, characterized by his rootlessness, mobility, and predisposition for commercial activities, alongside this figure, poor and visible in his unassimilated difference, was the parvenu, who labored under the illusion that he might be admitted into the ranks of the ruling classes by rejecting his own identity and tradition. Made up of leading citizens, bankers and financiers, a few influential industrialists, doctors and lawyers, journalists and cultural workers, liberal and left-wing politicians, this group of prominent assimilated Jews in these important areas enhanced their visibility despite their attempts at integration, and encouraged fears of Jewish domination. Antisemitism grew in response to the heightened success and visibility of assimilated Jews in the Weimar Republic. For a short time at least, there was a powerful renaissance of Jewish culture in Germany until the crisis of the Depression hit in 1929–1930 and antisemitism spread beyond the radical and traditional right. While the unassimilated Jews of the Scheunenviertel produced one kind of renaissance of Jewish culture, based on a thriving infrastructure of Yiddish-language community newspapers and institutions, assimilated German Jews participated more fully in mainstream society and rose to positions of prominence within the arts, sciences, professions and politics.

In *Trains I* and *Trains II* (1994–1995), Attie and his collaborator, Mathias Maile, projected more than four hundred monumental portraits of former assimilated Jewish residents of Hamburg and Dresden in the train stations of the city centers from which they were deported to their deaths in concentration camps, or from which they fled for their lives. In Hamburg, Attie was limited by the city government to hanging portraits from the station's ceilings for *Trains I.* Railroad authorities did not permit him to project images directly onto the trains or train tracks, as he had requested, because of specious fears that train drivers "might mistake the projections for real people" or be "blinded" by the slide projection beams, even though the projections would be coming from a forty-five degree angle above and behind the trains so that blinding was impossible. These restrictions, Attie felt, radically altered and compromised the project.[45]

Trains II opened at the Dresden Train Station on 9 November 1993, on the anniversary of Kristallnacht. Slide projections of former Jewish citizens of Dresden,

Fig. 6 *(top)*. Shimon Attie, Slide projection of former persecuted Dresden Jewish citizens, Dresden Central Train Station, from *Trains II*, 1993. Courtesy Jack Shainman Gallery, New York.

Fig. 7 *(right)*. Shimon Attie, Slide projection of Yiddish newspaper *The Future*, November 1923 issue, Dresden Central Train Station, from *Trains II*, 1993. Courtesy Jack Shainman Gallery, New York.

borrowed from the private archives of Jewish families in Dresden, were slide-projected onto trains, tracks, and station walls (fig. 6); in addition, the front page of a 1923 Yiddish-language newspaper with the English title *The Future* was projected onto the floor of the station near the main information board (fig. 7). For a period of two weeks, "images of handsome, smartly dressed young and middle-aged men and women shone brightly from the rafters of the station; other images of sad-eyed Jews peered up at travelers from the tracks, or stared down rebukingly from the walls, or confronted travelers face to face from the sides of trains," reminding travelers that on such train platforms and tracks, the Jews whose faces they saw "began to die."[46] The installation was on view at the height of a wave of neo-Nazi attacks against foreigners in Germany, many of which took place in or near Dresden.

But the monumental portraits of former professional and assimilated Jews were indistinguishable from gentile German citizens and unrecognizable as Jews to the contemporary population. In the Hamburg installation, a curious passerby asked Attie whether they were the pictures of the German Railway founders, causing him to realize that the people in the photographs could not be easily identified as Jews, and to mount large informational posters near the images. Despite the convergence of the photographs with the iconic symbolism of trains and train tracks, nobody could figure out who they were. There are no identifying characteristics. Precisely the unrecognizability of assimilated Jews compelled explanation and this didactic necessity rendered the project less successful than the Berlin project. In Dresden Attie put up identifying signs with the following text:

> Who are the people appearing in this station?
> Where do they come from?
> What do they want?
> They are former Jewish citizens of Dresden who were persecuted during national socialism [sic]. Most were deported on trains to the death camps, while others managed to emmigrate [sic] while there was still time.
> They are here to remind us of their fate, and to ask us to reflect on the current wave of hate sweeping Germany today.

Linking the victims directly to their fate, Attie inserts the past into the framework of the present in a far more pointed and obvious way. Yet the very obscurity of the project, which provoked the necessity of identifying signs, gives it a certain irony that highlights the disparity between a culture that once contained many Jews and the one that has taken its place. The very people once thought to be poisoning the body of the nation today look just like good Germans, while new waves of hatred target those whose difference is more obvious. The projection of *The Future* evokes the dark irony more explicitly, not only for most prewar Jews who didn't survive to see one, but also for the foreigners in Germany today, such as the Roma and Sinti (Gypsies), the Turks, Asians, Africans and Eastern Europeans, who are subject to sweeping forms of discrimination.

The German press commented on the resistance felt by many members of the public toward Attie's project. *The Dresdner Zeitung* noted that some travelers did not notice the black and white projections at all; one voyager joked that he wondered if they were farejumpers who had been arrested; his companion thought they were portraits of well-known personalities. Another thought the photos came close to being propaganda. The reviewer concludes, "Many, including the elderly, are not interested in the past, because they do not feel it concerns them. Or they do not want to see the contemporary problems."[47] The *Sächsische Zeitung* characterized a widespread sentiment as, "This happened so long ago. What do we, those born later, still have to do with it?" The reviewer comments, "The walls against memory grow higher" and describes the confrontation with the return of the disappeared as "shocking."[48] Perhaps the shock resides in the call to contemporary conscience beyond the mourning of an unalterable past.

Before the future was over for prewar Jews, the logic of assimilation meant that the parvenu Jew wanted to be accepted, or at least to be potentially acceptable, to antisemites. Therefore the parvenu, ironically, could not tolerate the Ostjuden, whose totalizing appearance of Jewish otherness undermined all his efforts at integration. Antisemites themselves preferred the Orthodox ghetto Jew to the parvenus, whose secularism and success contradicted two important myths about the Jew. The first was the religious myth of fundamentalist Christians who claimed that Jews clung to empty religious ritual. The second was the racist myth of the superiority of Germanic blood. The very existence of assimilated, secular Jews made it necessary to supplement traditional Christian myths with the racism of blood. "Liberalism" was denounced by racists as an "emanation of the Jewish spirit," and was attributed to assimilated, secular Jews as part of a drive to destroy Christianity and dominate society.[49] When Jewry was the topic of Hitler's lectures, attendance at his meetings in the 1920s soared.[50] It must have seemed intolerable to conservatives in prewar Germany that instead of Germany colonizing the East, large numbers of dirty Ostjuden came to Germany, either parasitically feeding off German society as pariahs, or, perhaps even worse, adopting German dress, language, and manners, and prominently integrating themselves into German cultural, intellectual, and economic life.

SITES UNSEEN

ATTIE'S QUEST TO bring the history of the Holocaust into the present as a site of resistance against contemporary atrocities continued in major installation projects in Copenhagen, Amsterdam, Cologne, and Krakow in the mid-1990s, which are collectively titled *Sites Unseen.* In Copenhagen, *Portraits of Exile* (June-July 1995) commemorated the fifty-year anniversary of the end of World War II and the liberation of Denmark from Nazi occupation. It both celebrates the Danish water rescue of thousands of Jews in 1943 and questions Denmark's far more ambivalent policies toward boat refugees from the Balkans and elsewhere today. Attie's project took the form of nine light boxes, each measuring 1.8 meters by 1.6 meters, about ten meters apart, with transparencies (dura-trans) submerged under water in the Borsgraven Canal surrounding the Danish Parliament building. The transparencies, parallel to the water surface where waves lap gently over the faces, show portraits of Danish Jews rescued during the war, as well as contemporary refugees (fig. 8). A Bosnian Muslim refugee, for example, is overlaid with the image of *Flotel Europa,* a notorious, floating hotel ship overcrowded with refugees waiting for asylum, some of them waiting for years, and moored just one canal away from the installation. Portraits are superimposed on maps of escape routes, passport entry visas, yellow stars, and fishing boats involved in the rescues of both eras, casting light, both figuratively and literally, on the less than heroic events of today by framing them with the events of the past. Even those events, utilized to construct the nation as an ideal refuge, elide less noble acts, such as Denmark's refusal to grant asylum to thousands of Jews attempting to flee Nazi Germany

Fig. 8. Shimon Attie, Installation shot, present-day refugee with dormitory ship (*Flotel Europa*) used to house refugees in Copenhagen harbor, from *Portraits of Exile*, Copenhagen, 1995. Dura-trans photograph mounted on light box submerged one meter under water, Borsgraven Canal. Courtesy Jack Shainman Gallery, New York.

before the war. To that extent, the present course of Denmark is consistent with their prewar policy. Denmark, of course, was not alone in taking this position, but as the preeminent rescuer nation, the complications of the past, alluded to in Attie's six-week project, raise questions about the complexities of humanitarian motives and the construction of national identity.

The Cologne project, *Brick by Brick* (November 1995), a project of the Cologne Kunstverein, also brings to light past history in the context of present events. Every year, one of Europe's most important commercial art events, *Art Cologne,* takes place, as it happens, on the anniversary of Kristallnacht, in a building that was once used as a slave labor camp and deportation site for Cologne's Jews, Roma and Sinti, and others who were persecuted. The massive Rheinhalle was also used to store furniture and goods confiscated from the victims; these goods were then auctioned to members of the Nazi party whose houses suffered damage from Allied bombing raids. During *Art Cologne 1995,* Attie projected images of furniture and other household items commonly found in middle-class German-Jewish households during the 1930s and 1940s onto the huge brick columns leading to the main entrance of the fair building, including images of a Singer sewing machine, a late-nineteenth-century commode, a Bauhaus menorah, and other objects whose design and period of production collectors and connoisseurs would recognize. Attie and his collaborator, Mathias Maile, passed out a handbill to visitors at the fair that pointed out the nefarious, complex, and unacknowledged past of the Cologne fair building. They reproduced an announcement for one of the furniture auctions held during the war, which included the information that at the end of 1942, a satellite camp of Buchenwald was established on the fair grounds, supplying approximately one thousand slave laborers to the nearby Rhenish factories.

Attie's installation places a dark cloud over the freewheeling commerce of contemporary antiques collectors, whose interest in provenance is minimal, raising the possibility that a table or a piece of silver bought during the war may have once belonged to a deported Jewish family. The project taints all such objects as possible emblems of death and complicity in the national disgrace of genocide, transforming any given object "from mere memento into an accusing memento mori."[51] The forgetfulness over provenance further converges with the forgetfulness of history in *Art Cologne,* evidenced through the choice of date for the annual festivities. On 9 November 1938, Kristallnacht became the most extensive orgy of destruction of Jewish property, businesses, and synagogues in Germany, with more than twenty thousand Jews arrested and dragged off to concentration camps. When the Berlin wall fell on 9 November 1989, Walter Momper, mayor of West Berlin, triumphantly announced, "The ninth of November will become part of history!" Clearly, the mayor had already forgotten the previous significance of this date. Enzo Traverso observes, "Nearly three generations born during and after World War II are confronted by the contradictions that spring from a double impossibility: the impossibility of remembering and the impossibility of forgetting."[52]

Attie's project *The Neighbor Next Door* (December 1995), funded by the Paradox Foundation in Amsterdam, addresses a nation known for its tolerance toward the Jewish community. Because of famous cases of hidden Jews, such as Anne Frank, the mythology of the "sheltering" Dutch has developed. Though there was an important Dutch resistance movement, and many hidden Jews, there were also those who collaborated with the Nazis and informed on their Jewish neighbors, including the Franks. More than 80 percent, an unusually high proportion of the Jewish population, was deported from Holland during the war, though this statistic is complicated by the difficulties of living in hiding within such dense urban populations during wartime scarcity. Today, an estimated 100,000 illegal immigrants are also in hiding in Amsterdam, fearing deportation, while the Netherlands grapples with the issue of meeting the needs of immigrants under a strained system of social services and resources.

The Neighbor Next Door was sited at three of the addresses on the canal street *Prinsengracht* where Jews and others were hidden during the war, including Anne Frank's family and an estimated 155 other groups. Projectors with 16mm film were placed inside a window at each former hiding place and portions of archival film footage, secretly shot from above during the years of Nazi occupation by hidden individuals, were projected as film loops into the street below for one week, from 5:00 p.m. in the evening to 1:00 a.m. in the morning. In one ten-second loop, a Nazi funeral cortege appears on its way to bury a Dutch Nazi collaborator assassinated by the resistance; in another, a military band with the insignia of the Dutch Nazi Party marches in a continuous six-second loop; in the final loop, filmed by Nazi propagandists, German soldiers give endlessly robotic Heil Hitler salutes on the sidewalk. Showing Dutch collaboration with the Nazis in the projections of the hidden Jews, Attie conveys the daily terror of hidden confinement and complicates the benign mythology of sheltering, while once again bringing the past into tension with the social pressures and policies of the present as a fertile departure point for renewed resistance to policies of social expedience.

Attie's final project in this series departs in conception from the others and takes a more rhetorical turn. After Steven Spielberg filmed *Schindler's List* in Krakow, Poland, the simulacrum of history created by the film sets left behind appears to be slowly displacing authentic history as local residents and tourists now have the option of choosing between guided tours to authentic historical sites or guided tours "Retracing the Filming of *Schindler's List*." Franciszek Palowski, a Polish journalist who had interviewed Spielberg for Polish television and later wrote a book on the filming of *Schindler's List*, has organized the film-set tours. Palowski is careful to distinguish between the sites of actual history and the sites of Spielberg's film; nevertheless, "it is one thing to add the history of the film to the history of events, another to displace the history of events with the history of the film."[53] In *Walk of Fame* (June-July 1996), Attie takes inspiration from Hollywood Boulevard's *Walk of Fame* in Los Angeles and produces a simulacrum in front of the Jewish Museum and former Old Synagogue on Szeroka Street in Krakow, using twenty-four five-pointed terrazzo stars, based on the originals in L.A. Szeroka Street was the site on which a mock version of the Krakow Ghetto was erected for the Spielberg film although the actual location was in the Podgorze district. In his sidewalk stars, Attie places the names, not of the movie stars in the film, but the actual Jews who were on the *real* Schindler's List, abbreviating their first names to protect their identities. Attie's project is a parody that mocks the insidious substitution of celebrity for history. At the same time it comments on the effects of Hollywood on even the most profound events of history, the dangerous confusion of historical fact and fiction, and the replacement of history by a simulacrum in which the real and the imagined are increasingly difficult to distinguish.

THE CODE OF "THE EAST"

HISTORIANS HAVE NOTED that when Germans thought about Jews they looked East, not West. The great mass of Polish Jewry was there on their doorstep, stigmatized by Germans in general, including German Jews, as primitive Ostjuden, living among the other primitive peoples of the East, for whom German nationalism had as much contempt as it did for the Jews. The East, in German thought and history, was in general a place of darkness, populated by Slavs, Mongols, Tartars, pagans, Gypsies, Jews, and other dirty, backward, dangerous peoples, waiting to be colonized and civilized by the Germans.[54]

A restructured geographical stereotype of the East arose once more in the 1986 Historians' Debate in Germany. This debate was prompted by the attempt on the part of conservative historians to revise the past through the critical move of separating Nazi territorial claims from Hitler's crimes against the Jews, that is, they advanced arguments to justify national expansionist goals while opposing the crime of genocide. Conservative historian Ernst Nolte suggested that the singularity of Hitler's crimes should be reconsidered. Auschwitz, according to Nolte, was not a German crime or product of German history but a deed imported from the East, an "Asiatic" deed, a reference that invokes the late nineteenth-century East-West discourse in which the West feared the East while seeing it as an object of imperialist desire. The East was regarded as the origin of Judaism and Byzantine mysticism; the rationalism of the West was counterpoised to the inscrutable empires of Asia, which were seen as the source of great wealth and Oriental luxuries. It has been argued that the German annexationist projects of both world wars were based largely on the desire for the East, the *Drang nach Osten*. In the twentieth century, the East also became the origins of Bolshevism, regarded as a specifically Jewish phenomenon.[55]

Since World War II, "the Asiatic" has constructed new subjects in Germany, most prominently the Turkish and Kurdish guest workers that were recruited in the 1960s to help fuel Germany's postwar economic boom. Turks have been integrated into the economy but segregated at the bottom and denied full citizenship rights. The Turks, like the Jews, can be construed as originating in the vast, murky East and practicing an exotic religion; they have been constituted by the Asiatic code as a threat to the German identity of the nation, a foreign and potentially subversive population. Racism stands as the counterpart to the desire for a homogeneous national identity based on blood ties rather than place of birth. Even well established Turks who have been in Germany for twenty to thirty years, no less than their recently arrived immigrant brethren, are viewed by conservatives as pariahs, along with Roma and Sinti, and subjected to right-wing attacks. Nor are the German-born children of emigrant Turks automatically considered citizens; instead, they are regarded as "immigrants by birth."[56] Enzo Traverso notes, "Today any Pole, Rumanian, or Russian whose ancestors were citizens of the Reich is warmly welcomed in Germany and automatically acquires German citizenship, whereas asylum is denied or doled out in driblets to Kurdish refugees. The *völkisch* ideology is no longer acceptable but in practice, some of its principles remain valid in defining what constitutes belonging to the nation."[57] Thus, the sometimes disturbing reception of Attie's work not only raises questions of continued German denial and resistance to the implications of the past but continuities with that past, in particular regarding contemporary attitudes toward today's minorities in Germany. Distinctions between assimilated and traditional, poor and bourgeois have as little impact as they did for the prewar Jewish collective. The Turks, like the Jews before them, cannot escape their status as other, foreign, and inassimilable, providing fresh impetus for questioning the nature of national identity, at the core of Attie's project of haunting the German present with the vanished victims of its past.

Ironically, there has been a surge of philosemitism in Germany, particularly in Berlin, among non-Jews in the last few years, though the Jewish population in all of Germany is about half of what it was in Berlin before the war. Although Jews never represented more than approximately 1 percent of Germany's overall population in the late nineteenth and early twentieth centuries, in 1925, according to some estimates, as many as 200,000 Jews or approximately 5 percent of the general population was living in Berlin in the interwar period. In the past decade, the number of Jews in Germany has reached about 100,000, mostly as a result of an influx of Jews from the former Soviet Union. The wave of philosemitism, however, has been countered by the radical right-wing backlash to immigration and economic recession after the fall of the Berlin wall in the early 1990s, expressed most violently through an increase of neo-Nazi attacks on foreigners, which has been accompanied by an increase of desecrations of Jewish cemeteries and memorials.[58]

Attie returned full circle to the destiny of the East European Jews who fled the pogroms of Russia and Poland at the end of the nineteenth century with his public project on the Lower East Side of New York City, *Between Dreams and History.* This street installation was produced by the nonprofit public-arts organization Creative Time, Inc., in New York City. For the project, Attie interviewed diverse neighborhood residents, asking them about the past and present of the community. They, in turn, wrote down "their memories of the neighborhood from their youth, their hopes for the future, dreams about the neighborhood, superstitions, and premonitions,"[59] producing a kind of "communal poetry in which neighborhood residents serve as their own witnesses."[60] In collaboration with the artist and technology expert, Norman Ballard, Attie used these handwritten passages to create laser light projections of the now culturally mixed communities who live on the Lower East Side, including Jews, Chinese, and Latinos. In English, Chinese, Spanish, Yiddish, or Hebrew, contemporary hopes, dreams, and anxieties were "written on the wall" in real time, letter by letter, at night (fig. 9). Attie projected the laser installation

Fig. 9. Shimon Attie, "I remember the Jewish church on Rivington. I was 17 years old when I saw it for the first time. I am 72 years old now." Lasers writing Latino senior's memory of Rivington Street Synagogue, from *Between Dreams and History*, New York, 1998. Courtesy Jack Shainman Gallery, New York.

onto tenement buildings and an old synagogue at the intersection of Ludlow and Rivington Streets for three weeks, following the opening on 22 October 1998. A half-hour video made by the film director Christopher Beaver of the interviews and experiments that went into the making of Attie's project was also shown in neighborhood businesses. Unlike the European projects, *Between Dreams and History* does not contain the same kind of provocative critique; it is meant to draw the neighborhood together rather than excavate a dark, buried past, though still offering poignant literary images of longing, loss, and a sense of displacement that compresses past, present and future.

Despite the contemporary ethnic mix, the Lower East Side is historically known as the former Jewish ghetto, which at one time constituted the single largest enclave in America of Eastern European Jewish working-class immigrants. For the American Protestant elite, the Jewish Lower East Side was viewed in negative class/racial terms. A *New York Times* commentator a century ago contemptuously described it:

> The neighborhood where these people live is absolutely impassable for wheeled vehicles other than their pushcarts. If a truck driver tries to get through where their pushcarts are standing they apply to him all kinds of vile and indecent epithets. The driver is fortunate if he gets out of the street without being hit with a stone or having a putrid fish or piece of meat thrown in his face. This neighborhood, peopled almost entirely by the people who claim to have been driven from Poland and Russia, is the eyesore of New York and perhaps the filthiest place on the western continent. It is impossible for a Christian to live there because he will be driven out, either by blows or the dirt and stench. Cleanliness is an unknown quantity to these people. They cannot be lifted up to a higher plane because they do not want to be. If the cholera should ever get among these people, they would scatter its germs as a sower does grain.[61]

Like Joseph Roth's description of the East European Jews in Berlin in the 1920s, which also found them dirty, unassimilable, and threatening, such views were part of mainstream American thinking in the early twentieth century, lending themselves to a scientifically based racism founded on eugenic notions of racial inferiority and the belief, by the 1920s, "that real Americans were white and that real whites came from northwest Europe."[62] East European Jews were constructed as nonwhite, and therefore, non-American.

Jews still haunt the Lower East Side. Even as the old Jewish Forward building is converted to condominiums (*The Forward* newspaper having moved uptown and converted to English from Yiddish), the Orthodox Eldridge Street Synagogue, the first house of worship in America built by Eastern European immigrants (where Eddie Cantor sang in the choir) is restored to its earlier glory in a multimillion dollar renovation project. As the living culture of Jewish life is more deeply integrated today into the mainstream, the synagogue, a signifier of Old World Orthodoxy, points to what was lost in the Shoah. Jonathan Rosen, culture editor of *The Forward,* observes: "There is also an added poignancy in the knowledge that so many of the European synagogues that inspired the Eldridge Street Synagogue were destroyed in the Holocaust; what was once merely the echo now seems the lonely voice itself."[63] Attie's work means to provide another kind of site of resistance: resistance to the loss of community and to the homogenization of difference. The struggles between assimilation and difference among the Jews on the Lower East Side have widened to include all the ethnic groups who have lived there for decades, peoples hoping to maintain a sense of cultural identity while realizing aspirations of national equality and democratic rights—hopes that arc through time from the butcher stores in the Scheunenviertel to the Chinese diners near Eldridge Street. While the prewar Jews have disappeared, their remnants and other ethnic communities are given a voice.

In *The Writing on the Wall,* Attie showed the eastern Jews not in their usual form as always already victims, but in their far lesser-known prewar immigrant life. In the photographic fragments he chose, they appear by turns destitute and dressed in rags, as scholars, or selling their goods, variously embodying the characteristics of the pariah. In his later projects, *Trains I* and *Trains II,* Attie employed prewar photographs of highly assimilated or bourgeois German Jews, presenting the flip side of the pariah stereotype, the parvenu, perhaps with less success. Nonetheless, using the paradigm of pariah and parvenu, Attie's images may be seen as tackling both stereotypes *in situ,* where the infamies to come were set in motion, although they are never directly represented. The approaching catastrophe and its long aftermath is evoked simply by making the invisible Jews of Germany present once more in a form that is at once both historical and imaginative. Shimon Attie's German projects poignantly seek to reactivate the memory of the Jewish role in the development of German society and demonstrate how the absence of such cultural memory through the loss of an ethnic population leads to a dangerously distorted sense of national identity—a lesson as important for America as for Germany.

CHAPTER THREE

THE REINVENTION OF MEMORY

■

"We can evoke situations of passivity: affliction; the final, crushing force of the totalitarian State, with its camps; the servitude of the slave bereft of a master, fallen beneath need; or dying, as forgetfulness of death. In all these cases we recognize, even though it be with a falsifying, approximating knowledge, common traits: anonymity, loss of self; loss of all sovereignty but also of all subordination; utter uprootedness, exile, the impossibility of presence, dispersion (separation)."

MAURICE BLANCHOT
from *The Writing of the Disaster* (1980), trans. by Ann Smock, 1995

■

AS WE HAVE SEEN in Shimon Attie's projects, the subjective positioning of the contemporary viewer in relation to the lost world of the prewar Jews stands in uneasy relation to the political conditions of the present. In the work of Vera Frenkel, the focus of this chapter, the relationship between the present and the past is explored through a presentation of open-ended possibilities that specifically confront the massive art theft of the Third Reich and the continuing effects of the "rape of Europa." Frenkel's project, especially its ongoing web version, provides spaces and opportunities for a proactive stance on the part of the secondary witness and sympathetic viewer in acts of resistance against the passivity of despair, inviting the continuous construction of the legacy of the past.

VERA FRENKEL: *BODY MISSING*

In her work *Body Missing,* Toronto-based multidisciplinary artist Vera Frenkel explores the processes set in motion by Hitler's *Kunstraub* (art theft), and especially his *Sonderauftrag Linz* (Special Assignment Linz), Hitler's plan to open in his own hometown a grand museum of works looted from Europe's art collections through theft and forced sale. The stolen works were stored at the Altaussee salt mines near Linz during the war. When the Allies first opened the mines after the war, they discovered that a large body of the inventoried work was missing. This absence is the point of departure of *Body Missing,* Frenkel's project on the collecting fever of the Third Reich, which takes the dual forms of a six-channel video and mixed media installation (1994) and a *Body Missing Website* (http://www.yorku.ca/BodyMissing) that is an expanded version of the installation (1995–ongoing).

Body Missing was first produced in 1994 as a site-specific installation at the former Wehrmacht prison (then the Offenes Kulturhaus, now the Center of Contemporary Art for Upper Austria) in Linz, Austria, during a period following Frenkel's residencies there and at the Akademie der bildenden Künste in Vienna, the art school which had twice rejected Hitler as a student, and where staff members later collaborated with his art theft policies. *Body Missing* was part of *Andere Körper* (Other Bodies; The Body of the Other), an exhibition and symposium organized by the Offenes Kulturhaus. It has been subsequently installed at sites internationally.[1]

The installation took place on several floors and included six monitors and six videotapes, each six minutes long, consisting of contemporaneous and archival images such as casual meetings, descents to the cellar, corridors of crates, hands raised in the Hitler salute in the Main Square of Linz with its famous monument to the plague, a mysterious painting in progress, as well as photographs, records and lists detailing Nazi art looting throughout occupied Europe during the Second World War.[2] The installation included wall texts and enlarged translucent photomurals of images from the videotapes that were placed in the windows of the building facade of the Offenes Kulturhaus (fig. 10). They were backlit from the outside so that on the inside, one could feel situated within the work itself. In the traveling version, the photographic transparencies were removed from the windows and mounted in light boxes with wall text (fig. 11).

Historical material in the *Body Missing* installations includes Hitler's urban development plans in Linz in the early 1940s, in which a Führermuseum as large as the Uffizi or even the Louvre was planned. It was meant to hold all the looted art of Europe, with Hitler imagining himself as chief curator. While second-in-command Hermann Goering was in charge of the actual looting, Hitler had first choice of all

Fig. 10. Vera Frenkel, *Body Missing*, six-channel video installation. Detail of façade integrating video footage and archival imagery regarding art theft policies of the Third Reich, Offenes Kulturhaus, Linz, Austria, 1994.

the gathered stolen artworks, more than six thousand paintings, among other objects of art.

The Nazi project of carting off the cultural capital of Europe's Jews, and particularly the great collections in France, the capital of the art world between 1939 and 1944, has been traced by several investigators.[3] Thousands of crates of paintings, including works by artists such as Vermeer, Rembrandt, Courbet, Degas, Cézanne, Picasso, Braque, and Leger, were shipped from France to Germany during the war, intended for the grand museum to be established in Linz, or for Goering's private collection. The Nazis looted an estimated $9 billion to $14 billion in art and other assets, the current value of which is about $90 billion to $140 billion. After the war, the Allies organized the return of thousands of looted works in Germany to their countries of origin. About sixty thousand works of art were sent back to France, some of which were put on display for four years so owners or their heirs could claim them. About forty-five thousand items were claimed. The French government auctioned off a few thousand, and some two thousand artworks and objects went to French museums, not as part of their collections, but under the category MNR—Musée National de Recupération (National Museum Recuperation). The works

Fig. 11. Vera Frenkel, Station 5, *Body Missing*, "Athena's Polished Shield." Installation view, Kungl Konsthogskolan, Stockholm, 1997. Photo: Olof Wallgren, Riksutställningar, Stockholm.

entrusted to the Louvre and other French museums for safekeeping included one thousand paintings by major twentieth-century artists. Charged with producing an inventory of these artworks and attempting to find their owners, the museums for fifty years failed to meet this obligation. Compounding the effects of the wartime Vichy regime's collaboration in the murder and dispossession of Jews, the administration of French national museums stonewalled efforts by journalist Hector Feliciano and even an official government commission attempting to ascertain information on these artworks. In response to the scandal unleashed by Feliciano's book, *The Lost Museum,* which details the fates of five important individual collections in France, the museums in 1997 made efforts to publicize the unclaimed works by staging two-week exhibitions at the Louvre, Centre Pompidou, Orsay, Versailles, and the Sèvres museums.

Feliciano and others have demonstrated that there was no free art market under the Nazis for Jews, who had no rights to property. Either they were forced to sell their artworks, or the works were looted by the Nazis and placed on the art market. Author Tom Bauer suggests that a likely reason for French resistance to finding Jewish heirs is the enormous amount of trade between occupied France and Switzerland during the war.[4] Records of that war trade are held by the French foreign ministry, which denies access to researchers and historians who are not working on active claims. According to Willi Korte, a war loot researcher, without access to these files it is difficult to develop individual claims and nearly impossible to establish an overall perspective on the scope of the problem.[5]

Feliciano has professed a certain amazement at the Nazi's blithe confiscations, which might be cynically understood as the inevitable spoils of war that have been exacted by victors against the vanquished since the looting of the Temple in Jerusalem by the Roman Emperor Titus. The vast amounts of art and cultural property displaced during World War II and still appearing on the art market and in private, museum, and state collections have raised questions of ownership that continue to be hotly debated and battled out in court, legislation, or negotiated in treaties.[6] Germany still has claims against Russia for the looting of cultural works by the Red Army at the end of World War II, including the gold treasures Heinrich Schliemann excavated in Troy in the late 1800s and evacuated to Germany, which the Russian parliament has declared state property. Turkey, the site of Schliemann's original excavations, also claims the Trojan antiquities. The debate has raged for years over the Elgin marbles as well, which have not yet been returned to Greece. And to whom do the works confiscated by Napoleon at the beginning of the nineteenth century and now in the Louvre belong? Despite this sordid record of war looting and appropriations by treasure hunters, however, Feliciano's surprise and outrage at Nazi confiscations of Jewish-owned collections is entirely justified, not only on principle, but also historically. What distinguishes Nazi looting, like the Holocaust itself, is its breathtaking scale, ruthlessness, and planning. Even the term "looting," with its implications of spontaneous ransacking, does not begin to describe the massive, systematic, and highly organized bureaucratic machine by which the Nazis thoroughly dispossessed the cultural property of Jews, as well as state property, not only in France, but all over Europe.

It should not be forgotten that there were laws against the confiscation of private property during warfare established at the Hague Convention in 1907; these laws prompted the Nazis to legalize their confiscations with decrees declaring cultural property to be abandoned by Jews who had fled, been arrested, or who had deposited their valuables in public institutions for safekeeping. Fifty years later, this twisted logic continues to embroil Jewish heirs seeking to reclaim stolen art in unresolved disputes over ownership.

Frenkel's *Body Missing* website, based on the installation, developed as part of the International Symposium on Electronic Arts in Montreal and includes archival documents, stories, poems, newly uncovered materials, memories, and images that are woven together in a complex tapestry that leads to many pathways. Frenkel both presents and undermines the work of historical narrative through her multimedia integration of historical events, personal experience, documents and memorabilia, weaving together different genres in a nonlinear narrative. "Narrative," asserts Frenkel, "is just one way of sustaining a network of tensions that invite the viewer to question what's being presented. To say we live in invented reality is a way of saying that we live in metaphor, but it's an invention that's just air without the evidence of the body and that evidence, in turn, concrete as it seems, has no meaning outside some form of narrative."[7] In the opening image, ". . . passing through the town," participants are invited, in four languages—Swedish, English, German, and French—to embark on one of many possible journeys. The welcome page defines the project as a three-point inquiry that explores the art theft policies of the Third Reich, the proposed Hitler museum, and the fate of artworks missing after World War II. The piano bar in an earlier work, . . . *from the Transit Bar,* has been incorporated into the *Body Missing* website, becoming the starting point for Internet visitors' wanderings and a virtual meeting place for "bar regulars"—participating artists—and visitors to gather.

Because of the continuity between works, a brief examination of . . . *from the Transit Bar* helps illuminate some of the issues that underlie *Body Missing.* Frenkel's work . . . *from the Transit Bar* is a six-channel video installation in the form of a working piano bar and six videodisk players with fourteen on-camera storytellers, initially installed at documenta IX in Kassel (1992).[8]

Fictively located on the real ground floor of the Offenes Kulturhaus in Linz, . . . *from the Transit Bar* is placed in a site that was also once a Wehrmacht prison (fig. 12). While lounging on bar stools and ordering drinks in the Transit Bar, visitors can watch monitors showing people telling different stories that address issues of war, uprootedness, exile, and emigration. The speakers on video monitors, situated against a background of moving trains, present the migrant's constant negotiation between strangeness and familiarity. Like the former Wehrmacht prison in which the viewers sit, the trains are redolent of dread, departure, disappearance, and transience. Through uncertainty, the narrators' monologues evoke the unmarked effect of trauma on everyday consciousness. The uncertainties extend to the viewers, who are unsure of whether they are hearing truth or fiction, watching actors or real exiles. Even the music, including Polish and Yiddish melodies, popular standards, and Frenkel's own original compositions, was programmed to produce "dissonances and silences to create another kind of uncertainty, one of many ways of feeling at home in uncertainty or of feeling that uncertainty *is* home."[9] When it comes to truth, there can be no closure. Frenkel plays on the instability of truth in the construction of the past. Truth relies both on what is remembered and what is imagined, neither of which is wholly reliable or unreliable, thus requiring, in Frenkel's words, "the acceptance of the lie in the truth and the truth in the lie."[10]

Fig. 12. Vera Frenkel, *. . . from the Transit Bar*, 1992, six-channel video-disk installation and functional piano bar, documenta IX, Kassel. Photo shows reconstruction, National Gallery of Canada, 1996. Photo: Charles Huppé, NGC, Ottawa.

The languages of the narrators are overdubbed with Polish and Yiddish, two languages not widely understood in the West. This choice of languages was intimately tied to the site. Explains Frenkel, "I thought it would be good to hear in that space the marginalized languages of those, like my grandparents, who spoke several Middle European languages but whose voices I'd never heard. The voice-over on three of the monitors is in Yiddish and on the other three, Polish—two of the many languages spoken by the grandparents I never had a chance to know. The subtitles alternate among English, French, and German so that if you don't speak either Yiddish or Polish, you can only catch a third of the narrative, unless you know all three languages."[11] Frenkel is less interested in translation than in recognition of the loss to which our lack of comprehension points. Thus, the feelings of displacement, strangeness and difference produced in viewers who sit in the transitory bar/installation setting parallel similar feelings conveyed by the narrators on the video monitors. In this way, Frenkel's concerns with displacement and its effects on identity are not merely represented but reproduced.[12]

In a parallel fashion, as visitors to the *Body Missing* website we must make our own way, faced with numerous choices, in a search for information and illumination like the website bar regulars who ultimately make some remarkable choices of their own. Artists from various countries have participated at different times, including Thomas Büsch and Reinhard Moeller, Peter Chin, Michel Daigneault, Catherine Duncanson, Claudia Eichbauer, Monica Haim, Gordon Jocelyn, Joanna Jones, Alexina Louie, Alice Mansell, Mickey Meads, Bernie Miller, Piotr Nathan, Daniel Olson, Basil Papademos, Karin Puck, Jeanne Randolph, Iain Robertson, Julian Samuel, Bernie Schiff, Stephen Schofield, Judith Schwarz, Betty Spackman, Barbara Sternberg, Eileen Thalenberg, Elyakim Taussig, Anja Westerfrölke, and Tim Whitten. As bar regulars, they enter into discussion on "the curious relation of art and politics." Frenkel herself is present as the bartender who overhears and ultimately orchestrates a self-styled art squad of historical interventionists who operate, as Elizabeth Legge notes, as "a network of bar regulars/artists/resistance workers/art restorers/spies," while Frenkel stays in the background, inconspicuously providing a framework for the various narrative threads from "the pose of neutral authority": "I write down everything just as I hear it . . . I hope you will excuse me if I remind you that what you are about to read is true."[13]

The project presents as its departure point the loss and migration of the looted works of art, raising the question: "What is to be the fate of all the missing artworks?" This question is critical to understanding the paradoxical nature of Frenkel's work, both rooted in history and entirely open-ended. The artworks, we know, are missing—how then can we play a role in determining their fate? What does it mean to even pose the question this way?

There are six major areas of the *Body Missing* website: artists, bartenders, beyond, piano players, sources, and video, all of them accessible through the Transit

Bar image maps and points of access that follow (fig. 13). A random sampling turns up an array of seemingly crucial information. If we click on Judith Schwartz, for example, we find our way to the date 1946; we click on this and "My Private Will" appears under the title "Collecting Fever," which turns out to be the last will and testament of Adolf Hitler:

> All I own—if any of it is of value—belongs to the Party, and if the latter should no longer exist, it belongs to the State, and if the latter should be destroyed as well no further decision on my part is needed.
>
> The paintings I have collected through the years were never meant for my private enjoyment but always for a gallery to be built in my native Linz on the Danube.
>
> That this request be met is my sincerest wish.
>
> As executor I appoint my most loyal Party Comrade, Martin Bormann, whom I hereby authorize to make all final decisions.
>
> Berlin, 29 April 1945, 4 a.m.
> Adolf Hitler
>
> as witnesses:
>
> Martin Bormann
> Dr. Goebbels
> Nicolaus von Below

This defeatist excerpt from Hitler's will provides final evidence of his remarkable fantasy obsession even on the eve of the Third Reich's demise and his own suicide.

Another click of the mouse turns up an excerpt from a document by Edward Breitenbach, American Chief of the Monuments and Fine Arts Section of the Historical Survey of the Activities of the Intelligence Department, dated 30 June 1949: "By the end of the second day, when the looting was finally stopped, all the pictures were gone. The loss was quite considerable. It included 259 items of the Schloss collection, perhaps the finest private collection of Dutch 17th century paintings, which the Nazis had looted from France, and about the same number of pictures which had been recently acquired for the Linz Museum, and which for lack of transportation had not been shipped for storage to the Alt Aussee mine (fig. 14)." Images of work piled up in storage also appear on the screen (fig. 15).

These images call to mind a number of cases that came to prominence in the media in the late 1990s. In 1997, for example, two paintings by Austrian artist Egon Schiele, *Portrait of Wally* and *Dead City III,* were detained in New York while the heirs of two Jewish families went to court against an Austrian state-funded museum that claimed ownership of them. The paintings came to the Museum of Modern Art as part of the exhibition "Egon Schiele: The Leopold Collection," and were lent by the Austrian museum, The Leopold, named after Dr. Rudolf Leopold, a Viennese ophthalmologist and collector who obtained them under questionable circumstances and sold his collection to the foundation in 1994. Leopold asserted that he acquired the paintings legally, while the Jewish families—heirs of Fritz Grünbaum, a Viennese cabaret artist who died in Dachau in 1941, and descendants of Lea Bondi Jaray, who fled Vienna in 1937—contend that their relatives lost them due to Nazi wartime plundering. When Manhattan District Attorney Robert M. Morgenthau issued a subpoena to MOMA, ordering it to refrain from returning the two borrowed Schiele paintings, American art museums were given a shock and forced to recognize the seriousness of the issue. By June 1998, the Association of American Art Museum Directors pledged that its member museums would begin a review of their collections in search of artworks illegally seized during the Nazi era, would question donors or art dealers about gaps in provenance records, and would conduct more scrupulous ownership research before acquiring works of art.

In another case, the heiress of Jacques Goudstikker, the Jewish prewar collector

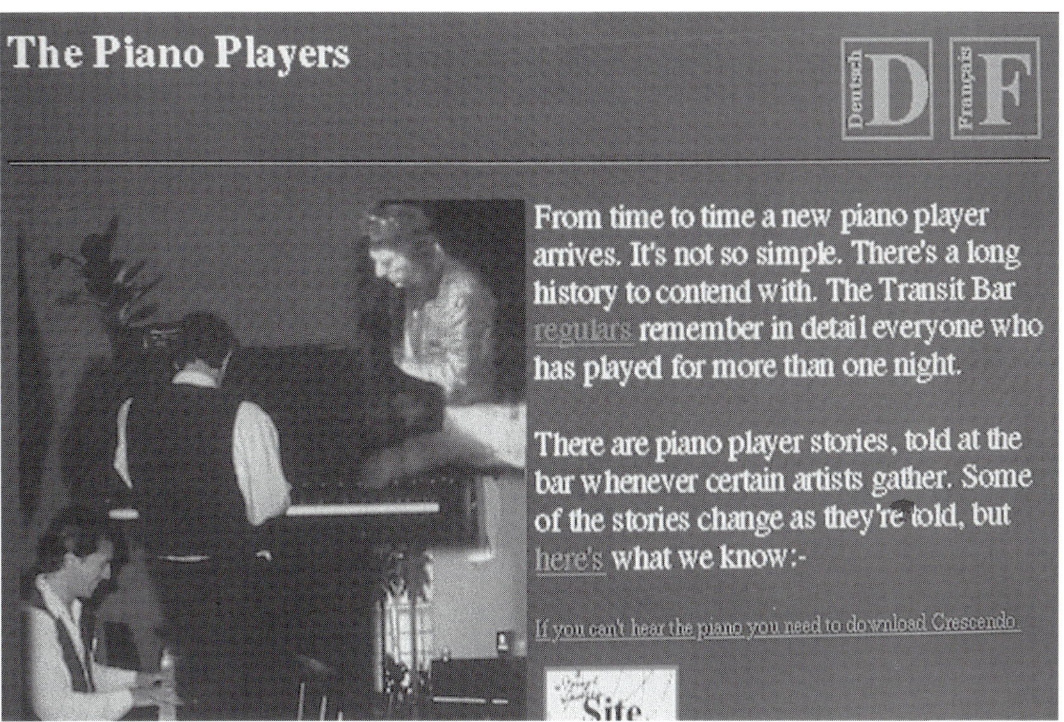

Fig. 13. Vera Frenkel, "And they had their histories..." Piano Players' page. *Body Missing Website* (http://www.yorku.ca/BodyMissing), 1995 and ongoing

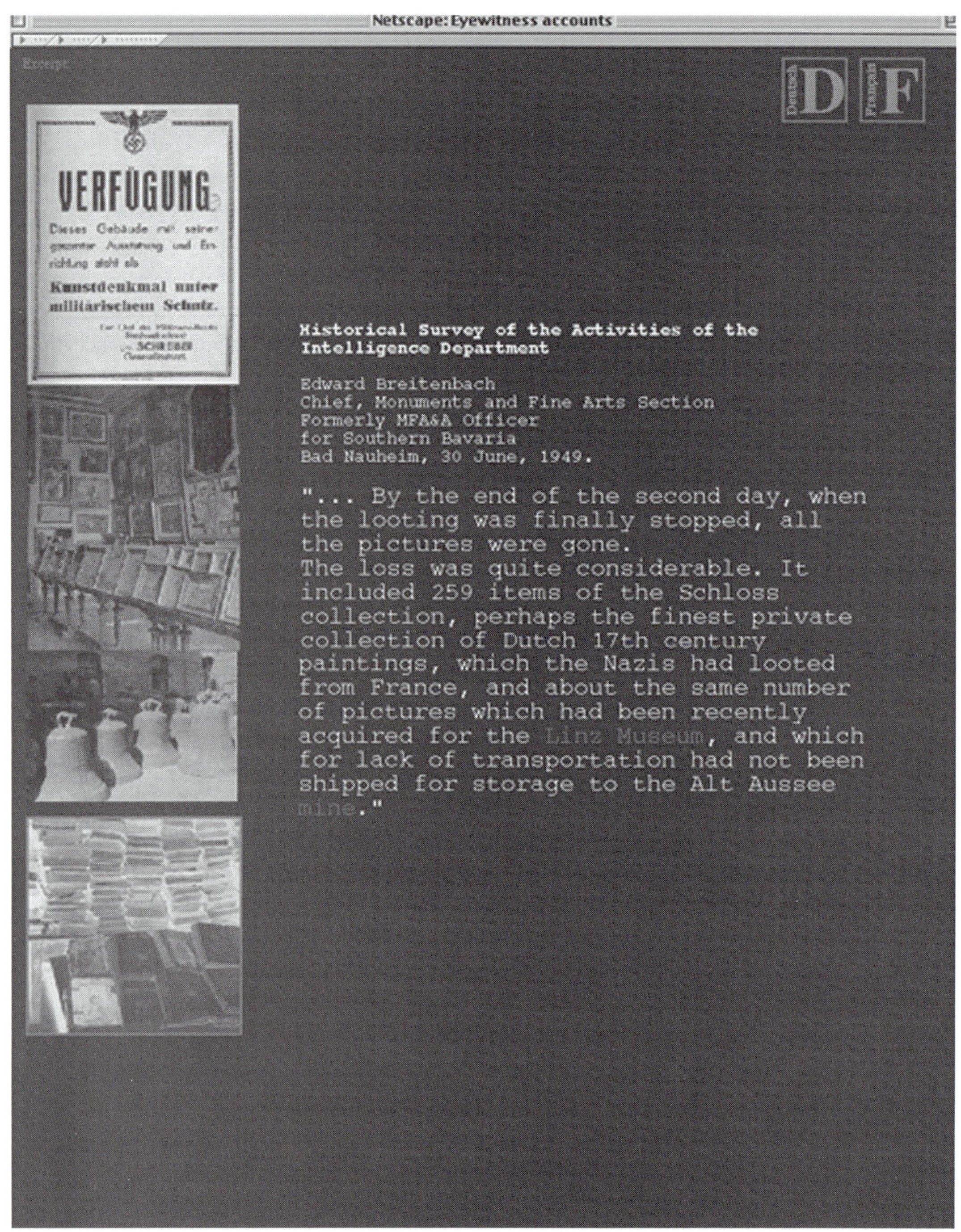

Fig. 14. Vera Frenkel, "Eyewitness Accounts," Web page. Edward Breitenbach Report for the U.S. Army, *Body Missing Website* (http://www.yorku.ca/BodyMissing), 1995 and ongoing.

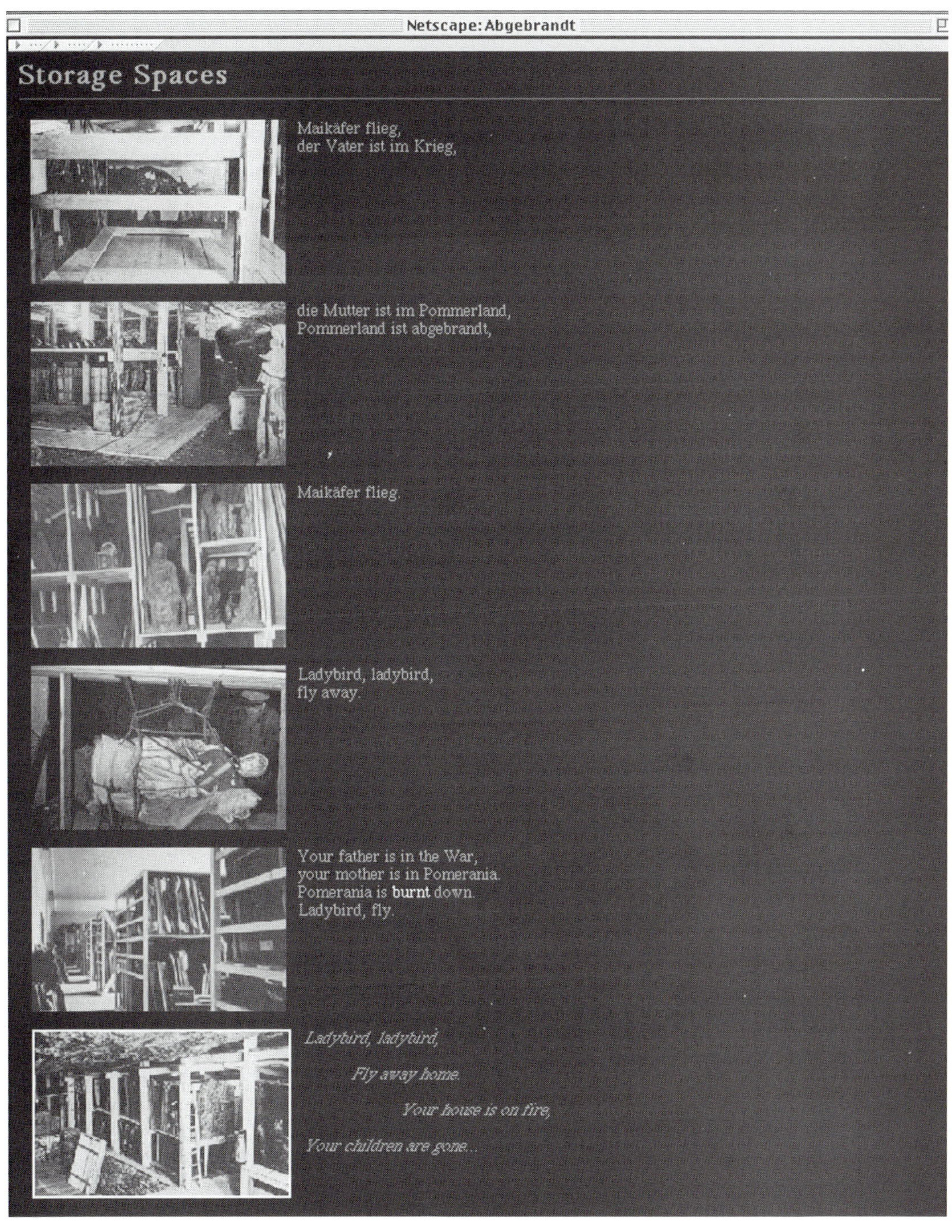

Fig. 15. Vera Frenkel, "Abgebrandt," Web page. Storage spaces, Altaussee salt mines and elsewhere; text of nursery rhyme/lullaby *Maikäfer Flieg*; link to Hitler's last will and testament, *Body Missing Website* (http://www.yorku.ca/BodyMissing), 1995 and ongoing.

and dealer in Amsterdam, sued the Dutch government over claims to paintings from her father-in-law's collection hanging in a dozen Dutch art museums. The Dutch government rejected her claims and even an offer of a settlement, arguing that it alone was the rightful owner of the collection, and reaffirming the stand taken by the government in the late 1940s when Goudstikker's widow tried to reclaim the gallery's holdings. Goudstikker's collection, which comprised 1,208 paintings, including works by Rembrandt, Goya, and Giotto, was sold voluntarily at a fraction of its worth, the government claims, to Herman Goering and his German agent Alois Meidl in 1940, when Goudstikker and his family fled Holland, and his Amsterdam art gallery was liquidated on orders from Miedl.[14] In other examples, a Rembrandt held by the Carnegie Museum of Art in Pittsburgh and thought to have been stolen by the Nazis turned out to be a fake, to the relief of the museum, with the real canvas turning up in Prague; Jacopo Zucchi's *The Bath of Bathsheba,* which had hung in the Wadsworth Atheneum in Hartford, Connecticut, since 1965, was returned to the Italian government in July 1998; *The Seamstress* by Berlin painter Lesser Ury was returned in July 1999 to Michael Loewenthal, whose grandfather, art collector Louis Loewenthal, lost everything when he fled Berlin at the beginning of World War II. Berlin art dealer Wolfgang Gurlitt, who later played a key role in Nazi efforts to sell degenerate art abroad and set up the Führermuseum in Linz, had insisted in 1950 that Louis Loewenthal's painting had been destroyed in a 1943 air raid. Gurlitt then sold the painting to the municipal museum in Linz in 1956. The Holocaust Claims Office returned the painting to Loewenthal's son after the Linz City Council voted to give it back.

The first dispute to be settled in the United States, in August 1998, involved a painting by Edgar Degas, *Landscape with Smokestacks.* Lili Gutman and her nephews, Nick and Simon Goodman, the daughter and grandsons of two Holocaust victims, came to an agreement with the last owner of the painting, Daniel C. Searle, the pharmaceutical company heir, who had bought the painting in 1987 in New York for $850,000. The case, which began in 1995, had bogged down entirely and was resolved in part through the intercession of Hector Feliciano who approached the Art Institute of Chicago on the Goodman's behalf. The Art Institute agreed to accession the work from both parties, paying the Goodman's half of the fair market value of the work, while Searle, a trustee of the Art Institute, agreed to donate his half-interest in the painting. The names of Friedrich and Louise Gutmann, who died in concentration camps, as well as that of Daniel Searle will be on the wall label. Since the agreement was first made, however, there has been renewed debate over the fair market value of the painting and the amount to be paid to the Goodmans. In another case, the Nazi-confiscated painting Odalisque by Henri Matisse turned up at the Seattle Art Museum after disappearing for decades, and was returned to the heirs of former Jewish art dealer Paul Rosenberg. The Seattle museum, in turn, is suing the Manhattan art dealer Knoedler & Company, which purchased the painting in Paris in 1954, claiming that Knoedler committed fraud, negligent misrepresentation and breach of warranty of title when it sold the work to Virginia and Prentice Bloedel, who eventually donated it to the Seattle Art Museum. This is only the second instance of an American museum returning a Nazi-looted painting to private owners since the Detroit Institute of Arts returned a Monet painting to a Jewish family in the 1950s.[15] In all of these cases, works were either plundered outright as Jews were hounded out of Europe or murdered in concentration camps, or were sold at ridiculously low prices by desperate Jews who needed cash to escape.

Many looted works have found their way across the Atlantic. The U.S. State Department and U.S. Holocaust Memorial Museum jointly sponsored a four-day conference in Washington, D.C., in December 1998, on "Holocaust-Era Assets" to address questions on Nazi-looted art and property. Ronald Lauder, chairman of the board of the Museum of Modern Art and an official with the World Jewish Congress, estimated that 110,000 pieces of art worth $10 billion to $30 billion were still missing and charged virtually every large museum, institution and private collection in the nation with containing some of these works. According to Lauder, a review of 225 museum catalogs over the summer of 1998 by his group found 1,700 looted pieces of art. The conference drew delegates from forty-five nations who attempted to reach a consensus on restitution for Holocaust-era art and other assets seized during World War II by establishing eleven nonbinding principles among participating nations. These included identifying art confiscated by the Nazis, opening relevant records and archives, making resources and personnel available to facilitate these tasks, publicizing confiscated art that has been identified, restituting it to prewar owners, creating a central registry of such information, and encouraging prewar owners to come forward to make known their claims.[16] The archive of prewar art is now in a condition that may be described as dispersed, disputable, fragmented, disappeared and lost—in short, a body missing.

Referring to the thousands of works stored in excellent condition in the caves at Altaussee for the museum that was never built, talk at the bar in *Body Missing* leads to thoughts about "fetishistic art collecting fever and war trophies; seeming disappearance versus outright loss; the possibility of reinventing, through cultural memory and fellow-feeling, a connection to earlier artists and absent work."[17] Frenkel draws the viewer into a shared, almost conspiratorial quest for knowledge, toward a confrontation with complacency and passivity. Remarkably, Frenkel achieves this intervention by inviting our complicity with the Transit Bar regulars who conspire to recreate works of art that went missing after the war, not as copies or reconstructions, but as gestures toward "an earlier artist and an absent work," as a way of keeping memory alive. This is the poignant gesture on which the project turns. The artists themselves seem taken aback by the idea, indicated by this excerpt from the dialogue found among the superimposed stories and images on the video monitors in the installation and in "Bar Talk" on the *Body Missing* website:

- I've spoken to Hannelore, Simone and Friedrich. They are ready. I left a message for Robert. Tomorrow I'll speak to Silvia.
- About the lost paintings?
- About each list. About painting the paintings.
- Sorry?
- It is very simple, she said quietly. Nothing to understand. It's a two part effort. We continue with or without the authorities, to try to find the art here or with the help of friends abroad. Those crates may be empty but somewhere are the crates that are filled. At the same time, until these are found, or in fact proved destroyed, we begin step by step to reconstruct the art that is missing, from memory, from pictures if any exist, from diary entries, by analysis, through invention.
- You can't reconstruct thousands of works of art even if you had the skill.
- Of course not. We just do one at a time. And we don't imitate or restore or pretend. We'll install them in some of the spaces at the Offenes Kulturhaus. It's more like saying: "Hello, I remember you."[18]

The viewer, as potential participant on the website, is also directly addressed:

> The participating artists (both those working privately and those whose studios are linked to this site) are interested in the fate of the works that have disappeared or have changed hands under unknown circumstances. If you know of the whereabouts of such a work, or have been offered a painting or drawing for sale under curious conditions, or have heard such a transaction referred to in conversation, we would be interested to learn more. *Mail us.*[19]

Alice Mansell and Mickey Meads are engaged in creating three stories about two missing Courbet paintings, each titled at various times *Venus and Psyche, Psyche Pursuing Venus,* and *The Awakening.* Their musings, as Elizabeth Legge observes, ponder "the psychosexual anxieties underlying Hitler's choice of a pilfered Courbet lesbian scene for his bunker under the chancellery; this is weighed against the puritan official meanings—health, sport, reproduction—attached to the nude by Nazi cultural theory" while also questioning why some works are considered masterpieces and others not.[20] Karin Puck produces a discussion of a Caspar David Friedrich painting with detailed reports of its state of decay and restoration; Daniel Olson tells war stories by his grandfather that are never quite believed; Bernie Miller draws attention to the modernist "decadent" art destroyed or auctioned off by the Nazis to finance their collection of Old Masters.

The postmodern love of naming and listing finds an apotheosis of purpose in the *Body Missing* website, which turns upon a core of lists that identify thousands of missing works of art with a code that has been lost. Frenkel compiles her own master list of the lists, which itself becomes a key to the rape of European art. The master list, from the notebook of the bartender, is as follows:

- what was collected
- what was stolen
- what was safeguarded
- what was transported by train
- what was shipped by truck
- what was hidden
- (list of all the better known hiding places)
- what was sold in Switzerland
- what arrived at the salt mine and on what dates
- what left the salt mine and when
- what was borrowed for party offices
- what was given as gifts
- what was insured
- what came from private collections
- what was once another country's treasure
- what the Allies found
- what the Russians took
- what now begins to appear at auction
- what was burned
- what crossed the ocean in strange ways
- what was saved
- what was brought back after the war by previous owners
- what never existed but was longed for
- what can be shown only privately
- what sits in the museums of Europe under new names
- items known to be in North and South America
- (list of vendors and sources)
- (list of the postwar collections, no questions asked)
- inventories of castles
- handwritten original lists
- typewritten collection point lists
- what has been returned and reinstated
- what is "heirless"
- what is still in dispute in the courts
- what was unsuccessfully claimed
- what is still missing

The *Body Missing* project addresses both the relationship between art and politics and the role of memory as a moral force and foundation for a civilizing opposition to tyranny, that is, a site of moral resistance. Frenkel describes *Body Missing* as raising

> questions about the nature of misguided power, the relationship between totalitarian regimes and invitations to collusion of those over whom they have power, another version of which might be the inherent conflict between bureaucracy and morality. In one way or another, all of my work has to do with the nature of citizenship, how we come to know what we know, and how we act on it. If . . . *from the Transit Bar* was about migration, displacement, deracination, memory, and exile, *Body Missing* is about the collecting fever that signals a

dehumanizing madness and about the role of memory as a basis for resistance in the face of that madness.[21]

Memory is counterposed to madness and madness is signaled, in part, by collecting fever, the obsession that haunted Hitler until his last moments.

Collecting fever might be regarded as a function of the acquisitive desire promoted by modern society itself, an impulse intensified by a capitalist culture predicated on a love of individual accumulation, the cult of genius, and the aura of value. The *Body Missing* project might be read as gesturing toward this development, from which the disastrous cultural greed and fetishistic appropriation of the cultural body of the Other has grown, while at the same time recognizing the unprecedented historical scope and destruction of the Nazi obsession with accumulation and its exceptional abuse of power.[22]

The issue of the urge toward accumulation and related structures of romance and consumerism have been employed by Frenkel in other works, such as the video installation *Messiah Speaking* (fig. 16). This project, produced during a residency at Newcastle Polytechnic, posed themes of war, romance, messianism, and consumerism as intersecting images and the related animation, *Messiah Speaking,* was first displayed as a five-month installation on the Spectacolor Board in the expensive shopping district of Piccadilly Circus (1990–1991). In both projects the "Messiah" urges the viewer to shop.

For Frenkel, however, the central metaphor for the Nazi art theft is a kind of ritualized cultural longing related to an entirely different form of cultural appropriation: the cargo cult. These quasi-religious practices were produced by the arrival of Western visitors bearing products of modern culture in previously isolated areas in the South Pacific, such as Papua-New Guinea. The cargo cults of South Sea islanders were based on a belief that the spirits of their ancestors were returning with supplies of marvelous modern goods, thus inaugurating a new golden age. Such practices were characterized by millenarian fantasies, the attribution of redemptive powers to certain objects and rituals, the generation of charismatic and destructive leaders, and by an attachment to the notion of the millennium itself, perceived, like the "thousand-year Reich," as a thousand years of bliss. Frenkel observes, "The forceful accumulation of cultural artifacts, a desire to own the strength of the other by swallowing its totems, is not a practice unique to National Socialism. It is a practice that has probably gone on since art began. . . . In thinking about the appropriation of art from other cultures, or *Kunstraub* of any kind, it seems to me that the practice of art-theft was and is a kind of cargo-cult practice in which the art serves as a kind of fetish for the world that is lost, or is longed for, and which others appear to have easy access to."[23] The metaphor of Nazi art theft as cargo-cult practice further provides a way of approaching the terror at the heart of the Nazi project: "[Siegfried] Kracauer, in discussing the Holocaust, alludes to the 'Mirror of Athena,' to finding a way of approaching and reflecting evil (the Gorgon) indirectly, without dying in the attempt. The concept of the cargo-cult is such a mirror, as is the *Kunstraub* policy itself."[24]

The master list, then, may be read as a kind of shadow list for a much larger moral horror, the other body missing that endows the Nazi *Kunstraub* policy with an intensified resonance of historical enormity. Kyo Maclear testifies to the palpable tension created between the given subject of Frenkel's project, with its lists, logs, and registers, and the unspeakable dominating master text, the bureaucratic efficiency of Hitler's genocidal program. While never directly referring to Hitler's murder of European Jewry, Frenkel's work gestures toward his "two lists, two sets of operating codes, two programs, which culminated in a vision defining both the destructible and the sanctifiable."[25]

The multivocal quality of Frenkel's project is another of its resonant dimensions. The multiple voices of the contributing artists not only allude to the many nationalities targeted by the genocide, but also parallel a long-standing Talmudic tradition in which the meaning of the biblical texts has been debated throughout the centuries, and in which the accretion of contributions assumes an authoritative weight and ethical framework not given to any one voice individually. The task of

Fig. 16. Vera Frenkel, "There's no rush," frame from *Messiah Speaking*, Piccadilly Circus Spectacolor Board Animation, London, 1990–91. Photo: Artangel Trust, London

the multivoiced dialogue, in relation to biblical interpretation, "is to keep open the mutual belonging of the text and those who hear it."[26] Frenkel's project similarly keeps open a sense of mutual belonging of the text and those who hear it, or view it, and goes further, encouraging those who wish it, to enter the text. This model of multiple voices operating through a historical framework constructs a narrative based on an accumulation of individual stories and events that continues not only to be relevant, but also to contain the potential for new meanings.

The *Body Missing* project, particularly as an evolving website, seduces the viewer into appreciating the historical specificity, complexity, and seriousness of the Nazi art theft while combining it with a highly provocative and imaginative contemporary response. The production of a dedicated group of artists parallels the work of the viewer who must also put together the pieces of the puzzle. This work of detection leads to the startlingly transgressive idea of becoming active players who intervene in this ongoing history, in effect reimagining cultural memory in order to bring it to life in contemporary form once again. *Body Missing,* then, constitutes the production of a new archive, a new body that is no less authentic than the cultural production of the past, a body that incorporates the memory of the body missing. It reads both back into the past and opens out into the future. At the same time, the nature of the archive is transformed from a discrete collection of objects stored in a specific place, which can only be accessed at certain times, to a continuous stream of images and ideas that can be accessed at any time through a global website.[27] It maintains continuity with the past yet projects the possibility of new meanings that recognize and include the history and implications of cultural despoliation. Regarding this open-endedness, Frenkel writes, "My work has been engaged since I can remember with a desire to prevent or preclude closure, preferring to establish a structure of exchanges or oscillations, a climate of uncertainty which is both axiomatic and nurturing."[28] The conversation continues, fertile, alert, and irresolvable. *Body Missing* is therefore not a work of mourning; rather, Frenkel posits the question, "What is to be the fate of all the missing art works?" in order to project the possibility of a future for the absences of the past. In *Body Missing,* memory is not a passive repository of longing but a catalyst to action.

At its core then, *Body Missing* calls for an active response to the historical enormity of the Holocaust. Like Art Spiegelman's *Maus*, Frenkel presumes a paradigm for history in which a narrative of historical events includes the present conditions under which they are being narrated, in which the past and present are not only linked but become inseparable, producing in the process a complex of memory effects that addresses cultural memory as the most responsible and meaningful basis for cultural identity and agency—"the nature of citizenship, how we come to know what we know, and how we act on it." Through an open-ended dialogue that precludes closure and revitalizes the archive through continuous construction, Frenkel's project appears to be no less than an attempt to save the future from the oblivion of the past—from what Maurice Blanchot calls "passivity" in the epigraph at the beginning of this chapter. Geoffrey Batchen has suggested that one of the primary goals of the archive is "the definition of national identity through the constant recall of a supposedly collective memory."[29] Let us assume that collective memory is not only supposed but also real in its public construction. If so, Frenkel's international website project by its very nature and by its appeal to global participation redefines collective memory from a form of nineteenth-century nationalism to a model of reimagined internationalism based on the conception of memory as a basis for resistance.

CHAPTER FOUR

APPROPRIATING THE TESTIMONIAL FORM

■

"Tell us, Mr. De-Nur, what's frightening you?" The voice comes reaching for me from every corner of Auschwitz. "What is frightening . . . frightening . . . frightening?"

Auschwitz is a flaming pyre. I know I have been summoned to witness the fire-belching sight. Ashmadai, King of Auschwitz. Here he is. I see him with my own eyes emerging from the furnace in his ascent from the chimney, from the hidden holies of his abode. Cloaked by the smoke, he wafts to the heights of heaven, with Shamhazai and Azael unfurling a canopy over his head. Mushroom-like, the specter looms in the sky: Shamhazai and Azael are about to anoint Ashmadai as the new King of Kings, lord of the universe. With blaring trumpets they declare to the four corners of the earth that the new name of this sovereign of the universe will no longer be Ashmadai, but Nucleus! His birthplace: The heart of the furnace in the mystery laboratory, Auschwitz. Manufactured from a new substance, altogether unique, Nucleus is the concentrate of the souls of one and one-half million living, breathing children.

KA-TZETNIK 135633 during LSD therapy, from *Shivitti: A Vision,* 1989

■

THE ARCHIVE OF MEMOIRS and videotaped survivor testimonies has rapidly expanded in the last decade, with testimony regarded as the primary and privileged arena of the Holocaust survivor. Thousands of videotaped testimonies have now been deposited with a number of archives, such as the Yale

Fortunoff Video Archives for Holocaust Testimony, Steven Spielberg's Survivors of the Shoah Visual History Foundation, and at the U.S. Holocaust Memorial Museum in Washington, D.C. Commentaries on survivor testimonies and/or the impact of trauma on narration and the psychic economy of primary witnesses have been written from widely varying disciplinary perspectives by observers such as Lawrence Langer, Cathy Caruth, Henry Krystal, Dori Laub, Shoshana Felman, Henry Greenspan, Ernst van Alphen, James Young, and Michael Rothberg, among others. If we recognize that secondary witnesses also may suffer forms of secondary trauma, it is reasonable to inquire into their relationship to these testimonies and the testimonial format as a forum for secondary witnessing. While identifying with survivors, secondary witnesses also resist and reject the pathos and abjectness that are associated with victimhood, often constructing the survivor in ways that create a tension between the horror of the past and the resilience to it that has brought them into the present. In this chapter, artist Jeffrey Wolin tells the stories of survivors through photographs on which Wolin himself writes their stories in his own hand, implicating himself in the construction of the narrative by implicitly making visible the presence of the listener, who inevitably affects how the stories are told. Artist Pier Marton videotapes the testimony of secondary witnesses directly, presenting his subject position openly by including himself among those who give testimony on the effects of intergenerational transmission of Holocaust experience, and the self-hatred, ambivalence, and trenchant resistance to the tropes of antisemitism that it generates.

JEFFREY WOLIN: *WRITTEN IN MEMORY: PORTRAITS OF THE HOLOCAUST*

Born in 1951, Jeffrey Wolin grew up with survivor grandparents whose families perished in the Holocaust. His project, begun in the 1980s, was produced with subjects in Bloomington, Indiana, where he teaches, as well as in Indianapolis, Chicago, Skokie, South Florida, and Paris. The survivors' experiences vary widely: some survivors were in the concentration camps, others were in hiding, some fled to America. For most, it is their first public telling of their story. First shown at the Catherine Edelman Gallery in Chicago, then as part of Holocaust exhibitions such as *Witness and Legacy,* Wolin's project was published as a book in 1997. By transfiguring the experiences of survivors into the high art of the gallery and museum, Wolin, in addition to the video testimonials of the Yale Archive, the Shoah Foundation, and the Holocaust Memorial Museum, has helped legitimize the Holocaust narrative and the right of survivors to tell it in public after decades of public silence.

Wolin videotaped survivors prior to making portraits with a still camera. At first, he rewrote their accounts onto the photographs in his own words. Subsequently, he excerpted whole chunks of their stories verbatim and, in many cases, hand-inscribed these excerpts directly onto the black and white portraits, blocking out their contemporary surroundings, or leaving only tenuous connections. Wolin thus makes the survivor's past visible as well as legible by visually immersing the survivors in their memories, mirroring the dual lives that many survivors lead, split between then and now. For many, their war experience is more real than their life afterwards, constituting what Lawrence Langer calls "deep memory" that lives beside "common" or narrative memory.[1] With the technique of writing the survivors' stories onto their images in his own hand, Wolin disrupts the reality effect of the photographic image with the graphic surround of handwritten text, signifying the constructedness of the archival document he has produced. At the same time, however, the implicit presence of the artist may be read as creating a kind of intrusiveness. That is, the words produce access to Holocaust experience while simultaneously representing the vicarious inscription of the artist into the survivor's world, and conversely, the entry of the survivor into the contemporary concerns of the photographer.

The subject, then, is not only the survivor and the testimony of the survivor, but also the testimony of the artist who has inscribed the survivor's words in, at times, his own voice, or own handwriting. The reinscription of the stories by Wolin makes apparent not only his desire to preserve the legacy of Holocaust experience and pass on the stories, but also to assert the present conditions in which they are told and recorded, including Wolin's role in creating the circumstances of the telling, a contingency that necessarily shapes the narratives.

The "inner compulsion to repeat the narratives," writes Lori Lefkovitz about the recounting of survivor accounts by the listeners, at first made her "feel like a medium through whom other voices speak, the puppet in a ventriloquist act. I now realize that part of my own conflict over reporting my parents' stories is shame over the unconscious wish to control their presentation, to cloak these sometimes awkward immigrants in my vocabulary. From puppet to puppeteer, in reciprocal ventriloquism."[2] Over half the stories in Wolin's book have quotation marks around them, suggesting they are reproduced verbatim in the voice of the survivor. In others, however, we might wonder to what extent Wolin intended to smooth out the rough edges of the immigrants' language by editing the survivors' stories and rewriting them in his own voice, in his desire to make sure their stories were clearly heard. As an extreme example of usurping the voice of the victim, Ruth Bettina Birn points to Daniel Goldhagen's *Hitler's Willing Executioners,* observing that the author "fills page after page with graphic descriptions of gruesome events during mass-murder actions and in camps." But Birn suggests, "There is an extensive collection of survivors' memoirs and testimonies, in which we can hear the voices of the victims themselves. In the approach Goldhagen advocates, the historian takes on the position of an intermediary who is not interpreting sources but retelling the events in light of his own imagination. It's his voice we hear!"[3]

A great deal of weight has been given to survivor testimonies as a form of representation closest to the historical truth. Yet the role of the interviewer-artist is of considerable importance in determining how the work is shaped and perceived. In the case of Claude Lanzmann's important film Shoah, Dominick LaCapra argues that Lanzmann was so keen to identify with the painful experiences of Holocaust victims that he only selected those subjects who were willing to relive or act-out their traumatic experiences before the camera, sometimes at the near sadistic insistence of Lanzmann in the face of their breakdown.[4] Lanzmann further chose those who were closest to death, dismissing interviews with those who refused to act-out or who led resistant actions. Wolin does not employ such techniques; nor do such techniques necessarily throw into question the validity of the narrative. Nonetheless, they reveal the construction of the narrative, the unavoidable biases. Wolin, whose photographic work constitutes a more delimited form of survivor testimony, also frames and guides the work in ways that affect the perception of survivor testimony by the viewer in order to achieve the desired emotional impact.

Some of Wolin's image/text constructions are particularly successful in capturing the dual aspect of time, the past and the present of the survivor. Mieczyslaw Weinberg, for example, born in Warsaw, became a body builder and mechanic (fig. 17).[5] Weinberg tells of returning home one night to the ghetto in time to see a Nazi soldier murder his friend on a dark street: "He got in one hand the revolver, a Luger, and in the other a flashlight. He shot my friend in his mouth, killed him. Then he bent down to see what he did and I saw I been at risk he kill me too. He will turn and he'll see me. So I hit him in his neck. I was a middleweight boxer, a karate man too, and then I lay down and with my leg on his throat I strangled him. We pulled him into the ghetto. We got to wash the blood from my friend off the ground so no one should see something happened here. And we disrobed the German. They got there in the ghetto hundreds of dead people each day from hunger. We put him on the wagon with the Jewish dead people and put maybe 25 or 30 dead Jews on him and took him to the Jewish cemetery, the Gesia cemetery." In Wolin's photograph, Weinberg tilts his head back, peering warily down into the viewer's eyes. His arm, bearing a faded tattooed number, lies across his torso like a talisman and a warning, revealing what is not narrated in the text: Weinberg was later sent to Auschwitz. The space between the tattoo and the vigilant eyes contains the implied and unspeakable complexities of Weinberg's story, what we may regard as the difficulty of asserting a definitive subject position for the survivor. Was he a subjective agent boldly acting on his own behalf or a helpless object of terrible circumstances? A Nazi-killer in the ghetto or a brutalized victim? The answer perhaps is both. Ernst van Alphen suggests that one of the difficulties for survivors in narrating their experiences is precisely that of definitively locating themselves in relation to events: "The actuality of the Holocaust was such that this distance from the action was not possible; there were no unambiguous roles of subject or object."[6] This painful ambiguity is one of the reasons many survivors find the Holocaust to be unrepresentable. Van Alphen argues that it is not so much a question of the inadequacy of language per se, but the inability to frame the role of the victim in situations and events for which there was no prior frame of cultural reference. In the photograph of Weinberg, the words form a screen behind him, acting as a metaphorical screen for the trauma that cannot be conveyed. His penetrating gaze seems to challenge the viewer to comprehend both what has and what has not been told: the acts of resistance and the force of subjugation.

Wolin reorders the traditional format of documentary photography by openly integrating the relationship between image and text, rather than maintaining the

Fig. 17. Jeffrey Wolin, *Mieczyslaw Weinberg, b. 1912, Warsaw, Poland*, from *Written in Memory: Portraits of the Holocaust*, 1997. Toned gelatin silver print with silver marker. © Jeffrey A. Wolin. Courtesy Catherine Edelman Gallery, Chicago.

fiction of an image that stands alone or is only supplemented by the caption. Yet the images here do not, in fact, illustrate the story. They present the survivors to the postwar generations not as they were then, when the events described took place, but as they are now, more than fifty years later. The words cannot bring about the full presence of the past. The words and images, then, are not a presentation of the past, but the past as it has become in the present. The history of the Shoah continues to be told, retold, and understood in the present conditions of the telling. These images become part of the ongoing archive of the Holocaust. On one hand, "by showing us whole human beings, however inwardly scarred they are, [they] rehumanize the survivors, and in so doing, rehumanize the murdered victims as well," suggests James Young, in relation to testimonial videotapes.[7] On the other hand, they bring the Holocaust experience into the contemporary moment as something quite different from what it was then, an experience that is in part constituted by the intersubjective presence of the secondary witness. After years of listening to Holocaust survivors, psychologist Henry Greenspan observes that "survivors anticipate what will be hearable by us as well as what is tellable by them, and both negotiations are reflected in what they do, in fact, retell."[8]

In another photograph Wolin narrates the story of Moses Wloski, who was sent on a transport to Auschwitz from his hometown in White Russia: "Then one morning the Blitzkrieg roared through and Moses Wloski found himself behind German lines. Eventually he was boarded onto a transport headed for Auschwitz with Wolkowisk's 2500 remaining Jews. Moses was one of only 250 men and women allowed into the camp—the rest were gassed" (fig. 18). The silver words on the black background of the photograph become like patterned echoes of the large and legible tattooed number on his arm, which Wloski holds up for the viewer, propping it with his fist, as if these numbers are the true repository of the story. The numbers 94250 signify that 94,249 prisoners preceded him since March 1942 when the tattoo practice at Auschwitz began. The tension between subject and object positions is represented by the tension between Wloski and the number 94250. The story skips over his time in Auschwitz, proceeding to events after. Wloski's portrait, however, belies this ordering of the story by framing his head with his arm and the five well-shaped numbers, the emblem of his traumatic experience.

In a more oblique manner, Mišo Vogel, born in Czechoslovakia, reveals his tattooed number by his rolled-up sleeves as he holds a small framed photograph of his father, who died in Auschwitz (fig. 19). The fingers of Vogel's hand placed flat on his chest are seemingly truncated by being partially hidden under his shirt, as if to signify the riven heart. At the same time, they covertly point toward the tattooed number, while both arms float on a sea of words. The words engulf most of his body, as if he has sunk into them permanently. Here, too, the story is told in the third person, written in the words of Wolin who thereby helps to constitute the story, listing the dates and names of the camps where Vogel's family was killed and recounting what happened after the war: "He was just 20 years old. After escaping from concentration camp deep inside Germany, Mišo joined the United States Army. On furlough at the end of the war, he returned to his hometown in Slovakia to obtain records (birth certificate, medical history, etc.) needed for U.S. citizenship. The same Slovaks who had appropriated his father's cattle business and family's home greeted him from the front door of his house. 'We thought you were gassed, thought you were burned like all the rest.' Mišo's records, all the records of the Jews, were, like the Jews themselves, gone forever from that part of the world."

Many witnesses hold up photographs of loved ones, sometimes with multiple figures in them. Ruminating on such photographs in videotaped testimonies, Langer writes, "We are prompted to ask by the subtext of the narrative whether the point is to remind us that they once were or no longer are alive. Is it an effort at rescue or an avowal of loss? Are we gazing at presence—or absence?"[9] But there is another

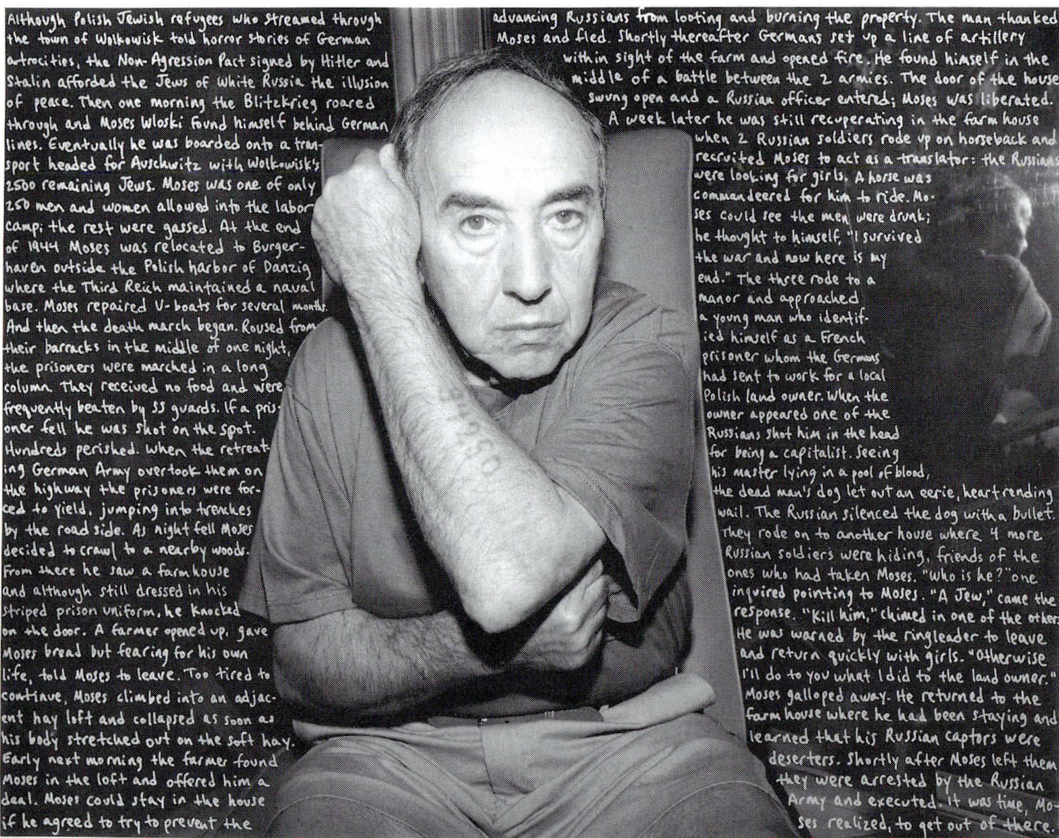

Fig. 18. Jeffrey Wolin, *Moses Wloski, b. 1921, Wolkowisk, White Russia*, from *Written in Memory: Portraits of the Holocaust*, 1997. Toned gelatin silver print with silver marker. © Jeffrey A. Wolin. Courtesy Catherine Edelman Gallery, Chicago.

aspect to holding up the photographs. This is the opportunity, consciously given by the survivors to the secondary witness, to perform the essential role of looking, of becoming secondary witnesses. Marianne Hirsch observes, "Photographs in their enduring 'umbilical' connection to life are precisely the medium connecting first- and second-generation remembrance, memory and postmemory. They are the leftovers, the fragmentary sources and building blocks, shot through with holes, of the work of postmemory."[10] The mutual interaction of primary and secondary witness through the act of showing and looking, like telling and hearing, produces what Hirsch calls "postmemory," or what I call memory effects. Critic Luc Sante suggests that photographs of the dead offer viewers "an excruciatingly intimate sight" along with "the burden of this intimacy. . . . The terrible gift that the dead make to the living is that of sight, which is to say foreknowledge; in return, they demand memory, which is to say acknowledgment."[11]

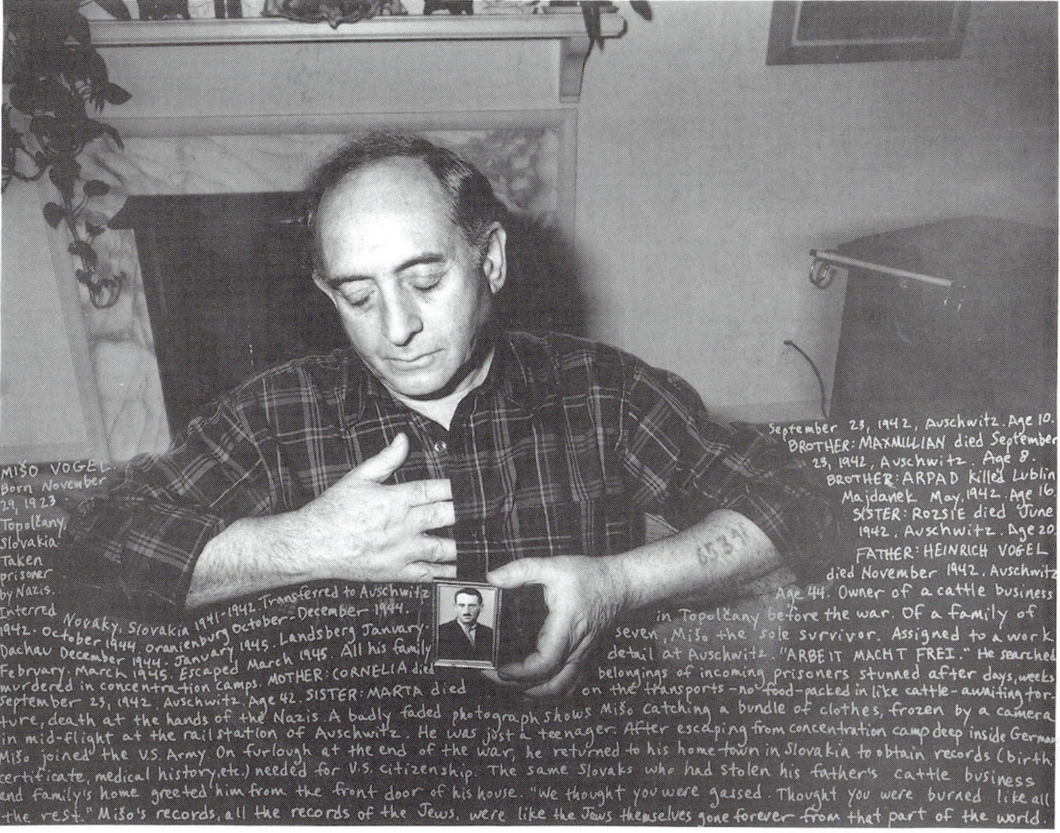

Fig. 19. Jeffrey Wolin, *Mišo Vogel, b. 1923, Topolcany, Slovakia*, from *Written in Memory: Portraits of the Holocaust*, 1997. Toned gelatin silver print with silver marker. © Jeffrey A. Wolin. Courtesy Catherine Edelman Gallery, Chicago.

On the facing pages of the survivor portraits, Wolin often includes pictures of the survivors in the early postwar years, or in some cases during the war years or before. These images show smiling, healthy people. The small size subordinates them to Wolin's own full-page photographs, suggesting that Wolin's images, taken fifty years later, are closer or truer to the Holocaust experience the subjects describe than the generally cheerful earlier pictures. It is easy to be persuaded that this is so, not only because the telling occurs in the present, but because the young smiling faces are more difficult to associate with the narratives than the contemporary faces. The pained, stoic, resilient looks on the faces of Wolin's subjects and the stories of their survival project a moral force that defies the effacement of memory and allows these photographs to be read as sites of resistance to the loss of history.

The differences between videotaped testimony and Wolin's photographs are more striking than the similarities, though these do exist. The most obvious difference is the ability to hear the voices of both witness and interviewer in the videotaped testimonies, allowing the viewer to be drawn with greater ease into the emotional texture of the narrative exchange, the shifting idioms and multiple voices that emerge from the witness. This provides greater access to the complexities of the victim who has survived and confronts us with our own false preconceptions and expectations. Wolin's photographs necessarily produce a greater emotional distance from the subject, obscuring the voice of the interviewer and modulating the voice of the witness, especially in the photographs in which Wolin retells the witness' story in the third person. Yet Wolin's photographs may be as effective as many videotaped testimonies in establishing a sense of the Holocaust experience as an ever-present part of the mental and emotional landscape of the witness, a physical presence that coexists with his or her daily life, as screens against feeling, a sea on which they float, or walls surrounding and enclosing the survivor.

In his portrait of Alice Friedman, Wolin effectively counters a commonly held misconception that survival constitutes "salvation" or "redemption" (fig. 20). Friedman's testimony illustrates with chilling clarity that survivor narratives generally do not end with a sense of liberation and triumph; she emphasizes discontinuity with the future, which is also the present. In this case, Friedman's testimony, in Wolin's handwriting, is reproduced in her own words:

> The Nazis came in the wee hours of the morning and this time they got my father . . . I remember them taking him and me sitting in the middle of the bed by myself crying so hard that I was throwing up. My mother was in the opposite corner of the room crying . . . I was alone for a long time . . . and much later I remember arms around me. And that was basically all I remembered for years and years. Every time I would try to bring anything back, I knew that this night has a profound effect on me. And whenever I would try to bring back what else I might have seen that night I would start to black out so I gave up. But a few

years ago I started being extremely self-destructive in subtle ways. I started realizing that it was like pus rising to the surface after festering for years. So I decided to go for counseling and I found a middle-aged Jewish woman who had some experience with Holocaust people. And so until recently I thought maybe they beat my father and that's what I saw and blocked out or they raped my mother. It turned out to be nothing like that at all. What was inside me all these years were the thoughts I had that night. And there were three different thoughts. One was: Why love my father? No, not why love my father—that I better not love him because it's not safe. The second one was: If they took him, how do I know they're not coming back for my mother? Believe it or not that thought was like a lifetime of fear. Well, everything is fear. However, as far as with my mother, I loved my mother terribly and we were very close. And when she died, which is now twenty seven years ago, I went into terrible mourning

Fig. 20. Jeffrey Wolin, *Alice Friedman, b. 1934, Vienna, Austria*, from *Written in Memory: Portraits of the Holocaust*, 1997. Toned gelatin silver print with silver marker. © Jeffrey A. Wolin. Courtesy Catherine Edelman Gallery, Chicago.

> for about a week and then I felt a weird kind of relief and I could never understand why until I was in counseling. The relief was the fact that I didn't have to be afraid of losing her anymore. The third thought was the hardest of all and that is the fear that I think will never go away, especially with the world situation. And I figure that it's just something I have to learn to live with and cope with rather than erase. And that was the thought that when I grow up they're going to come and get me.[12]

Wolin visually portrays Friedman's words as a dark wave threatening to wash over her like a black tide. The background plane consists of books stamped with the names and dates of Jewish families; Friedman eyes are cast obliquely into the past while holding up her postwar passport with a photograph of herself as a child. Only the child's gaze and the woman's hand break through the picture's surface. The words in the foreground are on the same plane as the child's image, generated by the experiences of the child. It was not the content of those memories but their very unrecoverability that produced the black shadow. Recovery, however, does not cause the wave to recede. In ways that dissolve the border between "documentary" and art, Wolin here imaginatively achieves what is more difficult to convey in the videotaped testimonies: a moving visual evocation of how the past dwells in the present in the lives of survivors—how the traumatized child lives alongside the adult, perhaps more vividly than the adult. Langer has sought to expose commonplace assumptions about "the strength and optimism that regulate our image of the heroic spirit."[13] Friedman describes a life shadowed by fear.

On the endleaf of Primo Levi's posthumously published book *The Drowned and the Saved,* a note "About the Author" briefly outlines the facts of Levi's life, his arrest and deportation to Auschwitz in 1944, the names of his books, and his death in 1987. The final paragraph suggests that Levi's writings "offer a wondrous celebration of life" and remain "a testament to the indomitability of the human spirit and mankind's capacity to defeat death through meaningful work, morality and art." That Primo Levi died by committing suicide at the age of sixty-seven is not mentioned. That the theme and mood of *The Drowned and the Saved* is profoundly pessimistic, sadly certain that the world has learned nothing from the Holocaust and that the gap of understanding widens the further we get from the actual events is dismissed by such cheering words as "wondrous celebration" and "indomitability." In his conclusion, Levi writes: "It happened, therefore it can happen again: this is the core of what we have to say." Levi's words are cast aside by the unquenchable desire for a happy ending. Members of the postwar generations often cling to reassuring affirmations of strength and the triumph of the spirit, while survivors are often left with an unmitigated sense of loss, discontinuity, unresolved fear, a diminished sense of self, or an inability to love.[14]

"INTELLIGENT, ARTICULATE, FEARLESS, AND OFTEN VERY GOOD LOOKING"

ARTIST PIER MARTON explores the many phases of coming to terms with a Jewish identity, from a recognition of pariah status, disgust, denial, puzzlement, to an uneasy pride as a form of solidarity with a long history and as a foundation for resistance against the suppression and loss of cultural identity. Marton inscribes himself directly, as one of the participants, into his videotaped interviews with secondary witnesses. A second-generation Jew born in France after the war, his father was in the French Resistance, helping to hide a French deserter, producing fake I.D. papers/official rubber stamps, and was involved in ambushes against the Germans in Paris; his mother was in hiding in Hungary. Two of his grandparents were murdered in Auschwitz, the other two in Budapest. As an adult, Marton became absorbed with the problem of Jewish identity: "I met a Dutch woman who, at age twenty-one, after much of her own prodding, had finally been told she was Jewish; her father had tried to 'shield her' by telling her she was *of no particular religion.* That story echoed an encounter I had had earlier with a British man who had found out he was Jewish when he was thirteen. All of these stories felt like more dramatic enactments of the same unease I had grown up with."[15] Obsessed with the question of how others coped with the problem of "being Jewish in Europe," Marton attended a Children of Survivors conference in New York City and advertised for individuals born and raised in Europe who were willing to tell their story on camera. He found a number of volunteers.[16]

A marathon of talking heads, Marton's 28-minute video *Say I'm a Jew* (1985) compensates for what it lacks in production values by a head-on confrontation with the issue that matters most to him: How strong are the pressures to assimilate and deny an identity seemingly founded on negative stereotypes? How strong is the compulsion to embrace and reconstruct Jewish identity? Marton appropriates the model of the videotaped survivor testimonial to interview sixteen second-generation subjects from nine different countries, including Germany, France, Poland, Romania, Holland, Belgium, Austria, Hungary, and Yugoslavia. The responses reveal a deep ambivalence about each subject's ethnic identity. The narratives interweave stories about growing up Jewish in Europe, absorbing an impending sense of doom from their survivor parents, experiencing painful incidents of antisemitism, internalizing antisemitic stereotypes, raging against the deep unhappiness of their parents, experiencing Jewishness as a negative identity and shame at being Jewish, finding it is easier to be a Jew in America, and finally, coming to grips with a positive, if still ambivalent, sense of Jewish identity. One woman born in Germany, who emigrated to America with her family, recounts that her passport was stamped by the Germans "Homeless Foreigner." "I still feel that way," she observes. Others embrace their Jewish identity more wholeheartedly after a youthful estrangement. All of them attest to the painful challenge of coming out Jewish. As Jon Stratton observes: "It seems as if, for some of my generation, born in a Europe which could not even begin to talk clearly about what had been done to the Jews, and often of parents whose not necessarily conscious response to the Holocaust was that it was a visitation for not assimilating enough, the ability to acknowledge one's Jewishness in a public fashion has been difficult in the extreme."[17]

The pressure to assimilate and the continued existence of anti-Jewish stereotypes, in subtle forms, may be read as the premise of the video, in which the troubled subject position of the narrators in relation to antisemitism takes as its first goal the simple ability to "say 'I'm a Jew.'" For these secondary witnesses, the traumatic Holocaust experiences of their parents were a profound influence on their lives and their sense of Jewishness is based on a negative identity founded on genocide. At the same time, the multiple voices of the participants relentlessly scrutinize the identification of the second generation with their parents, sorting out what has been internalized as part of the structure of feeling of their parents' world from their own experience of the contemporary world. Jewishness is understood as both a source of oppressive misery and as a source of pride. Lori Lefkovitz relates a story about a friend that captures this ironic contradiction, in which pride and oppression stem from the same source: "Kathryn came upon an old dictaphone tape on which her father's reporting of a case is interrupted by quarreling children in the background. To distract them the father offers to interview the children on his machine, and the young Kathryn reports that she is five years old and will soon be off to Hebrew School. When asked why Hebrew School is important, the little voice confidently replies: 'Because Jews were burned in ovens.'"[18]

An interesting aspect of this project is its reception by critic John Russell. In a review for the *New York Times*,, quoted on the back of the videotape, Russell praises the work for its honesty and uplifting ending: "Not a moment is wasted, nor a word. The speakers are intelligent, articulate, fearless, and often very good looking. What they think, they say. What they feel is written on their faces . . . It is the wonder of Mr. Marton's film that his young people heal their wounds almost before our eyes. They end not as victims, but as exemplary human beings. And we leave convinced that—to quote from Mr. Marton—'nothing short of complete healing is required of all of us.'"[19] Russell's remarks are a redemptive gloss that includes the seemingly innocuous observation that "the speakers are intelligent, articulate, fearless, *and often very good looking*" (emphasis added). There is something troubling about this notion. While movie stars are regularly discussed in entertainment columns in terms of their looks and screen appeal, a reference to the speakers' good looks in this video work about the Jewish children of Holocaust survivors raised in Europe and now living in the United States seems rather inappropriate. What appears to have crept into this review in one of the major liberal organs in the United States is the old European stereotype of the ugly Jew, here implicitly acknowledged, albeit rejected. These particular Jews, the statement implies, who are "often very good looking," do not fit the stereotype. But the stereotype itself remains unchallenged.

The irony is that the stereotype is at the heart of the anguished soul-searching by the participants on the video, who regard it as one of the main sources of their bifurcated sense of self. One of the interviewees, the brother of Marton, enumerates the traits of the ugly Jew: "We're different, we're not pure, Europeans are pure, we're not as white as Europeans, we have curly hair, hooked noses, darker skin." Sander Gilman has written extensively on the construction of the Jewish stereotype, analyzing these and other common features of the anti-Jewish image, including flat feet, bowed legs, beady eyes and big noses. Commenting on the effect and consequences of stereotyping, Gilman writes, "The goal of studying stereotypes is not to stop the production of images of the Other, images that demean and, by demeaning, control. This would be the task of Sisyphus. We need these stereotypes to structure the world. We need crude representations of difference to localize our anxiety, to prove to ourselves that what we fear does not lie within. . . . We view our own images, our own mirages, our own stereotypes as embodying qualities that exist in the world.

Fig. 21. Pier Marton, Installation view of *JEW* at the Judah Magnus Museum, Berkeley, 1994. Courtesy Pier Marton.

And we act upon them."[20] The *New York Times* critic merely turns the stereotype on its head, from negative to positive, and reads the determination of the secondary witnesses to embrace and defend Jewish identity against demeaning stereotypes as an all-encompassing healing rather than a political, cultural and ethical stance: "They end not as victims, but as exemplary human beings" and "heal their wounds almost before our eyes." Victims, then, are structured as the opposite of exemplary human beings. In this reading, the apparent transcendence of victimization by this group of young Jews not only allows for the inversion of the stereotype but also allows for an easy dismissal of the victimization itself, even while recognizing the radical resistance embodied in this form of secondary witnessing.

Say I'm A Jew subsequently became the centerpiece of an installation entitled *JEW,* marked in large Hebrew-style letters.[21] For the installation, Marton placed the video in a room designed as a cattle car with wooden benches for viewing (fig. 21). In a black-walled hallway outside the cattle car, including inset photographs of some of the video participants, viewers were invited to write comments in white chalk (fig. 22). With the testimonial format and simulated cattle car, Marton bluntly appropriates the signifiers of Holocaust experience to legitimate the traumatic expe-

Fig. 22. Pier Marton, Installation view of *JEW* at the Judah Magnus Museum, Berkeley, 1994. Courtesy Pier Marton.

rience of secondary witnessing; the black walls invite the complicity of those who interact with the installation through their epistolary participation while the oversize title shouts the source of Marton's shame and pride in a highly provocative confrontation with the spectator. While Jeffrey Wolin searches for ways to get into the narratives of his survivor subjects, Marton presents the angry, anguished narratives of the children of survivors who testify to a world of experience they have tried to avoid and deny, ultimately recognizing the possibility of using it to build a foundation for the voluntary embrace of difference.

CHAPTER FIVE

LANDSCAPE AND THE SEARCH FOR MEMORY

■

Sitting on a rock, Yukel watched the sea leaf through the world's book of water.

We are constantly in touch with the work, as salt is in touch with the sand, as air with water, secretly in touch as scales are with the echo, as silence is with signs.

Lived moments, faithfully recorded. The patient work of death.

There are no trees for the dead earth.

There are no stars for dead skies.

Light from beyond the crests, the grooves.

It engulfs heaven and earth.

EDMOND JABÈS
from *The Book of Questions,* vol. 1, 1972

■

As we saw in the previous chapter, secondary witnesses engage in forms of both overidentification with and resistance to the experience of primary witnesses; they also are subject to internalized stereotypes that further shape a troubled and conflicted sense of identity. Many secondary witnesses attempt to work through their relationship to the past by retracing the lives of their parents, grandparents, or unknown ancestors in some way, or even performing the role of Nazi victim. Pilgrimages to the European birthplaces of ancestors and/or to the locations of death camps made by succeeding generations as journeys of discovery often end in perplexity. At the same time, they shift the focus of witnessing from the devastating events themselves to the reconstruction of those events in the present through fresh interrogations of the public archive, examinations of traces and remains, and renewed attention to the contemporary contingencies of culture and politics. The four artists discussed in this chapter each returned to the European landscape in a search for clues to the contemporary structure of knowledge about the Holocaust and its continuing effects; at the same time, their representations themselves contribute to the structuring of that knowledge, suggesting an inability to recuperate the past even as the compulsion for reenactment, and even impersonation, drives their projects forward toward a more enlightened encounter with the future.

JAMES FRIEDMAN: *12 NAZI CONCENTRATION CAMPS*

JAMES FRIEDMAN, whose awareness of the Holocaust began at age four when he saw a black and white newsreel showing Jewish victims of the Nazis, uses the postwar visual archive as a foil for his own autobiographical, postmodernist archive. Born in 1950 to assimilated American parents, Friedman connected to European Jewry through his Orthodox grandfather and felt the effects of antisemitism firsthand growing up in Columbus, Ohio. As a child, Friedman was witness to the hanging of the family dog by neighboring kids; a few years later an antisemitic German neighbor doused the house with gasoline and tried to set it on fire; in the following decades the house was damaged several times by gunfire.[1]

As a graduate student, Friedman studied with Minor White at MIT and was an assistant to Imogen Cunningham at San Francisco State University. In 1981 he traveled to Europe to photograph the Nazi concentration camps and subcamps in Austria (Mauthausen), Belgium (Fort Breendonck), Czechoslovakia (Theresienstadt), France (Natzweiler-Struthof), and Germany (Bergen-Belsen, Bisingen, Dachau, Flossenbürg, and Vaihingen). He canceled his visit to Poland when it came under martial law during the Solidarity crisis and the U.S. State Department could not guarantee safe passage out of the country once entered, making a return trip in 1983 to photograph Auschwitz-Birkenau, Majdanek, and Treblinka. In 1988, thirty of Friedman's camp photographs were turned into a traveling exhibition, *James Friedman: 12 Nazi Concentration Camps, Color Photographs, 1981 and 1983*, organized by the Visual Studies Workshop in Rochester, New York; in the same year, an exhibition of nineteen photographs, *Concerning a Personal Project: Photographs of Nazi Concentration Camp Sites,* was shown by the University Gallery/Wexner Center for the Visual Arts at Ohio State University in Columbus.

Friedman's visits to the camps in the early 1980s, especially to Poland during the Stalinist era, made him one of the few pilgrims from the West at that time. In some of the camps there was nothing left but a field or memorial sculpture or facsimile barracks to replace the ones that had disappeared; in others, the effects of tourism had left their mark. Friedman's photographs make no attempt to travel back in time; instead, they unsettle viewers' expectations, presenting such startling elements as concession stands, maintenance workers and tourists who wander through the grounds of the camps or pose for the camera in front of monuments to the dead. By shortening the focal length of the lens, a dark circle surrounds many of the images, producing vignettes that are constant reminders of the camera's presence and disrupting the conceit of omniscience in documentary photography. In one photograph, men at a survivors' reunion at Natzweiler-Struthof stroll into the viewfinder wearing suits and ties, binoculars and ascots; in another, a German family, the mother wearing white plastic boots, stands in front of a monument at Bergen-Belsen (Plate 4). The simplicity of this image in the context of any ordinary tourist site would be unremarkable; yet the blank stares of the German family posi-

Fig. 23. James Friedman, *Delivery truck, Mauthausen concentration camp, Austria*, 1981, from *12 Nazi Concentration Camps*. Courtesy James Friedman.

tioned before a Holocaust monument on a sunny day evokes an air of unreality to the image that makes the convergence of setting and actors seem both slightly ridiculous and vaguely disturbing. At Mauthausen a truck delivers cheerfully colorful cases of soda pop to the concession stand (fig. 23); at Dachau, a teenager takes advantage of the parking lot space to run his remote-controlled, miniature racing car (fig. 24). Some photographs include arrangements of ambiguous, personal, talismanic objects belonging to Friedman, colored markers and small cameras, handwritten notations about the sites, the cherrywood frame of his camera set, his own hands, his own shadow, and even himself as one of the many figures who wander through the landscape or pose for the camera (fig. 25). "The world that Friedman found and photographed," comments Jonathan Green, "was not a world of grim reminders of man's inhumanity but slices of banal normality; everyday life at a series of tourist attractions."[2] Friedman's modus operandi for photographing the camps is a rejection of the somber, aestheticized modernist compositions devoid of people and shot in black and white that we have come to associate with the photo-

Fig. 24. James Friedman, *Parking lot, Dachau concentration camp*, 1981, from *12 Nazi Concentration Camps*. Courtesy James Friedman.

graphic archive of the concentration camps. In effect, his photographs constitute a critique of such an approach, instead depending on strategies that challenge documentary photographs as transparently timeless windows into history.

A recent successful example of the modernist approach is the work of Erich Hartmann, former president of Magnum Photos. Hartmann was a German Jew who fled Germany when he was sixteen and survived the war in England. He moved to the United States and returned to Europe fifty years later to photograph the concentration camps and subcamps. After a two-month period of photographing in 1993, Hartmann's work was exhibited at various galleries around the United States and reproduced in book form as *In the Camps* (1995).[3] Even before we read the titles that identify the sites in the black and white photographs, we know where we are. Hartmann captures the oft-repeated icons of Holocaust imagery: worm's-eye and bird's-eye views of train tracks, entrance gates with the sign *Arbeit macht frei* (fig. 26), guard towers, barracks, mounds of shoes, mounds of suitcases, artificial limbs,

Fig. 25. James Friedman, *Local resident, photographer, and shepherd, Bisingen (subcamp of Natzweiler-Struthof concentration camp)*, 1981, from *12 Nazi Concentration Camps.* Courtesy James Friedman.

Fig. 26. Erich Hartmann, *Entrance gate to prisoner cells. Theresienstadt Gestapo prison; Terezin, Czech Republic*, 1993. ©Erich Hartmann/Magnum Photos, Inc.

barbed wire, and crematoria ovens. The photographic frontispiece to *In the Camps,* "Barbed wire. Majdanek KZ; near Lublin, Poland," portrays the silhouette of a bird perched on a wire; in the last photograph, the same bird takes flight, in an obvious metaphoric gesture of liberation (fig. 27 and 28). The arc of the photographic text,

Figs. 27. Erich Hartmann, *Barbed wire. Majdanek KZ; near Lublin, Poland,* 1993. ©Erich Hartmann/Magnum Photos, Inc.

which moves toward this redemptive moment, parallels Hartmann's modernist aesthetic: unpeopled sites in somber shades of black and gray, often creating starkly beautiful compositions of carefully considered formal values, and allusive religious iconography that evokes shining crosses of light at the center of prison bars, or inti-

Figs. 28. Erich Hartmann, *Barbed wire. Majdanek KZ; near Lublin, Poland*, 1993. ©Erich Hartmann/Magnum Photos, Inc.

mations of the last supper in a Gestapo sentencing chamber (fig. 29). The overtones of sacrifice and death culminate in the gesture of spiritual freedom.

In the afterword to his book, Hartmann indicates a primary motivation for his project: "Soon the entire physical fabric—buildings and authentic objects—will have disintegrated and will have had to be completely replaced by reconstructions, as for instance the seemingly endless miles of rusting barbed wire are already having to be replaced every few years. Hence, the functions of the camp sites will change from being mainly places of memory and reminder to becoming mainly museums and educational sites, their physical area to be reduced in many places. Photographs such as these may not be possible much longer."[4] To address his concern that the camps will become reduced, sterile sites with sanitized forms of documentation, Hartmann focused his energy on documenting the physical fabric of the camps in the belief that simulated replacements and reconstructions cannot carry the aura of the originals. His work, nonetheless, raises questions about Holocaust aestheticization, even dark romanticization, and the resulting emotional distancing from camp realities that so moved him. The imagined authenticity of Hartmann's photographs, it may be argued, can no more preserve the lost experience of the camps than the sanitized museums he fears, with their potential for fetishized objects.

Fig. 29. Erich Hartmann, *Gestapo courtroom in death bunker. Auschwitz KZ; Oswiecim*, Poland, 1993. ©Erich Hartmann/Magnum Photos, Inc.

Indeed, the beautifully composed photographs may become a screen for memory, which both elides the past and receives all imaginative projections.

Friedman, in fact, documents the very thing that Hartmann feared and anticipated: a site in which the search for memory of a historically specific past becomes difficult if not impossible. At the entrance to the Natzweiler-Struthof concentration camp near Strasbourg, we see evidence of the camp reconstructions: a brand new wooden fence has been erected (Plate 5). Moreover, Friedman shortens the focal length, tilts the angle, and shoots into a glorious burst of clouds and blue sky, making the guard tower appear squatter than it might be, in opposition to the more familiar tendency to monumentalize. Like Hartmann, yet in a very different way, Friedman raises disturbing questions about the functions of these camps today. Hartmann's photographs aspire to convey the invisible horror of what occurred, like an omniscient window onto the past, while ultimately evoking a hope for spiritual transcendence; Friedman's photographs relentlessly evince the shrouding of the past by the depredations of the present with a deliberate and self-conscious irony. Friedman records the faces of contemporary survivors as they revisit the scenes of crimes against them; Hartmann's photographs convey a sense of loss and catastrophe veiled forever in the distant past. Friedman reveals the concentration camps as the tourist sites they are today, Hartmann carefully effaces the present, producing images that effectively continue the look and feel of postwar archival imagery, projecting a view of "the way it was then." It is as if they were taken fifty years ago. Yet Hartmann's photographs were shot ten years later than Friedman's. Friedman portrays what is left of the camps, using an approach that might be characterized as disruptive, openly pointing to the impossibility of recuperation, compared to the sacralized aura of Hartmann's works.

THE ARCHIVE/ACTING AGAINST THE GRAIN

THE ARCHIVAL FEEL of Hartmann's photographs is, in turn, conditioned by the work of others. Much of the archive of the Shoah that has shaped public memory consists of lens-based images taken either by the perpetrators or the liberators during or immediately after the war. Photographs taken by participants inside the ghettos were rare, and nonexistent in the camps.[5] Images of the ghettos and camps were mostly taken by the Nazis themselves and published during the war in works such as *Signal,* their main international propaganda magazine, which was translated into more than twenty languages. But it was photographs of the camps taken at the end of the war by the Allies, predominantly British and American military and press photographers, in addition to film footage, that has had the greatest impact. Ironically, the photograph that is now perhaps most associated with the camps, of male prisoners behind barbed wire at Buchenwald, taken in 1945 by Margaret Bourke-White, only became well known years later, and is a relatively benign representation (fig. 30). Though Bourke-White was a *Life* magazine photographer at the time, her photograph was not published in *Life,* but in the 1946 book *"Dear Fatherland, Rest Quietly"*; the photograph only appeared in *Life* in a 1960 collection marking its twenty-five-year anniversary.[6] It has become one of the most recycled images of survivors, appearing in dozens of Holocaust retrospectives and anniversary issues of journals, magazines, and overviews of photojournalism. In 1989, according to Barbie Zelizer, "Time selected the photo as one of the ten great iconic images of photojournalism because it 'informed the world about the true nature of the Holocaust,'" a claim made shortly before the Eichmann trial and the documentary footage of mounds of corpses shown in the film *Judgement at Nuremberg* the following year.[7]

Immediately after the war, it was primarily weekly photos in the press that bore witness to the atrocities of the Holocaust and served to convince an incredulous public about what had happened. Susan Sontag expressed a widely felt sentiment when she described her reaction on first seeing photographs of Bergen-Belsen and Dachau: "Nothing I have seen—in photographs or in real life—ever cut me as

Fig. 30. *Buchenwald, April 1945.* Margaret Bourke-White/TimePix.

sharply, deeply, instantaneously. Indeed, it seems plausible to me to divide my life into two parts, before I saw those photographs (I was twelve) and after, though it was several years before I understood fully what they were about."[8] Black and white stills have appeared in many periodicals since then, along with archival film footage in Holocaust centers and museums around the nation, and in documentaries and films on the war, such as Alain Resnais's *Night and Fog* (1955) and Stanley Kramer's *Judgement at Nuremberg* (1961), and have been fictively recreated based on the look of the postwar archive in television films such as *Holocaust* (1978), *Playing for Time* (which also inserts documentary images, 1980), *Escape from Sobibor* (1987), and *Schindler's List* (1993), to name just a few.

James Friedman effectively announced his intentions to act against the grain of the archive by choosing an 8 x 10 view camera and color film to produce large-format dye-transfer prints. Although color imagery was produced at the end of the war, we have learned to recognize the Holocaust only in black and white. In addition, Friedman disorders our expectations by capturing the cool ordinariness of these scenes. In another image, a child in blue jeans and a bright blue sweater stands in front of a bullet-pocked wall where Jewish prisoners were executed at Theresienstadt (Plate 6). As part of the present-day room numbering system, camp officials affixed the number 37, in blue, to the wall above the child, who patiently poses for his photograph. The uneasiness evoked by this photograph is not just from the juxtaposition of the child and the execution wall, but, as with the German family posing at Bergen-Belsen and Friedman's other photographs, the coexistence of the ordinary and the extreme, what Michael Rothberg has called traumatic realism. Echoing the making of a "souvenir," but at a murder site, the absurd banality is made apparent by the visible shadows of the view camera and the photographer whose hand holds a large film plate.

One of the places Friedman chose to photograph is the little known Belgian camp of Breendonck, where tourists stand about, pose for the camera, or lounge in comfortable chairs on the patio at the Restaurant Breendonck (fig. 31). The area is clean and paved and visitors can sit at tables shaded by festive umbrellas. Breendonck, halfway between Brussels and Antwerp, was a fortress during World War I and the last headquarters of Brussels' King Leopold during World War II. Today a Belgian National Museum, under German occupation it became a reception camp for those suspected of being in the Belgian Resistance, and was the place where Austrian writer Jean Améry was imprisoned and tortured.

Born in Vienna as Hans Meyer, Améry was the only child of a Catholic mother and a Jewish father. He left Vienna to join the Resistance in Belgium and was arrested by the Gestapo in July 1943. Describing the torture he suffered in "Reception Camp Breendonck" at the hands of the SS, Améry writes:

> In the bunker there hung from the vaulted ceiling a chain that above ran into a

roll. At its bottom end it bore a heavy, broadly curved iron hook. I was led to the instrument. The hook gripped into the shackle that held my hands together behind my back. Then I was raised with the chain until I hung about a meter over the floor. In such a position, or rather, when hanging this way, with your hands behind your back, for a short time you can hold at a half-oblique through muscular force. During these few minutes, when you are already expending your utmost strength, when sweat has already appeared on your forehead and lips, and you are breathing in gasps, you will not answer any questions. Accomplices? Addresses? Meeting places? You hardly hear it. All your life is gathered in a single, limited area of the body, the shoulder joints, and it does not react; for it exhausts itself completely in the expenditure of energy. But this cannot last long, even with people who have a strong physical constitution. As for me, I had to give up rather quickly. And now there was a crackling and splintering in my shoulders that my body has not forgotten until this hour. The ball sprang from their sockets. My own body weight caused luxation; I fell into a void and

Fig. 31. James Friedman, *Restaurant Breendonck, Breendonck concentration camp, near Antwerp, Belgium,* 1981, from *12 Nazi Concentration Camps.* Courtesy James Friedman.

hung by my dislocated arms, which had been torn high from behind and were now twisted over my head. Torture, from Latin *torquere,* to twist. What visual instruction in etymology! At the same time, the blows from the horsewhip showered down on my body, and some of them sliced cleanly through the light summer trousers that I was wearing on the twenty-third of July 1943.[9]

Améry concludes, "Whoever has succumbed to torture can no longer feel at home in the world."[10]

The impossibility of conveying traumatic Holocaust experience is mutely evident in Friedman's photograph, *Mannequin of political prisoner,* in which the head and upper torso of a mannequin protected in a display case is shown wearing a light-colored shirt and khaki jacket (fig. 32). Yet another mannequin wears an SS uniform (fig. 33), while a third mannequin in a display case wears striped prison clothes, bear-

Fig. 32. James Friedman, *Mannequin of political prisoner, Breendonck concentration camp, Belgium*, 1981, from *12 Nazi Concentration Camps*. Courtesy James Friedman.

ing the bizarre label, *Mannequin of religious zealot* (fig. 34). How are we to infer episodes of torture and cruelty from such unmarked spaces, benign displays, and misleadingly labeled mannequins? Here is an extreme version of the sanitized museum site into which Erich Hartmann feared the camps would be transformed.

THE MEANINGS OF AUSCHWITZ

WITH CAMPS IN the former Eastern Bloc, in particular Auschwitz, it is important to realize that these sites were maintained for a local Polish audience for decades before they were opened to Western visitors. "Auschwitz" did not exist for the Poles—only a place called Oswiecim, which had a very different signification that marginalized the memory of the Jews and

Fig. 33. James Friedman, *Mannequin of Nazi SS officer, Breendonck concentration camp, Belgium, 1981,* from *12 Nazi Concentration Camps*. Courtesy James Friedman.

sanctified Auschwitz as a site of Polish suffering and victimization. Thus, no signs, symbols or markers indicating that Jews were murdered in Auschwitz-Birkenau appear in Friedman's 1983 images because they did not yet exist. Controversy erupted in the 1980s, however, most prominently over a convent erected by a group of Carmelite nuns at the concentration camp.[11] This occurred at a moment when Polish isolation behind the Iron Curtain began to be broken and there was a reassertion of interest in Jewish tradition and culture among an elite group of Jews, half-Jews, spouses of Jews and sympathetic non-Jews. In 1980 Pope John Paul II, formerly Karol Wojtyla, the archbishop of Kraków, visited Auschwitz and spoke to millions of Poles in words that were reprinted and hailed throughout Poland. John Paul asked his listeners to "pause . . . for a moment *at the plaque with an inscription in the Hebrew language.* This inscription evokes the memory of the nation whose sons and daughters were intended for complete extermination . . . . It is not permissible for anyone to pass this plaque with indifference."[12] These sentiments became a focus of expanding interest in Poland, but as historian Michael Steinlauf comments, there was another, contradictory aspect to the Pope's visit. John Paul's statement about Jews came after his eulogy for Maximilian Kolbe, a Franciscan priest impris-

Fig. 34. James Friedman, *Mannequin of religious zealot, Breendonck concentration camp, Belgium*, 1981, from *12 Nazi Concentration Camps*. Courtesy James Friedman.

oned at Auschwitz who exchanged his life for that of another Christian prisoner he did not know, a father with children. John Paul's description of Kolbe's act as a "victory through faith and love" hints, Steinlauf suggests, that "the meaning of Auschwitz could be encompassed by a Catholic paradigm."[13] Kolbe's sacrifice fits the traditional notion of martyrdom that gives meaning to such a willful act, but has nothing to do with the murder of the Jews. Historians Debórah Dwork and Robert Jan van Pelt comment:

> Father Kolbe's death was exceptional because, ultimately, he died a free man while nearly all the other millions of victims never had a choice at all. In a fundamental way his memorial in block 11 fits the conventional, chivalric ideology of a hero who fights and dies on behalf of someone else. Pervasive and dominant, this concept of heroism is reflected in the official symbol of the memorial camp, a shield with two drawn swords, and the official banner which flies over block 11 in Auschwitz I and the monument in Birkenau, the red triangle of the gentile political prisoners superimposed on the uniform motif of vertical blue and white stripes. There is no room in this ideology for women like Mrs. Zucker [a Jewish mother], who during the selection in Birkenau on 22 August 1944, held fast to the hand of a little girl she knew. As her then fifteen-year-old daughter, Esther, recalled, "This was the last time I saw my mother. She went with that neighbor's child. So when we talk about heroes, mind you, this was a hero: a woman who would not let a four-year-old child go by herself."[14]

It was later discovered that Father Kolbe, whom the pope canonized in 1982, had been the publisher from 1935 to 1939 of the virulently antisemitic Catholic tabloid *Maly Dziennik* (*Little Daily*), the largest circulation daily newspaper in Poland.[15]

When Westerners in the 1980s discovered Auschwitz as a real place, it was a site already visited annually by hundreds of thousands of people, 90 percent of whom were Polish tourists. Only five million of the twenty-two million people who have visited Auschwitz over the past fifty years have come from outside Poland; only since the fall of communism have 50 percent of the visitors been non-Polish, primarily Germans and Jews from all over the world.[16] In the weeks before ceremonies took place, commemorating the fiftieth anniversary of the liberation of Auschwitz in 1995, a public opinion poll in Poland found that 47 percent of those polled believed that Auschwitz was primarily a place of Polish martyrdom, while only 8 percent believed that most of its victims were Jews.[17] Weeks after the ceremonies, a new survey found that those associating Auschwitz with Polish suffering dropped to 32 percent while those identifying it with Jews more than doubled (but remained less than a quarter of the population). Thus, it was possible for Lech

Walesa, during the commemoration ceremonies on 26 January 1995, to deliver a long speech in Kraków without once mentioning Jews.

Since the fall of communism in 1989, there has been both a greater proliferation of antisemitic graffiti, vandalism, and publications, as well as, for the first time in postwar history, public discussion of antisemitism. The first public opinion polls reveal higher levels of anti-Jewish sentiment in Poland than elsewhere in Europe except Slovakia.[18] In response to the increased numbers of Western and particularly Jewish visitors during celebrations of the fiftieth anniversary of the liberation of Auschwitz, the post-communist government in Poland initiated a number of changes at Auschwitz. These included the recaptioning of photographic displays with information about Jewish victims, the translation of captions into Hebrew alongside other languages, and the retraining of some of the guides. A permanent International Auschwitz Advisory Council has been organized to address the problem of the progressive deterioration of the grounds and exhibits at Auschwitz.

Friedman's photographs of Treblinka, Majdanek, and Auschwitz, taken two years after his first visit to European camps, evidence a shift in his working method: the forms of self-referentiality became either more subtle or more direct. Friedman speculates, in hindsight, that perhaps two years later he was more "anaesthetized," yet at the same time more deeply committed to the project that he knew would not be complete without Poland. He "began to believe," he says, "more in the power of the straight photograph" and was chastened by a constant awareness of soldiers brandishing machine guns wherever he went. In *Local resident with scythe, photographer, Auschwitz-Birkenau concentration camp, Poland,* 1983, Friedman appears facing the camera behind a local farmer posing with his scythe in his hand (fig. 35). The city government had given local residents part of the land inside the concentration camp to care for. The old man mowed the grass with his scythe; in return he could bring it home to feed his cattle. A translator told him about Friedman's project, whereupon the old man told of how he had helped Jews escape during the war. Whether true or not, he was clearly sympathetic, while other townspeople Friedman met were hostile, some openly declaring that more Jews should have been killed.[19] The peasant with his scythe occupies the foreground of the image, bracketed by chimneys and a barracks. The position of the photographer may be read as both trapped and protected behind the looming blade and the unflinching face of its owner, adumbrating the position of many Polish Jews fifty years earlier who were either saved by the altruism of their Polish neighbors or condemned by them. The resonance with a history of rescue or betrayal overcomes a more kitsch reference to the grim reaper by its context: this is Auschwitz in the full light of day; *three million Jews died here.* The real and not the symbolic Auschwitz stands against a flood of meanings produced by different individuals, groups and nationalities. Auschwitz has stood unchanged for decades in the Western historical imagination, but can do so no longer. By resisting the tropes of the modernist archive, Friedman's photographs resist the sacralized, fixed and fictive conception of the concentration camps today.

Over a decade after Friedman photographed Auschwitz, a visiting reporter captured in words the contradictions Friedman captures in images:

> In the big parking lot colored buses stand in a row. One hears the multilingual buzz of groups waiting for their guides. Taking advantage of a free moment, tourists line up to change money or buy ice cream or address postcards. Tired travelers stretch out on the lawn. A teacher scolds some overly noisy children. A group of young Israelis unfurl national flags. Several Germans emerge from the flower shop with wreaths. A bright red truck with a Coca-Cola sign arrives at the restaurant, just behind it a green bus marked [in English] "Kraków—Wieliczka—Auschwitz. Every day at 6 p.m." We are in Auschwitz—a real place on the earth. Thirty kilometers from Katowice, sixty from Kraków. We find ourselves in a place that is exceptionally problematic.[20]

Fig. 35. James Friedman, *Local resident with scythe, photographer, Auschwitz-Birkenau concentration camp, Poland*, 1983, from *12 Nazi Concentration Camps*. Courtesy James Friedman.

By making the hand of the photographer apparent at every turn, the effect of Friedman's approach goes beyond a postmodernist challenge to the objectivity of the documentary method; Friedman makes the producer, the identity behind the camera, the secondary witness, as much a subject of the photographs as the barracks, execution walls, landscapes, and returning survivors. The separation of the space before the camera and the space of the unseen photographer, demarcated by the camera lens, is the way in which the assertion of objectivity has been traditionally produced. The space of the photographer thereby has been undefined, invisible, and by implication, irrelevant. Friedman's visibility as the photographer overtly implicates him in decisions of framing, distancing, and a myriad of other choices. His presence marks him as a subjective participant, an agent who influences what is seen before the camera. This approach runs counter to the usual non-participatory positioning of documentary photographers, including photojournalists who, for example, photograph atrocities as they are being committed.

Friedman avoids the presumption of speaking for the witnesses or seeing what they saw. By filtering the presence of the camps through contemporary consciousness, Friedman constructs a bridge from the past to the present, dropping the pretense of "going back in time" to capture the past as it exists today. The contrived and contingent effects, the subjective awareness, the pervasive intrusion of contemporary culture and personal objects, and the refusal of "timeless truth" convey, in their jarring effects, a difficult and uncomfortable sense of commemoration that reflects on the paradox of memorializing in order to forget. While searching for traumatic memory, the photographer instead seems to experience a crisis of secondary witnessing—an inability to lift the veil from the face of oblivion. Friedman's camera reveals an extraordinary ordinariness that defies our vision of the Holocaust as occurring in a suspended sphere of no-man's-land, a place beyond time, an airless space. Here, where millions suffered and died wretchedly, well-fed sightseers in casual, contemporary dress stroll around under sunny, blue skies, where groundsmen mow green lawns and new wooden fences are erected. This is not the melodrama of train tracks and chimneys in grim shades of gray, but the world of the secondary witness who "refuses to disappear from the pictures, refuses to correct off-perpendicular angles, refuses to give his subjects the entirety of the picture frame, and in short, refuses to allow the viewer to forget that these pictures are photographic constructions," as Vincent Leo remarks. Referring to the controversial television film *Holocaust,* Leo continues, "In so doing, Friedman acts to prevent the possible glamorization of the subject, a terrible problem with the historically realistic docudramas now on TV. The viewer is never allowed to construct an objectified and unmediated reality from which to isolate and/or fetishize fascist symbols or actions."[21]

Many of the visitors in Friedman's photographs seem to wander aimlessly, searching for memory and history like a lost pair of glasses. Friedman does not exempt the secondary witness from this process, also positioning himself as a tourist at the site of memory, searching for a heritage to which there is no easy access, and walking through his own photographs with the unidentified others. The photographs implicitly interrogate the landscape as historical site: Can cultural identity be recuperated from the site of events that lie beyond the borders of memory, which exist only as memory effects?

And yet, the photographs still manage to evoke a sense of profound loss. Because we *do* know where these photographs were taken, because the ghost of the postwar archive haunts them, the very casualness of the scene with its peaceful, pastoral face provokes a creeping sense of dislocation and unexpected sense of horror. In more than one hundred and thirty photographs, Friedman quietly informs the viewer with captions such as, "Wall where Jewish prisoners were shot, Theresienstadt concentration camp, Czechoslovakia, 1983," and "Tourists, execution area, Fort Breendonck concentration camp, Belgium, 1981." The atrocities referred to in the matter-of-fact captions, juxtaposed with sunny settings, become all the more unnerving: we are challenged to imagine what we have never seen, to will ourselves into this history, to resist forgetfulness. The camps cannot evoke the past on their own, but only if "the will to remember," in Pierre Nora's words, already exists. The ruins project no meaning without the intention of visitors to recognize their significance; indeed, the lax or uninformed visitor might be seduced by the beauty of the landscape. Simon Schama observed: "In our mind's eye we are accustomed to think of the Holocaust as having no landscape—or at best one emptied of features and color, shrouded in night and fog, blanketed by perpetual winter, collapsed into shades of dun and gray; the gray of smoke, of ash, of pulverized bones, of quicklime. It is shocking, then, to realize that Treblinka, too, belongs to a brilliantly vivid countryside; the riverland of the Bug and the Vistula; rolling, gentle land, lined by avenues of poplar and aspen."[22]

Friedman's photographs capture the paradox between the horror of the past and the beauty of the present. In short, the works do not pretend to offer the definitive version of the Holocaust revisited, but, in an idiosyncratic personal style, attempt to instill memory by representing a singular view of a specific place and time, the undisguised subjective experience of a secondary witness. "Friedman refuses to assign the Holocaust a place in the comfortable past, just as he refuses to assign the viewer a comfortable ideological or historical position from which to view this past."[23] If writing poetry after Auschwitz once seemed unthinkable, how much more uncomfortable it seems to lounge under colorful umbrellas, drink soda pop, or watch teenagers play with toy cars in the parking lot.

SELF-PORTRAITS WITH JEWISH NOSE WANDERING IN A GENTILE WORLD

FRIEDMAN CAME TO SEE his 1983 experience of the Polish camps as an ironic commentary on his life as a Jew because in 1982 he was denied tenure in the Department of Photography and Cinema at Ohio State University because he was Jewish.[24] These events made finishing his concentration camp project more urgent, deepening a sense of "not feeling safe" in the world that had begun, in his own lifetime, with antisemitic acts of violence in his childhood.[25]

In a later series of photographs, *Self-Portraits with Jewish Nose Wandering in a Gentile World,* Friedman includes self-portraits taken from 1954 to the present, focusing on photographs produced in the last twenty years, and addressing the question of how to find one's place in the world as a Jew. In a self-portrait taken in 1982, Friedman poses between a pillar and a wall at a junior high school fifty-three yards from his front door on which a graffiti worker has scrawled two swastikas (fig. 36). The photograph functions as evidence of a continuing form of secondary Holocaust trauma.

Fig. 36. James Friedman, *Untitled (Swastikas fifty-three yards from my front door)*, Columbus, Ohio, 1982, from *Self-Portrait with Jewish Nose Wandering in a Gentile World*. Courtesy James Friedman.

Years later, Friedman had a striped prisoner's uniform made to order and arranged a series of photo shoots of himself wearing the uniform in public, in Columbus, Ohio, where he lives, beginning in March 2001 (fig. 37).[26] Does Friedman, as secondary witness, overidentify with the survivors he has photographed, as one who has also been targeted and victimized? Is this an example of surrogacy caught in the breach of melancholia or a struggle through the meaning of victimization—in Freudian terms, acting out or working through? These psychoanalytic categories, however, do not seem adequate to explain artistic representation. Friedman's photograph of himself about town, in this example standing next to two young girls, one of whom presents the camera with a pained expression of complex emotion, is both poignant and self-mocking. While the striped uniform seems to have a self-affirming effect on its wearer, like the figure who inspired it, a woman at a survivor's reunion in Majdanek (fig. 38), it also has an alienating and slightly ludicrous effect. The real survivor, having endured three concentration camps, poses before the camera in a striped prisoner's shirt bedecked with a large red and white sash and a group of medals and patches. Her authenticity overcomes a possible sense of the ludicrous, as she emanates the quiet strength of "a victim who has now become a victor."[27]

Friedman, in emulation of this pose, may be said to engage in a form of mimesis, a concept put forth by Theodor Adorno and elaborated by Andreas Huyssen in relation to Holocaust representation in general and Art Spiegelman's *Maus* in particular. Huyssen likens mimesis to "a becoming or making similar, a movement toward, never a reaching of a goal. It is not identity, nor can it be reduced to compassion or empathy. It rather requires of us to think identity and non-identity together as non-identical similitude and in unresolvable tension with each other."[28] The context and wry self-consciousness of Friedman's pose expresses both similarity and difference from the real concentration camp prisoner, making it impossible for anyone to mistake this photograph as one documenting an authentic camp survivor. Rather, it performs, in Huyssen's words, a "mimetic approximation," based on secondary trauma.

Spiegelman also portrayed himself in the striped uniform, in comic book format, in "Prisoner on the Hell Planet," produced in response to his mother's suicide and reproduced as part of *Maus*. Huyssen suggests that Spiegelman draws himself in striped prisoner garb to perform "a compulsive imaginary mimesis of Auschwitz as a space of imprisonment and murder" and argues that the more estranging mode of *Maus,* in which animals stand in for people, overcomes the "paralyzing effects of a mimesis of memory-terror."[29] Similarly, Friedman's mimetic performance overcomes the paralyzing effects of memory-terror through irony and black humor, qualities that Huyssen identifies as constitutive of narrative strategies of Holocaust representation that overcome "official memorial culture." This "intensely personal, experiential dimension" to Holocaust representation prompts Huyssen to comment: "Prerequisite for any mimetic approximation (of the artist/reader/viewer) is

Fig. 37 *(top)*. James Friedman, *Untitled*, Columbus, Ohio, 2001, from *Self-Portraits with Jewish Nose Wandering in a Gentile World*. Courtesy James Friedman.

Fig. 38 *(bottom)*. James Friedman, *Survivor of Three Nazi Concentration Camps, Survivors' Reunion, Majdanek concentration camp, near Lublin, Poland*, 1983, from *12 Nazi Concentration Camps*. Courtesy James Friedman.

the liberation from the rituals of mourning and of guilt. . . . All this requires new narrative and figurative strategies including irony, shock, black humor, even cynicism."[30] Like Spiegelman, Friedman is always conscious of the porousness between past and present, and the limitations of official Holocaust memory.

SUSAN SILAS: *WE'RE NOT OUT OF THE WOODS YET*

In the summer and fall of 1969, Anselm Kiefer produced a series of photographs titled *Besetzungen (Occupations),* consisting of his performing Hitler salutes in sites around Italy and France. Kiefer's *Sieg heil* performances have been interpreted by many observers as satirical gestures meant to deliver a shock to the processes of normalization in Germany, where the post-Auschwitz generation had not yet begun to deal with the Nazi past. The sites he "occupied" were associated with Roman history, which the Nazis claimed as their own, and thus they refer to the Nazi appropriation and occupation of these places. Kiefer's performances assume a fantasmatic identification with Hitler, which, on a larger plane, represents a surrogate subject position for all Germans, identifying them with the Nazi perpetrators. At the same time, it is understood that Kiefer critically mimics, even ridicules German psychic involvement with Nazism. In his ironic and faintly preposterous posturings, the *Sieg heils* of the *Occupations* series have nonetheless made critics uneasy. Andreas Huyssen comments, "Are irony and satire really the appropriate mode for dealing with fascist terror? Doesn't this series of photographs belittle the very real terror which the Sieg heil gesture conjures up for a historically informed memory?"[31] Similarly, for G. Roger Denson, they evoke an "ambiguity that ends by diminishing the effects of imperialism and terror."[32] The ambiguity lies between identification and repudiation, complicity and innocence, history and mythology. Kiefer himself explained, "I do not identify with Nero or Hitler, but I have to reenact what they did just a little bit in order to understand the madness. That is why I make these attempts to become a fascist."[33] Lisa Saltzman, in her book, *Anselm Kiefer and Art after Auschwitz,* argues that Kiefer's project grapples with the repressed national loss of a paternal ego ideal (Hitler) and the resulting impoverished sense of national self-identity that is the legacy of postwar generations following the Third Reich. Alexander and Margarete Mitscherlich, in their 1967 study *The Inability to Mourn,* describe this as the central trauma for Germans. Saltzman suggests that Kiefer "took up the paternal legacy and the role of the father as a means of negotiating his own identity in relation to history."[34] She also points to a general conflation in Kiefer's work of the two kinds of losses that resulted from the war—the trauma of repressed history and the trauma of annihilation.

This conflation is at the heart of a response by American artist Susan Silas to Kiefer's *Occupations* series, for although the traumas at the core of both troubled subject positions—German and Jewish—appear to be irresolvable, they are not, her work suggests, commensurable.[35] In her 1990 photographic work, Silas reacts to Kiefer's ironical identification with the subject position of the perpetrators by emphatically counterposing an alternative identification with the subject position of the victims in a rereading of Margaret Bourke-White's famous Buchenwald photograph (fig. 39). Enlarging the Bourke-White photograph to life-size proportions and setting it in a woodland on Bear Mountain, Silas cut out a hole and inserted her own face in place of one of the prisoners, then had the entire scene photographed in black and white, like the Kiefer print. In the presentation of this work, Kiefer's photograph appears side by side with Silas's own as if on the facing page of a book, and the entire image is placed within a steel frame.

In Kiefer's work, he stands atop a neoclassical monument in Nazi salute with the open space behind him framed by two boughs of a tree, bringing the legacy of the Nazi past into the present. The Buchenwald photograph, now altered and framed by a contemporary landscape, also brings the events into the present. Silas's photograph, wittily titled *We're Not Out of the Woods Yet,* is in part a response to the fall of the Berlin wall, the unification of Germany, and the ensuing fear of a greater Germany that this evoked among Europeans.[36] Paired with Kiefer's print, the tight,

Fig. 39. Susan Silas, *We're Not Out of the Woods Yet*, 1990. Courtesy Susan Silas.

barbed-wire enclosure of the Jews in the sun-dappled landscape not only sets in opposition perpetrators and victims, but contrasts the political and metaphorical uses of public spaces, and matches Kiefer and Silas as contemporary secondary witnesses whose perspectives are still at odds. The consequences of Nazi ideology raised by Kiefer as absurdly grandiose gestures of power are transformed by the counterposed Silas image from an examination of the effects of that ideology on postwar German male identity to its effects on its targeted victims. Denson observes, "The resulting image of deprivation and brutal confinement in the midst of a natural landscape which National Socialism had mythically elevated as the birthright of the wholesome, upright, and purebred Aryan race cuts deeply. By placing her photo next to that of Kiefer's arrogantly buffoonish fascist, Silas emphasizes Kiefer's neglect of the very history he is supposed to be recalling—in the extermination of six million Jews. By contrast, the picturing of the two living individuals—Kiefer and Silas—underscores the fact that the inheritors of German and Jewish identity must now face one another"[37] Whereas Kiefer presents an ambivalent monumentalized parody of Nazism, Silas parodies Kiefer's assumed subject position. Her own assumption of a prisoner identity is also marked as an ironical appropriation, reminiscent of a "carnival image of the fat lady whose body you can adopt by sticking your face inside the hole."[38] The carnivalesque gesture underlines her distrust of Kiefer's own provocative gesture. It is worth remembering, however, that Kiefer's posture of confronting the legacy of Nazism in contemporary Germany was met with great hostility within Germany when the *Occupations* series was first published in 1975 in the pages of *interfunktionen,* then edited by Benjamin Buchloh. The photographs proved to be so offensive that the journal was boycotted.[39]

THE DEATH CAMPS

After World War II ended, documents by prisoners were unearthed around the former death camp Chelmno. One such document, dated 9 January 1945, was written by the last group of forced laborers, who were executed 17 January 1945. An excerpt reads, "This is written by Israel Ziegelman, who lived in Lodz, in Wolczenska Street, number 159, and later on Wrubla Street, number 10 . . . In the camp I work as a tailor and usually I get along well, because I eat, but any food I take to my mouth is like poison to me, because this is nothing but a death camp. Two years ago they brought here all the children from the ghetto of Lodz, they gassed them and then burnt down their bodies. What do you have to say about this?"[40]

Susan Silas has something to say. For a decade since the late 1980s, she has focused her work on the cultural reception and interpretation of the Holocaust in artworks, films, literature, and television. In 1998 her treatment of the Holocaust became more direct with two projects based on work in Germany and Poland. Using lens-based imagery, Silas employs an approach that is different from that of both Erich Hartmann and James Friedman, in which she explores the altered postwar experience of landscape as a site of traumatic experience. In Poland, Silas videotaped scenes from the four exclusive-function death camps—Chelmno, Sobibor, Belzec, and Treblinka—and slowly drains them of color and ambient sound filled with birdsong until only the (added) sound of film going through a film projector gate can be heard (mimicking the sound archival film would make) (fig. 40).[41] On its most obvious level reproducing the loss of the lifeworld that the Judeocide represented, the loss of color and sound also replicates the way that the Holocaust archive has shaped public memory of the genocide. By slowly draining color and sound from the video footage of the camps, Silas interrogates the tropes of collective memory. Her project reenacts, in a rather chilling way, the loss of history and the postwar generations' estrangement from the past, reproducing the aura of distant, exotic otherness, while resisting this effect by calling attention to it. Silas's video performs at a double remove from history, constructing the past through the means of a contemporary simulacrum that forms a continuum with it and stands in for it, but is not identical with it. She uses no archival footage and does not, therefore, literally "go back in

Fig. 40. Susan Silas, *Untitled*, video still of Sobibor, 11–14 May 1998. Courtesy Susan Silas.

time." The video takes the viewer back metaphorically, by recreating the aura of the public archive, the site of the production of collective memory, invoking the way in which we think we know the past, because we have seen the archival images so often, and have shared those images with millions. Anton Kaes, commenting on World War II films presented on television, observes, "Future representations of World War II will be compared to the images from these television films, just as these films use countless images from earlier representations. Thus images of images circulate in an eternal cycle, an endless loop. They validate and reconfirm each other, 'swiftly spreading identical memories over the earth.'"[42] But Silas's project *cannot* refer to an actual visual archive of the four death camps contemporaneous with events, since one does not exist. Instead, her contribution helps to produce the archive, creating representations as contemporary remnants of a vanished past that may yet remind us of the murdered children of Lodz. Though the death camps have taken on the appearance of beautiful pastoral landscapes rather than sites of terror, Silas's documentation of them in itself constitutes an act of resistance to their obliteration in memory, confirming their existence as real locations in the world today.

The death camps were established with the sole purpose of functioning as killing centers. The Nazis made a distinction between exclusive killing centers and other concentration camps. The four death camps, designed to kill all who entered as quickly as possible, were located in Poland. Auschwitz/Birkenau and Majdanek were also in Poland, functioning as both labor and extermination complexes. Historians speculate that the death camps were established in Poland because of its highly developed train system, which stopped at even the smallest towns, because isolated sites surrounded by forests could be found which allowed for greater secrecy, and because the SS was already well established in Eastern Poland, where most of the death camps were located.[43] It is no accident that Claude Lanzmann begins *Shoah* with a tale of the truck gassings at Chelmno in December 1941. Here was the first camp in which the Judeocide began to be carried out in a systematic way, which was expanded to include the Operation Reinhard camps, Belzec, Sobibor, and Treblinka, named after Reinhard Heydrich, head of the *Reichssicherheitshauptamt* (Central Reich Security Office), after his assassination. No one knows exactly how many Jews were murdered in the four death camps which were closed down by 1943. Only two men survived Chelmno. Only five are known to have survived Belzec. Chelmno was the pilot death camp project, for which preparations were begun two months before the Wannsee Conference, followed by the Operation Reinhard camps.

Historian Konnilyn Feig describes the setup: "Operation Reinhard German camp workers were not told of the program goals and their precise duties until they reached the centers. Upon their arrival the SS officers oriented them by comparing center goals with the euthanasia program, which was very familiar to the workers. Then the SS swore them to absolute secrecy."[44] The Nazis were at pains to keep the killing centers secret and to a great extent succeeded even after the war. They have been the least visited memory sites in Poland, though a third of the Jews and many Gypsies killed in the Shoah died in them, a total of perhaps two million Jews and five thousand Gypsies, one-third of whom were children. None of the death camps existed longer than seventeen months. In the concentration camps, which also had gas chambers, crematoria, shootings, beatings, medical experiments, slave labor, starvation, disease, and mass graves, there was still a slim chance of survival. In the killing centers the only inmates kept alive for more than a few hours were those selected to process the bodies of their fellow Jews. Then, they in turn were killed. Subsequently the very depths of the Holocaust must remain veiled in darkness, blind and voiceless. Primo Levi observed, "At a distance of years one can today definitely affirm that the history of the Lagers has been written almost exclusively by those who, like myself, never fathomed them to the bottom. Those who did so did not return, or their capacity for observation was paralyzed by suffering and incomprehension."[45]

Chelmno, as the pilot extermination project, used only gas vans to murder victims brought there, a technique borrowed from the *Einsatzgruppen* on the Eastern Front. Bodies were then dumped into mass graves in the woods. Belzec followed with diesel-run gas chambers, and burned the bodies in open-pits. Sobibor followed suit and Treblinka, the most efficient, came last. Following a prisoner revolt at Sobibor, Heinrich Himmler, head of Nazi police forces, ordered all the killing centers closed in 1943.

In 1996 historian Martin Gilbert made a journey with eleven graduate students and a survivor to the sites of ghettos, concentration camps and death camps, and recorded their experiences and impressions, as well as the written and oral evidence that has survived and that he read at the various sites. His journal of the experience was published as *Holocaust Journey: Travelling in Search of the Past.* The group's arrival at Chelmno is described simply and provides the stark evidence of the Nazi's success in removing most traces of the gruesome operations: "We walk away from the road into a large clearing. . . . It is the field of ash that acts as the overwhelming monument here; that, and the dense, dark forest on all sides, and the track through the forest—a broad swathe of grass—along which the gas vans came. We are all deeply affected by the mass graves, and also by the curious colour of the grass, a disturbing mixture of pale green and pale russet."[46] One of the survivors of Belzec, Chaim Hirszman, gave this account, which Gilbert read at the site:

> I and some other men were appointed to take the people to the kiln. I was sent with the women. The Ukrainian Schmidt, an Ethnic German, was standing at the entrance to the gas chamber and hitting with a knout—a knotted whip—every entering woman. Before the door was closed, he fired a few shots from his revolver and the door closed automatically and forty minutes later we went in and carried the bodies out to a special ramp. We shaved the hair off the bodies,

> which was afterwards packed into sacks and taken away by Germans. The children were thrown into the chamber simply on the women's heads. In one of the "transports" taken out of the gas chamber, I found the body of my wife and I had to shave her hair.[47]

When the group left Belzec, Gilbert recorded the following in his journal:

> I stand for a few moments just outside the gate looking again at the forester's house, which has been built there since my last visit. A young child plays at the front gate facing the entrance to the camp. A turkey and her chicks cross the yard. A small boy comes out of the house and chases the turkey with a stick. His mother gathers the young chicks with a broom. There is a water pump in the yard. There are pretty potted plants around the house, and lace curtains in the window. Marie later wrote to me of what she called "my feeling of disgust, or was it pity (?) for the children in the house who were playing in the garden. I didn't even want to imagine what it would be like to grow up next to a death camp."[48]

When the group arrived in Sobibor, Gilbert again remarked on the near annihilation of all traces of the horrific events that had taken place there: "We walk along what is now a grass path. The Germans called it 'the route to heaven.' We pass the area in which the deportees were forced to undress, then the area in which the clothing barracks stood. Then we turn through what is now thick woodland, past what was once one of the final stops on the 'route to heaven': the building where the women had their hair cut off." The only archive which the intrepid travelers have available to them are schematic maps of the area. Gilbert continues, "When the camp was deliberately obliterated in the autumn of 1943, trees were planted all over this area. Now they are sturdy, half-century-old mature trees. We push on through the wood and reach the site of the gas chambers and the cremation pyres. In front of us is a low mound of ash, and around the mound, to the left and right, fields of ash."[49] On 30 April 1943, two thousand unarmed Jews attacked the SS at arrival at the unloading ramp at Sobibor. All of them were killed by grenades and machine-gun fire. On 14 October 1943 there was a more successful armed revolt by Jewish prisoners led by Red Army men who had been captured in the fighting on the Eastern Front and brought to the camp as slave laborers. Their leader, Alexander Pechersky, was a composer before the war who had written music for plays in his hometown, Rostov-on-Don. Of the six hundred prisoners in Camp I, three hundred managed to overpower the Germans and escape. Of the remaining three hundred, two hundred were killed trying to break out and the rest were murdered in the camp. The Germans hunted down most of those who had escaped, but sixty-four survived. Gilbert records in his journal: "Yesterday afternoon at Belzec and this afternoon at Sobibor we have been to two places where almost a million Jews were murdered in the space of twelve months. Mike tells us that at Belzec the locals still have picnics on the site."[50]

Jacques Derrida's conception of "archivization" as "a movement of the promise and of the future no less than of recording the past," already mentioned in relation to the work of Shimon Attie, takes on another dimension in relation to the visual archive of the concentration camps, both in the imagery of James Friedman and in Susan Silas's video footage of the death camps. Both constitute a continuation of the Holocaust archive. In both visual and literary form, there are few descriptions of the death camps—by the few SS witnesses willing to testify, or the rare survivor, or in the testimony of modern-day pilgrims. Thus, the very concept of the archive we have assumed up until now, as a closed body of images referring to the past, is seen to be too narrow and incomplete. We must understand the archive as open-ended, ever-forming, and opening out into the future. "The archivist produces more archive, and that is why the archive is never closed."[51] Silas and Friedman continue to produce the archive even as they produce a critical awareness of the effects of the archive.

HELMBRECHTS WALK, 1998

From 13 April to 5 May 1998, Susan Silas walked the route of the Helmbrechts death march, a twenty-two-day journey of 195 miles from Helmbrechts, a concentration camp in Germany, to Prachatice, a town in former Czechoslavkia. The original death march took place precisely fifty-three years earlier from 13 April to 5 May 1945. Of the 580 Jews on this march, the majority were Hungarian Jewish women. Using detailed information on the events of each day provided in courtroom testimony by the camp commandant, Alois Dörr, at his 1969 trial in Germany, Silas began and ended each day in the same location as the women in the death march, photographing the landscape as she walked and videotaping it in a reverse journey by car. Like Friedman, Silas successfully employs a realist mode, yet one that is complex and paradoxical. The realist emphasis on documentary value is subverted by the postmodern conceptual framework on which the project rests, disdaining conventional pretense toward documentary by conveying the contemporary circumstances in which the past is performed and inviting a meditative focus on landscape as a source for both traumatic memory and Nazi romantic ideology (figs. 41–42).

Daniel Goldhagen has described the Helmbrechts death march in his book *Hitler's Willing Executioners*. Despite criticism of the book as a whole, and a critique of specific aspects of his description of the Helmbrechts march by Ruth Bettina Birn in *A Nation on Trial: The Goldhagen Thesis and Historical Truth,* Goldhagen's basic discussion of the death march remains the most comprehensive. The Helmbrechts camp was a satellite of the Flossenbürg camp and was founded in the summer of 1944, close to the border of Czechoslovakia and what was to become East Germany. Located on the edge of the town of Helmbrechts, the camp was small, with fifty-four guards arriving at different times and working under the camp commander Alois Dörr. Half the guards were women and half men, but the camp inmates were all women prisoners. Between 670 and 680 women were non-Jewish Polish and Russian protective custody prisoners, who worked in the Neumeyer armaments factory. Twenty-five of these were German women, incarcerated mostly for consorting with prisoners of war or foreign workers, or for insulting the Reich or aiding Jews. Conditions for these women were somewhat better than for the Jewish women prisoners, primarily Hungarian Jews, who were segregated in separate barracks and lived under brutal conditions. In five weeks, forty-four Jews died, before the camp was evacuated on 13 April 1945, less than four weeks before the war's end. At the start of the death march, the guards set out with about 580 Jewish prisoners and about 590 non-Jewish prisoners, escorted by an estimated forty-seven guards. Of the non-Jewish group, the Polish and Russian women were left behind at another camp after seven days; the twenty-five German women marched to the end, but at some point were also made to function as guards of the Jewish women during the march.[52]

Fig. 41. Susan Silas, *Helmbrecht's Walk, 1998 (day seven, the road between Zwodau and Lauterbach)*. Courtesy Susan Silas.

The Jewish women received food only once a day—sometimes not at all—consisting of a little bread, or a little soup, or a small portion of potato, so that the women were starving to death. When townspeople offered food and water, the prisoners were prevented from taking it by the guards. "On the eighth day of the march, part of the column paused for a while in the town of Sangerberg, during which time the Jews communicated to the townspeople standing nearby that they were suffering from hunger: 'A few women from Sangerberg tried to pass to the prisoners some bread. At once, however, the nearby SS women prevented it. A male guard threatened one of the women who wanted to distribute food that he would shoot her if she should try again to pass food to the prisoners. In two cases, the guard struck with his rifle butt prisoners who wanted to accept foodstuffs. A female guard cast bread, which had been intended for the prisoners, to chickens.'"[53] The march lasted for twenty-two days and many of the women were killed, or died from starvation, disease, and exhaustion along the way. The official death toll is 178, but the unofficial death toll is approximately 275, which means that 30 percent of the women died in three weeks. Of the ones who survived, an American physician estimated that 50 percent would have died within days without the intensive medical care provided after liberation.[54]

Fig. 42. Susan Silas, *Helmbrecht's Walk, 1998 (day eight, the road between Lauterbach and Hammerhof)*. Courtesy Susan Silas.

Silas, born in 1953 to Hungarian Jewish parents, sought out survivors of the Helmbrechts death march and interviewed several for her project, an excerpt of which was shown as part of the exhibition *Intersecting Identities: Jewishness at the Crossroads* at the State University of New York at Stony Brook. Projected slides of photographs taken along the path of the death march were accompanied by a sound piece called, *In the Waiting Room of Death, Reflections on the Warsaw Ghetto,* in which Silas reads an essay of the same title by Jean Améry, written to accompany a photographic exhibition of images on the Warsaw Ghetto.[55]

Silas views her works as portable memorials that avoid the problems of large public memorials, which allow a certain forgetfulness by becoming repositories for memory that displace the actual memory sites. Jane Kramer has observed that Germans "prefer the symbolic simplicities of objectification—the monuments, memorials, and 'commemorative sites' that take memory and deposit it, so to speak, in the landscape, where it can be visited at appropriate ceremonial moments, but where it does not interfere unduly with the business of life at hand."[56] Berlin Jews, she notes, worry that the huge memorial monuments "are slowly replacing the real *lieux de mémoire*—the camps themselves. They think it is only a matter of time before those camps are turned over to developers and supermarket chains."[57] Ravensbrück and Sachsenhausen camps have already effectively filed for bankruptcy.

But the photographs and video footage of the Helmbrechts walk may be seen as a byproduct of the project, which was centrally about the obsessive act of retracing the steps of the victims, performed by the secondary witness. Silas herself has said of *Helmbrechts Walk,* "In the way of 70's conceptual art, the act of walking the walk in time and space is probably the work . . . and everything else is genuinely something else."[58] Conceptualism may be defined as a forum for philosophical thought. Thomas Crow observes, "In a culture where philosophy has been largely withdrawn into technical exchanges between academic professionals, artistic practice in the Duchampian tradition has come to provide the most important venue in which demanding philosophical issues can be aired before a substantial lay public. It has provided another kind of academy, an almost antique variety analogous with those associations for learned amateurs which sprang up across Europe during the Enlightenment."[59] Conceptual art does not confine its meaning to an image or discrete object. Rather, it sets aside the assumed primacy of visual illusion as central to the making and understanding of a work of art. For conceptual art to be successful, "it must document a capacity for significant reference to the world beyond the most proximate institutions of artistic display and consumption."[60] Conceptual art, therefore, is regarded by many as more adequate to the task of a complex, ambivalent presentation of the Nazi genocide, especially given the postmodernist mistrust of art's ability to describe the indescribable. This mistrust has been conditioned by the rejection of traditional pictorial and sculptural forms, as well as the rejection of mimetic approaches developed by artists in the decades immediately after the war. Conceptualism provides a method for avoiding the easy pitfalls of sentimentality and fetishization fostered by the use of overly literal imagery, allowing artists as secondary witnesses to explore their relationship, both belated and afflicted, to the events they stage and reenact. This relationship is the real subject of the work. Silas's "walking the walk" attempts to connect to the death march experience, a mimetic approximation of that which cannot be adequately visualized or understood by the postwar generations who have been, nonetheless, unwilling to part with the burden of memory. By producing visual representations, the images become a site of resistance to the loss of memory and historical specificity even as they fail to recapture memory and history.

Some of the images from Silas's reenactment of the walk include self-portraits in round convex mirrors placed at sharp turns in the road (placed so that present-day motorists can see cars coming around the corner). The mirrored, distorted self-representation not only reflects the performance of the walk, but reproduces the conceptual nature of the project, that is, the relationship between the secondary witness and the site of memory at a remove (fig. 43). It also unsettles our expectations of the landscape itself, juxtaposing one scene in the mirror with the very different land-

Fig. 43. Susan Silas, *Helmbrecht's Walk, 1998 (day twelve, the road between Straz and Vilkanov)*. Courtesy Susan Silas.

scape in which the mirror itself is positioned. From one side of the road to the other, the world seems to change, just as it has between then and now. Like Friedman and Attie, Silas employs a paradoxical realist mode, rejecting the conventional pretense toward documentary by conveying the contemporary circumstances in which the past is performed.

MIKAEL LEVIN: *WAR STORY*

OTHER ARTISTS HAVE FELT the compulsion to find lost tracks as well. Photographer Mikael Levin, in 1995, retraced the steps of his father's journey through the battlefields and concentration camps of Europe in 1944–45 as an American war correspondent. Levin's father was Meyer Levin who later became famous for his obsession with bringing the diary of Anne Frank to the stage.[61] The elder Levin embarked on his journey with jeep mate and photographer Eric Schwab, who not only photographed the war and liberation of the concentration camps that Levin wrote about, but searched for his mother who had been deported in 1943. The elder Levin later wrote an autobiography, *In Search,* describing his experiences, which the younger Levin reproduced as text panels along with his own photographs taken fifty years later, often in the same spots, in the project *War Story* (1995–1996), exhibited at the International Center of Photography in New York in 1997. The father's text was also reproduced, along with press reports, in the accompanying book that includes a selection of Eric Schwab's photographs.[62] As a war correspondent, Meyer Levin was one of the first to focus on Jewish communities during the war in Belgium, France, Holland, and Germany. Along with Schwab's early photographs, Levin filed some of the first eyewitness accounts of the Nazi extermination camps. His son Mikael not only retraces the father's journey, beginning in Drancy and continuing through Buchenwald, Dachau, and Theresienstadt, but also photographs the specific locales described in his father's dispatches and later autobiographical writings. Yet the son's photographs do not quite illustrate the father's text; the vivid wartime narratives of the father are not evident in the cityscapes, fields, roads, and rural landscapes of the 1990s. There are only traces in the countryside, ironic signs in the cities, which can easily pass by undetected. Mikael Levin's unpeopled, black and white images of present-day Europe portray sites swept clean of rubble and death, rebuilt and grown verdant. Thus, one must look with a will to remember and a keen eye to find a legible past.

In one of a series of photos of Nordlager Ohrdruf, in Germany, for example, we see an overgrown dirt road leading up a hill and beyond a clump of trees (fig. 44). The son's caption recounts the history of this seemingly unremarkable site: "This area had been part of a military base before the war, and following the war it was occupied by the Soviet Army. The hill on which the concentration camp had been located was used by the Russians for war games—nothing at all remains of the camp. Today the Soviets are gone and the huge facility they built is deserted, but the whole area remains a closed military zone. A recent local publication detailing the 100-year history of the base only mentions in passing the existence of the concentration camp."[63] The text written by Levin's father fifty years earlier tells a different story and is worth quoting at length:

> There was more to see, the Pole told us. His German was inadequate, but he kept motioning up the hill, beyond the camp, and finally we got into the jeep and he guided us again. There was no road. He seemed uncertain of the way, and yet persisted passionately we had to go. He alone remained to show us. Death commando. The other workers had been killed.
>
> On top of the hill there was a rut that gave out, and then nothing. We began to get jumpy again. There might be mines. And there might be a bitter-end SS who could pot us off. We were going to turn back when the Pole suddenly got his bearings and motioned to a clump of trees. We saw nothing special. There was indeed a half-dug pit as large as a swimming pool, filled with ooze. Some sort of work had been going on there. Perhaps excavation for a building foundation. A section of narrow-gauge track lay beside the pit, reaching from nowhere to nowhere. There were some shovels and other work tools lying on the ground, all muddied over with the gray ooze.
>
> The Pole was talking excitedly. He pointed beside the tracks, and in the mud we saw a few striped rags from prisoners' uniforms, and little heaps of cinders, then bits of bone, a half-charred body, a skull.
>
> There was a pile of logs for fuel. Now we comprehended. The track with the logs laid across simply became a grate.
>
> The survivor had picked up a long pole terminating in a grappling hook, and now he was pushing it around in the ooze in the pit. Presently he levered it up just far enough for us to see what was on the hook. Then he let the half-decayed human body fall back into the slime.
>
> Now we understood. In the last weeks the SS commanders of the camp had forced a group of slaves to exhume these bodies and burn them, to destroy the evidence . . .
>
> It was to the edge of this pit, some days later, that the army brought the mayor and other dignitaries of the city of Ohrdruf, good Germans who "had not known" what was being done in their land. The mayor went home and shot himself.[64]

Ordruf was a labor camp that had been opened late in the war to enable a future army command center, in the event of a retreat from Berlin, to be built underground

Fig. 44. Mikael Levin, *Nordlager-Ordruf*, from *War Story*, 1995. Courtesy Mikael Levin.

Plate 1. Shimon Attie, *Mulackstrasse 37, Former Jewish Residents (ca. 1932)*, from *The Writing on the Wall*, Berlin, 1992. Courtesy Jack Shainman Gallery, New York.

Plate 2. Shimon Attie, *Linienstrasse 137, Police Raid on Former Jewish Residents (1920)*, from *The Writing on the Wall*, Berlin, 1992. Courtesy Jack Shainman Gallery, New York.

Plate 3. Shimon Attie, *Almstadtstrasse (formerly Grenadierstrasse)/Corner Schendelgasse, Religious Book Salesman (1930)*, from *The Writing on the Wall*, Berlin, 1992. Courtesy Jack Shainman Gallery, New York.

Plate 4. James Friedman, *German family, Bergen-Belsen concentration camp*, 1981, from *12 Nazi Concentration Camps*. Courtesy James Friedman.

Plate 5. James Friedman, *Entrance, Natzweiler-Struthof concentration camp, near Strasbourg, France*, 1981, from *12 Nazi Concentration Camps*. Courtesy James Friedman.

Plate 6. James Friedman, *Wall where Jewish prisoners were shot, Theresienstadt concentration camp*, 1981, from *12 Nazi Concentration Camps*. Courtesy James Friedman.

by tens of thousands of Jewish slave laborers who had been evacuated from the east. As American and British forces pressed in from the west, the Jews were evacuated again by train to Bergen-Belsen, Dachau, Leitmeritz, Theresienstadt, and Ebensee. In each of these camps, wracked by starvation, typhus, and terrible living conditions, hundreds died every day. In Ordruf, 4,000 camp inmates died or were murdered in the three months prior to the arrival of the Allies; hundreds more were shot on the eve of the American arrival in April 1945 and found in mass graves. Victims included Jews, Poles and Russian prisoners-of-war.[65]

Though we, unlike the mayor, are not implicated in what occurred at Ohrdruf, a difficult kind of confrontation is nonetheless demanded. The muddy hole, the path up the hill, the trees that shield the events that took place here become suffused with a horror that the son can only gesture toward using the words of the father. As viewers we become uncomfortable witnesses to a disappearing history and the very threat of its ultimate invisibility is central to the dread these pictures evoke. What are the responsibilities and requirements of memory? How should forgetfulness be resisted? Observers have noted the troubled visibility of the past in other photographs by Levin: "Amid the new buildings that have risen on the site of the former Jewish quarter in Frankfurt . . . we can make out a poster, savagely torn, that demands a memorial to the city's deported Jewish children. At Dachau we glimpse, quietly disappearing beneath grass and leaves, the last remnants of the railway tracks over which prisoners packed into boxcars once rolled to their deaths."[66] With the accretion of innocent-seeming pastoral photos and their frequent juxtaposition to photographs of the same sites taken by Eric Schwab, showing the dead and emaciated victims that he and Levin discovered there, every image begins to assume a portentous aura, as if the catastrophe were not only lurking just below the surface, but still waiting to happen.

Levin's work has had a charged effect on audiences in Germany, creating what he calls a "third frame" for the events of the Holocaust, that is, the journey of the original witness, the journey of the secondary witness in retracing those steps, and the journey of the resulting project, which takes on an independent life and creates its own effects, especially on those who know little of the events.[67] As an example, when Levin showed *War Story* at Innsbruck, the sponsors of the exhibition, a group of journalists, conducted an inquiry into the village of Itter, one of the sites revisited in the book. They researched the role of the castle, which had been a prison during the war, and the village itself, interviewing residents, organizing a discussion in the village about attitudes to the war and to the Holocaust, and creating an archive on the subject for the village. The resulting "Itter Project" report was presented to a European-wide conference on racism.[68] For the showing of *War Story* in Berlin (titled *Suche* [Search]), Levin produced an accompanying exhibition, *The Burden of Identity* (1998), consisting of twenty portraits of contemporary Jews living in Berlin interspersed with seven narrow views of the city (fig. 45). The exhibition provided a new context for *War Story* that specifically addressed Berlin audiences, and presented a kind of "wall of the living" that alludes to the walls of old family pictures often displayed in Holocaust memorials. "On the one hand," asserts Levin, "I was saying that even in Berlin there can today exist a Jewish community . . . but I was also engaging in what is essentially a very internal German-Jewish dialogue about who are the Jews of Germany today, portraying, as I was, mostly Jews coming from regions of the former Soviet Union, as opposed to 'German' Jews."[69] In the exhibition catalog, Levin lists the birthplaces of all his subjects (from whom the twenty were chosen) and where they lived before coming to Berlin, some from Greece, the U.S., Poland, Israel, as well as Germany. Either peering directly into the camera lens or averting their gaze, many of the subjects convey a melancholy loneliness.

A wall installation with fifteen photographs from *War Story* opened in September 2001 at the Jewish Museum in Berlin, designed by Daniel Liebeskind. The installation includes a display case containing wartime objects and documents belonging to Meyer Levin and Eric Schwab, including Levin's typewriter, Schwab's camera, copies of Levin's typescript dispatches, vintage prints of Schwab's photographs and

Fig. 45. Mikael Levin, *The Burden of Identity*, installation view, Berlin, 1998. Courtesy Mikael Levin.

other objects. Other works by Mikael Levin include *Border Project* (1993–94), which examines the changing political significance of borders in Western Europe, including such crucial transit points for immigrants as airports and railway stations. The project was produced following the first dismantling of border controls within the European Union. In *Common Places* (1998), Levin examines how cultural identity is manifested in ordinary urban spaces through a series of photographs of four cities: Katrineholm, Cambrai, Erfurt, and Thessaloniki, shown at the Storefront for Art and Architecture in New York in May 2000.[70]

Both Levin's and Silas's visual projects, in a sense, constitute the aftereffects of their conceptual projects. Neither sets out to represent the past, but to resist the loss of the past by documenting its disappearing traces and invisibility in the landscape. Levin does not presume to reproduce his father's experience, just as Silas does not presume to reproduce the experience of women on a death march; rather, both give the viewer pictures of their attempts to imagine the past from a distance of fifty years, documenting their own experience of trying to connect to the experience of their relatives and ancestors through the landscape. The awareness of the historical present heightens the viewer's sense of the act of will that is required to reanimate the past, supported by the voices of primary witnesses. The memorialization of an invisible history documents the substantial loss of this history and the difficulty of recuperation. After completing her journey, Silas observed ironically, "I didn't find it easier to imagine the plight of these women but harder to imagine."[71] Both Silas's and Levin's work, too, continues the archive as a living entity.

MATTHEW GIRSON: COUNTERLANDSCAPES

In a different approach, painter Matthew Girson also addresses the difficulty of comprehending, and therefore remembering, the concentration camps through the public archive of images. In 1994, Girson produced a series of landscape paintings of the camps based on photographs of Auschwitz, Birkenau, Bergen-Belsen, Dachau, Mauthausen, and Treblinka. Small, pale gray likenesses of pastoral scenes were placed in the center of a five-foot white circle within a white square, in a nod to Kazimir Malevich's *White on White*. Spectral images, the landscapes lie coolly behind pale glazes on the surface of the canvas, defying depth of field, as if made of ashes disintegrating within a void of space/ knowledge/ time, into the painterly surface of abstraction. They also recall the words of Paul Celan describing his poetry, in which, he wrote, he sought "a 'greyer' language," one distrustful of "beauty" but trying to be "truthful."[72]

Girson's concentration camp series were followed a year later by *Not a Forest*, a series of nearly identical paintings of an obsessively repeated, isolated ambiguous form that resembles a tree but is actually the shape of a plume of smoke photographed during the Treblinka uprising of 1943, the subject of one of Girson's earlier concentration camp paintings. The individual works in *Not a Forest* are untitled except for one presented as a lectern with a light-table built into it, ironically titled, "The Tree of Knowledge Was a Puff of Smoke in Nazi Germany, 1943." Like the earlier grisaille landscapes, the tree/plume of smoke exists within a seeming void. In another series, the tree/plume is itself transformed into a pale grey void collaged onto the center of color reproductions of "old master paintings." The suspended recognition of the tree/plume image causes both it and the old master painting to

Fig. 46. Matthew Girson, *Untitled (Vermeer)*, collage with color photocopy, 1995. Courtesy Matthew Girson.

be made "strange" (fig. 46). The collaged forms are like "scars or brands" irredeemably marking "the cultural trophies of western painting."[73]

In 1998, Girson produced a series of eighteen landscapes, each within a 20-inch white square. Nine represent the place of his birth and those of his parents (in America) as well as his four grandparents and two great grandparents in Hungary, Lithuania, and Ukraine. The other nine represent the places of birth of nine continental philosophers: Descartes, Kant, Hegel, Marx, Nietzsche, Husserl, Wittgenstein, Heidegger, and Sartre. Both groups were installed as formally identical grids at the Zolla/Lieberman Gallery in Chicago. Like the periodic table on which Primo Levi drew for inspiration in his book *The Periodic Table,* Girson's modernist grids also recall that of the chemical elements that illustrate the periodic law of recurrence. But how does the grid of European philosophy map itself onto that of the Eastern Europe of the Jews? Eastern European Jews in particular were regarded as inassimilable. Girson searches for a Jewish place, for a way to recover the sense of displacement following the migration of the grandparents and their generation, which distances the secondary witness from those origins that will never look the same upon return. As Jon Stratton observes: "Some Yiddish-background people return to visit the camps where their relatives died. Some look for the *shtetlach,* the small towns where their ancestors lived. Nowhere seems like home any more . . ."[74] Parallel, separate, yet connected, Girson's grids recall Jonathan Boyarin's observation that the ideological construction of Europe has historically excluded the voice of the Jewish collectivity. Addressing the question of the place of the Jews in Europe, Girson's painting installation points to this ambivalent history, inspiring the question, after Boyarin, "Is there a Jewish place in Europe, beyond Otherness?"[75] Girson observes:

> My intention was to use landscape to construct a family tree on the one hand, a history of continental thought on the other, and a relation between my family memories and history *and* our public history (read: Western society) in between. Those philosophers set the table for the values and beliefs that have carried us from the Enlightenment, through the Modern period, to today, and my family delivered me to that table. The events of one domain (why my Jewish family moved out of Eastern Europe? Why no buildings stand on the site in Grinkiskis, Lithuania [birthplace of my paternal grand and great grandmothers] represented in two paintings of the first grid) are "implicitly" affected by the influence of the other domain (systems of judgment and critique, notions of progress and value, etc.).[76]

Girson questions the failure of Enlightenment philosophy to ultimately prevent the construction of a falsely homogeneous Christian Europe, which may only hold a place for the postwar Jew as the "imaginary Jew" of Alain Finkielkraut or the "non-Jewish Jew" described by Isaac Deutscher.[77]

The landscape grids were followed by a series of twenty-four graphite wash drawings that Girson defines as "counterlandscapes," again made very pale, disallowing depth (fig. 47). Cloud-filled skies meeting fields or bodies of water are punctured by a white square in the center, disrupting the inevitable evocation of Romantic landscape painting (which originated in Germany) with an alienating effect that evokes the artifice of culture rather than the transparency of nature. Girson describes the white square as "a hole-in-the-image/ground/completeness/knowability."[78] For the secondary witness, all knowledge today is knowledge that comes "after Auschwitz."[79] Paul Celan put it another way: "Perhaps we can say that every poem is marked by its own '20th of January'?" (referring to the codification of the "Final Solution" at the Wannsee Conference on 20 January 1942).[80] Girson's paintings, following Celan, are also marked by their own "20th of January."

Fig. 47. Matthew Girson, *Untitled*, graphite wash on paper, 2000. Courtesy Matthew Girson.

The counterlandscapes evoke the rhetoric of countermonuments, which disappear and become invisible, returning the burden of memory to the contemporary viewer and disallowing the object to become a convenient repository for memory in which historical forgetfulness is not prevented but, perhaps, secured.[81] In a related fashion, the counterlandscapes disrupt our viewing pleasure, instead reminding us of the German cult of nature (as true for the Nazis as for the nature-worshipping *Wandervogel* earlier in the century), the Nordic myths, and the *Blut und Boden* (blood and soil) rhetoric that paved the way for Nazi redemptive mythology, powerfully reified in works such as Hans Jürgen Syberberg's 1977 film *Hitler, a Film from Germany.*[82] The counterlandscapes also evoke Paul Celan's *Gegenwort,* or counterword, the word of poetry. Celan described "a word against the grain, the word which cuts the 'string,' which does not bow to the 'bystanders and old warhorses of history.' It is an act of freedom. It is a step." It is also "a terrifying silence."[83] The square white hole in the image is also an act "against the grain" and a "terrifying silence." Thus, as with Malevich (and the abstract art movement of Suprematism that he pioneered), the painted surface in Girson's counterlandscapes is not only an autonomous form, but also another form of reality, a "painterly realism,"[84] in which the square white hole is the void at the heart of the twentieth century, the forgetfulness slipping into it, and the signal to remember.

CHAPTER SIX

FETISHIZED NAZISM AND EROTIC FANTASY

■

"In fact, an analysis of the new discourse, in revealing a deep structure based on the coexistence of the adoration of power with a dream of final explosion—the annulment of all power—puts us on the track of certain foundations of the psychological hold of Nazism itself, of a particular kind of bondage nourished by the simultaneous desires for absolute submission and total freedom."

SAUL FRIEDLÄNDER
from *Reflections of Nazism: An Essay on Kitsch and Death,* 1993

■

WE HAVE SEEN how artists reached back toward Europe, the external site of the disaster, in a search for meaning about the Holocaust. The body, sexuality, and the psychic economy of control and surrender offer internalized sites for the construction of knowledge. In both this and the following chapter, the body as memory site becomes a terrain for more personal expressions of a reinvented Jewish identity that resists the status of victimhood while manifesting new difficulties in bridging the rift between experience and representation.

. . .

Video artist Rachel Schreiber examines the effects of traumatic memory of the Shoah on contemporary erotic fantasy and desire. Her videos explore the body of the

Jew, usually her own, in an effort to understand "how the genealogy and cultural memory [of the Holocaust] makes itself a part of your body, and how to look at it not in terms of victimhood."[1] By framing her work "not in terms of victimhood" Schreiber acknowledges victimhood as a baseline of Holocaust experience, yet asserts the possibility of other forms of experience, particularly oppositional experience. "I have long had an obsession with the topic of women in the Resistance, because I believe that contemporary American Jewish culture relies on a Holocaust memory that is based in a history of victimization, and is largely unaware of the history of the Resistance (this is quite different in Israel). This history is also one of the points in Jewish history where women have been most active. . . . I employ specific historical accounts, in order to counter what I see in contemporary culture as a move to invest the Holocaust with a generalized sense of the unrepresentable."[2]

In her eleven-minute black and white 1994 video, *This is Not Erotica,* Schreiber combines a contemporary erotic love story with three accounts of Jewish women who fought in the Resistance in World War II.[3] The love story is about two teenagers, told in the first person, who have grown up together in a Jewish community and make love for the first time in the basement of the girl's parents' house. During their lovemaking, the girl tells her lover to tie her up. It seems, however, that only the fantasy of bondage is necessary to what is both an assertion and disavowal of control (fig. 48). The girl imagines that the two lovers are in the Resistance together, "sometimes in the past, sometimes in the present," producing a fantasmatic experience of extremity in which they still have the possibility of agency. The narrator continues, through voice-over, to relate the stories of the resistance heroines, all of whom exhibit extreme courage and skill in finding ways to sabotage or kill Nazis, ultimately ending, however, in the capture and execution of the women. As the narrator's voice is heard, her lover's tongue sensually explores the swells and curves of her body. At one moment, actually bound hands are glimpsed. At other moments, Schreiber interweaves family photographs from previous generations, wondering aloud how the Russian immigrants photographed by her grandfather would look in modern clothes, another way of seeing the past through the filter of the present. The black-and-white, close-up, grainy results of Schreiber's super-8 camera transposed to video render the visual presentation of lovemaking as dreamlike. Combined with her narrative of the women saboteurs, the video imagery eroticizes the excitement of political danger and resistance. The experience of the bound/unbound victim/lover evokes Friedländer's notion of "the simultaneous desires for absolute submission and total freedom." The next day the couple watch a film about the Holocaust together and the girl is transported to the night before, to the time of their lovemaking, underscoring the link between historical trauma, sexuality, and desire.

Schreiber not only eroticizes resistance experience but also the imagined memory of family history by showing photographs of her grandfather's trip abroad in 1937 as she describes her lover's body in voice-over. Thus, the imagined memory of both the acts of resistance heroines and the prewar experiences of family members may be seen as *fetishized* in the language of erotic fantasy and desire. When the voice-over describes mounds of Jewish corpses, however, the screen goes dark. Life-threatening action, but not death, is eroticized. The true horror of the Holocaust cannot be pictured.

The voluptuous bodies that surface in Schreiber's video have a luminous presence, even as they evoke the extinguished glow of those other bodies that also yearned with desire before growing thin, cold, and sexless. The sense of empowerment gained from identifying with strong female models, the intensity of the identification with the heroines, and their eroticization, coupled with an identification with family members who were alive in Europe before the war, may be recognized as experiences that, for Schreiber, "make [themselves] part of your body . . . not in terms of victimhood." The resistance heroines in particular represent a search for positive models in the world of Holocaust experience. Indeed, there has been an effacement of certain forms of organized resistance in U.S. Holocaust museums, in part, perhaps, due to the communist origins of much organized resistance both in Nazi-occupied Europe and in the death camps where such organized resistance existed, and in part, perhaps, because many of the texts are available only in Hebrew

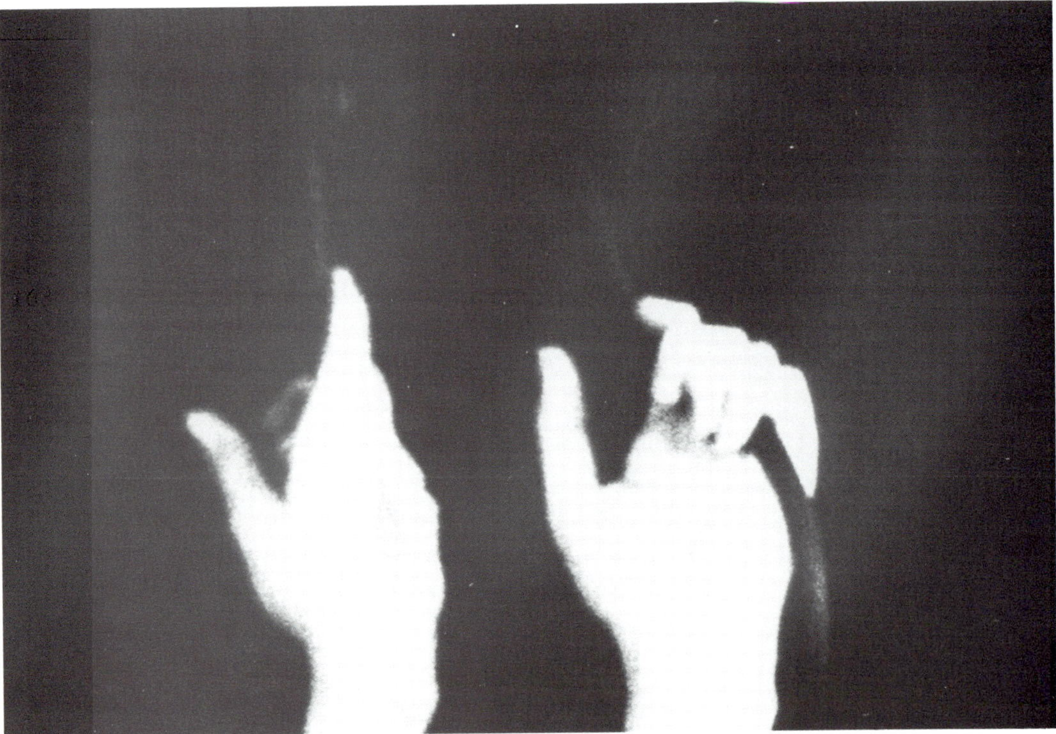

Fig. 48. Rachel Schreiber, *This is Not Erotica*, video still, 1995. © Rachel Schreiber.

or Yiddish. Schreiber, however, is not concerned with the political nuances of resistance history, but with an emphasis on the subjective experiences of resistance and the role that women played as individuals. As exemplary models, they provide a liberatory sense of inspiration.

Yet Schreiber's eroticized fascination with feminine heroines may also be read as cultivating a potentially troubling redemptive romanticism. The eroticized scenes provide a form of heightened pleasure and evocative desire as we hear of the exploits of the resistance heroines. Their ultimate torture and death is redeemed by their acts of resistance, which offers a vicarious form of redemptive experience for the viewer, too. (But if *This is Not Erotica* attempts to transform an adolescent fantasy into the possibility of a positive identity that is romantic and ennobling, as well as sexually gratifying, we might also recognize that for others, a post-Holocaust identity based exclusively on victimhood may also become a fetishized, fixed and ennobling condition.)

Schreiber's search for forms of positive identification leads not to the dead in the gas chambers and mass graves, but further back, to the living, who once throbbed with life. Believing that contemporary American Jewish culture relies too heavily on a Holocaust memory of victimization, Schreiber's focus on the largely unknown history of the Resistance effectively brings an Israeli perspective to the United States, which attempts to balance the memories of victimization with memories of acts of opposition. Having spent her summers growing up in Israel, Schreiber is familiar with the Israeli perspective and frank about her desire to structure a sense of Jewish identity around a positive model, rather than an empty center of defeat and loss.[4] This model resonates with the dominant forms of fighters and martyrs in Israeli Holocaust representation. The essential dichotomy between fighters and victims, writes James Young, referring to the early founders' task of state building, is resolved "by the ubiquitous twinning of martyrs and heroes in Israel's memorial iconography."[5] Schreiber also conflates martyrs and heroes in the figures of resistance fighters for whom the contemporary lovers become doubles, a reenactment of Holocaust experience that becomes "sexy."

Schreiber carries her exploration of the theme of traumatic memory and erotic desire to a logical extreme in her ten-minute 1996 black-and-white video, *Please Kill Me; I'm a Faggot Nigger Jew,* in which Nazi-fetish-based sadomasochistic fantasies are described anonymously on the Internet by self-proclaimed practitioners in response to a questionnaire posted by Schreiber on sites for s/m (sadomasochistic) chat groups. Schreiber's questionnaire investigates how the Holocaust is filtered into this specific form of outré contemporary sexuality. Some of the practitioners who responded exhibited surprising historical sophistication by constructing SA/SS conflicts and SS/Russian partisan revenge fantasies. Others engaged in the expected fare of Nazi tormentor and Jewish victim. One pair of female s/m partners described "loving the symbols": boots, uniforms, Hitler's speeches in German (without understanding the language). Schreiber interweaves these descriptions, both as voice-over and as typewritten texts on a computer screen, with personal histories. The result is a chilling, transgressive form of erotic practice that includes identification with the perpetrators as well as the victims. As in Israeli artist Roee Rosen's installation and artist's book *Live and Die as Eva Braun,* in which Rosen asks the viewers to "perform" and identify with the role of Hitler's mistress, Eva Braun, as she makes love with Hitler in his bunker for the last time before he kills her, the viewer must confront the "continual tension between desire and its limits"[6] or "the highly uncomfortable intersection between desire and terror."[7]

The various s/m narratives presented by Schreiber raise questions about the internalization of themes of force and control that arguably complicate all sexual desire, but reach their extremes in the "simultaneous desires for absolute submission and total freedom," which may be applied to s/m practice. More specifically, Schreiber's subjects spotlight the issue of fetishizing Nazism. In its simplest terms, fetishism may be understood as a libidinal investment in an object indispensable for sexual gratification. But if the chosen object is a Nazi emblem, how should we understand the significance of this? Historically, the word fetishism, from *fetisso,* came into being as a Portuguese trading term associated with "small wares" and "magic charms" used for barter between blacks and whites, thus introducing a magical valence to capital as a mask for black objects in a white society.[8] This fetishization of the Other, which began as a colonialist discourse, endows the Other with a split subjectivity, both positive and negative, alienating and desirable. The Other in s/m practice may also participate in a fetishistic exchange, whereby the kinds of pleasure offered by fantasies of power, traditionally the preserve of the dominant white or colonialist partner, become available to both parties involved, and are charged with both positive and negative valences. We may ask, then, is Western Nazi-fetish-based s/m practice exemplary of a postmodern infatuation with racial transgression, an eroticisation of power, or an ironic, aestheticized appropriation of demonized emblems?

Staying within a cultural rather than a psychoanalytic explanation of fetishism, I am relying on a materialist approach as defined by anthropological theorist William Pietz. Pietz has described the fetish as a "historical" object that necessarily engenders a "personal" attachment quite apart from the value the object holds in collective society:

> The fetish is always a meaningful fixation of a singular event; it is above all a "historical" object, the enduring material form and force of an unrepeatable event. This object is "territorialized" in material space (an earthly matrix), whether in the form of a geographical locality, a marked site on the surface of the human body, or a medium of inscription or configuration defined by some portable or wearable thing. . . . This reified, territorialized historical object is

> also "personalized" in the sense that beyond its status as a collective social object it evokes an intensely personal response from individuals. This intense relation to the individual's experience of his or her own living self through an impassioned response to the fetish object is always incommensurable with (whether in a way that reinforces or undercuts) the social value codes within which the fetish holds the status of a material signifier. It is in these "disavowals" and "perspectives of flight" whose possibility is opened in the clash of this incommensurable difference that the fetish might be identified as the site of both the formation and the revelation of ideology and value-consciousness.[9]

The actual referent for the fetish, then, is understood as incommensurable with the response to the fetish, or the meanings with which its users endow it: the impassioned personal response of fetish-users is always at variance with the significance of the fetish object in society, whether in a way that reinforces or undercuts. Fetishes therefore do not articulate the Real, but are only displaced representations, which, nonetheless, relate back to the forces that have generated them. Using this definition of fetishism, the possible meanings for Nazi-fetish-based s/m practice may include, depending on the practitioners, any of the three possibilities posited above, or all of them.[10]

At the conclusion of *Please Kill Me,* Schreiber's screen persona ("Justine," in a reference to the writings of the Marquis de Sade) cuts and shaves her pubic hair and in grainy close-up slowly writes the word *Jude* with a fountain pen on her pubis (fig. 49 a, b). The shaving sequence evokes the memory of women shorn of their hair as punishment for sleeping with the German enemy, as well as women stripped of

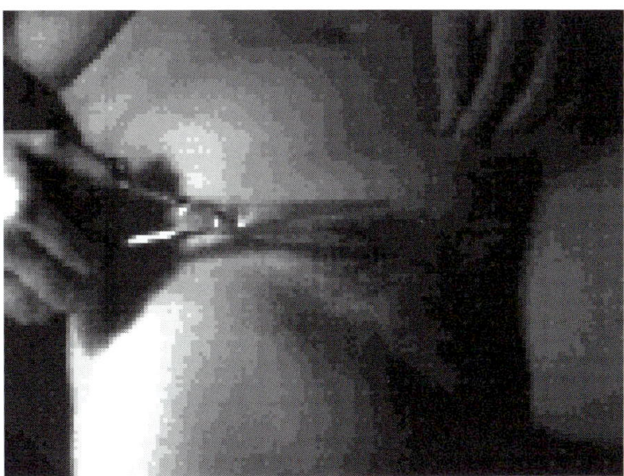

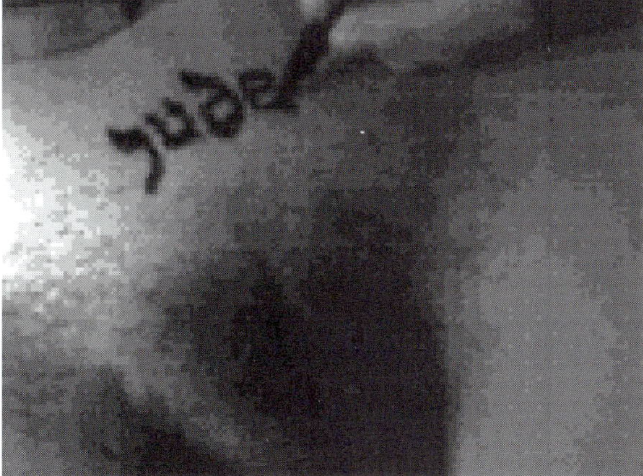

Fig. 49 a, b. Rachel Schreiber, *Please Kill Me; I'm a Faggot Nigger Jew*, video stills, 1996. ©Rachel Schreiber.

their sexuality in the camps as they wasted away.[11] On the whole, however, explicit sexuality does not figure in Holocaust memoirs, except in reference to those who gave themselves in desperation for an extra morsel of food or cigarettes (see Fania Fénelon, *Playing for Time*), who were forced into sexual play by their kapos (see Charlotte Delbo, *Auschwitz and After*), who were forced into prostitution, or were raped. For the most part, these were non-Jewish prisoners, as Germans in the camps were forbidden to have sexual relations with Jewish women. Many women's memoirs and testimonies also attest to the fact that women in hiding, in the ghetto, and in the camps, were terrorized by rumors and threats of rape. Yet not that much is known about its occurrence, in part because many of those who were raped were also murdered, and, in part, because of those women who survived, many have been reluctant to talk about it, to bring into view another level of degradation, just as interviewers have been reluctant to inquire about it.[12] The references to explicit sexuality are made in passing or absent altogether in survivor accounts. In many fictional accounts, however, as Rebecca Scherr observes, "eroticism emerges as the central trope for examining the difficult subject of Holocaust experience and memory. These fictional works of art replace the absence of sexuality characteristic of memoirs of camp experience with an overabundance of erotic imagery, a sign that indicates a general discomfort with the historical facts or methods one can employ to represent the Holocaust. Moreover, it is the female body which becomes the site for displaying this erotic impulse."[13] For Schreiber, too, the female body becomes a stage for the reenactment of Holocaust experience.

It may also be read as inscribing herself into the traumatic experience of the past, underscored by the strains of *Wenn ich mir was wünschen dürfte,* sung by Marlene Dietrich in the final moments of the video. Dietrich's version recalls the same song sung by a beautiful concentration camp inmate, played by Charlotte Rampling, in Liliana Cavani's 1974 film *The Night Porter.* The story takes place after the war, when Rampling's character, Lucia, becomes reabsorbed in a consuming sexual relationship with her former SS tormentor, Max, played by Dirk Bogarde. At one point, in a flashback, she is half-nude at an SS men's club when she is presented with the severed head of another inmate whom the SS officer had murdered because he thought it would please her. An unwilling Salome, she then sings the melancholy *Wenn ich mir was wünschen dürfte* (If I Were to Wish for Something) to the SS officers. The recapitulation of the song at the end of *Please Kill Me* evokes a kind of longing for the sadness of the past as an aspect of secondary witnessing. At the end of *The Night Porter,* the only way out for the former prisoner and the former SS guard is a decline into physical degradation and death, as they are pursued by an organization of former Nazis. As a couple, they are marked as equally victimized in their hopelessly obsessive and fatal bond. Scherr critiques the falsely eroticized nature of Holocaust experience that the film conveys: "*The Night Porter* turns the concentration camp memory into a memory of sexual play, a place where prisoners and the film spectators watch Max and Lucia enact their psychosexual drama. In effect, Cavani transforms the memory of the camp into a 'sexy memory,' which, through the depiction of eroticism and the sexualized female body, elicits a reaction of pleasure in the spectator, completely warping the historical facts of the Holocaust: in particular, the fact that the Holocaust was by no means, in any way, sexy."[14]

Schreiber's screen persona, in marking her body with the term Jude, runs the risk of making it "sexy" while utilizing a signifier of death, in this context, in an attempt to master it and subvert its power. The privilege of claiming the lethal, Nazi-tainted identity of Jude is appropriated by a contemporary Jew much the way other oppressed groups have appropriated racial epithets to hollow out their degrading power. The act of writing Jude on her shaved pubis attempts to break the lure of obsessive victimization, evidenced in *The Night Porter,* by performing an act of private opposition through self-naming. The humiliation of the Jews by the Nazis is reclaimed but, at the same time, fetishized by inscribing it on the sexualized body. This act of fetishization is an attempt to personalize the reified phenomenon of Nazi terror. Schreiber attempts to connect to the acts of courage and martyrdom performed by Jewish women in crisis during the Nazi genocide. Yet the act simultaneously undermines itself. By eroticizing Jude in the act of writing it in Germanic script on the female pubis, the fetishized female body of the "Jewess" in Nazi ideology is also in danger of being reified, along with the Nazi stereotype of her fatally seductive powers.

Schreiber's video does not replicate the double victimization of victim and perpetrator found in *The Night Porter*. Liliana Cavani declared that "we are all victims or murderers, and we accept these roles voluntarily," and further, "in every environment, in every relationship, there is a victim-executioner dynamism more or less clearly expressed and generally lived on an unconscious level."[15] Indeed, it has become fashionable to suggest that we are all potentially capable of barbaric deeds, of finding, if we search, the Nazi in ourselves. Psychology, however, has established that if aggressive impulses are innate, so, too, are altruistic ones. Therefore the presence of either fails to account for the choices made, which rely less on instinct than on cognitive and situational factors. It is thus not a question of some universal psychology that transcends social conditions and cultures, but rather the very specific historical circumstances of Germany that led to the Third Reich, that is, to what people actually did do, not what anyone might have done but did not. The genocide of European Jews was the culmination of a specific confluence of forces that led to an ideology of death, an organized program of murder on a scale without precedent. In each case of genocide in the twentieth century we must look to the specific histories and circumstances that drive peoples into murderous campaigns, rather than search for transcendental causes that dehistoricize and ultimately trivialize the realities of such events. Primo Levi thus responded to Cavani, "I do not know, and it does not much interest me to know, whether in my depths there lurks a murderer, but I do know that I was a guiltless victim and I was not a murderer. I know that the murderers existed, not only in Germany, and still exist, retired or on active duty, and that to confuse them with their victims is a moral disease or an aesthetic affectation or a sinister sign of complicity; above all, it is a precious service rendered (intentionally or not) to the negators of truth."[16]

Lawrence Langer has analyzed the testimony of survivors whose selves are split as a result of their experiences in the camps, creating an ambiguous subjectivity in which the self oscillates between object and subject positions, between responsibility and victimhood. As one survivor commented, "I'm thinking of it now . . . how I split myself. That it wasn't *me* there. It was somebody else."[17] Ernst van Alphen has elaborated on this phenomenon, suggesting that the difficulty experienced by Holocaust survivors in narrating their stories is not so much the inadequacy of language, but the difficulty of occupying a secure subject position: "They have difficulty experiencing the events they were part of because the language at their disposal offered them only two possibilities: to take the role of either subject or object in relation to the events. But the actuality of the Holocaust was such that this distance from the action was not possible; there were no unambiguous roles of subject or object. This is one reason the Holocaust was not 'experienceable' and hence, later, not narratable or otherwise representable."[18]

Schreiber searches for the assertion of more unambiguous subject positions, in which subjective agency can be grasped and stabilized, as in the actions of resistance heroines. In *Please Kill Me,* which was first shown at the 1996 San Francisco Jewish Film Festival, however, the fetishized object is not so much the daring or courage of female resistance fighters as the Nazi terror itself, which has been territorialized, domesticated, and contained on the surface of the body in the form of self-inscription. Schreiber further employs historical accounts in her work in order both to counter the move to invest the Holocaust with a generalized sense of the unrepresentable and in a search for usable meaning in relation to contemporary Jewish identity. Though she stands in danger of romanticizing the true nature of the disaster that engulfed the vast majority, her videos attempt to reinvent Jewish identity in America based on an understanding of Holocaust experience that encompasses more than absence and loss, venturing into the complex territory of sexuality and desire through an exploration of the effects of historical trauma on contemporary erotic practice. Much, however, remains to be explored in the relationship between Holocaust representation and eroticism.

CHAPTER SEVEN

THE TATTOOED JEW

■

"I believe that the catastrophe story, whoever may tell it, represents a constructive and positive act by the imagination rather than a negative one, an attempt to confront the terrifying void of a patently meaningless universe by challenging it at its own game, to remake zero by provoking it in every conceivable way."

J. G. BALLARD
from the introduction to *Apocalypse Culture,* 1990

■

IN AN EDITORIAL ON Judaism and body modification posted on the website of Body Modification Ezine in January 1996, twenty-three-year-old Joshua Burgin posed the following question: "Can a proper Jew practice body modification?"[1] Leaving aside the nettlesome question of what a "proper" Jew might be, we are left to ask, "What does being Jewish have to do with whether or not one practices this increasingly popular form of adornment among the young?"[2] Permanently marking or making cuts on the body is prohibited by the Hebrew Bible. (This does not include circumcision, which is regarded as a covenant with God.) Burgin, a Haverford philosophy major and Reform Jew who is familiar with the scriptures, nevertheless practices body modification, sporting a Star of David tattoo and brand on his arm, created by tattoo artist Raelyn Gallina in 1995 (fig. 50). Burgin's apparent contradiction—of being both, in his terms, a proper Jew and in violation of Jewish law (*Halacha*)—has brought about some trying chastisements for him, including unsolicited reminders from observers that tattooed Jews cannot be buried in Jewish cemeteries. Burgin counters, "For me to take the Star of David as a Jewish symbol of identity and mark myself permanently with it, makes me feel more Jewish than I ever felt before."[3]

The decision to be branded a Jew immediately evokes the historical trauma of Jewish persecution, from the pogroms of the Middle Ages to the catastrophe of the Holocaust. Precisely because Jews, in effect, have been branded historically as Other, for Burgin the voluntary and literal self-identification through branding represents a reclamation of the chastened body and enforced identity of the Jew by and as the Other. The Star of David is, of course, particularly significant as a symbol of ethnic identification because Jews were indeed historically marked with it, from fifteenth-century Spain to the yellow Star of David patches worn on arms and chests during the Third Reich. Jewish prisoners in Auschwitz were then forcibly tattooed and their identities wretchedly reduced to the blue numbers on their arms. This is the burdened history to which Burgin commits himself when he says, "For me to take the Star of David as a Jewish symbol of identity and mark myself permanently with it, makes me feel more Jewish than I ever felt before." In his desire to visibly bind himself more closely to a public Jewish identity, Burgin participates in a larger revival of ethnic consciousness among many young American Jews.

Traditional Jewish law forbidding tattoos is found in Leviticus (19:28), where the relevant line reads: "Ye shall not make any cuttings in your flesh for the dead, nor print any marks upon you." Many Reform Jews, including Burgin, believe the Bible should not be interpreted literally; indeed, the heads of the Reform Jewish Council of America agree that the Bible should be understood in the context in which it was written, that is, six thousand years ago, and therefore Reform Jews (and Conservative Jews, but to a lesser degree) are called upon to interpret the Bible and give it meaning for their own lives.[4]

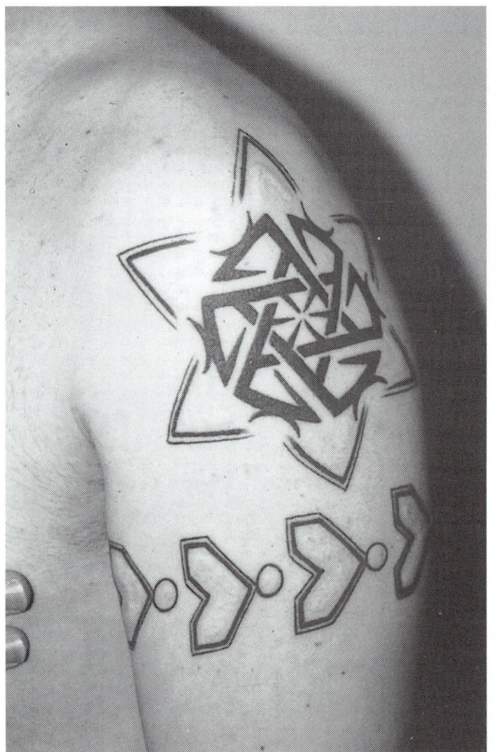

Fig. 50. Joshua Burgin's Star of David tattoo and arm brand, created by Raelyn Gallina, 1995. Photo: Amy Jay. Courtesy Joshua Burgin.

Burgin suggests that this also facilitates Reform Judaism's acceptance or tolerance of other such alleged sins as homosexuality, premarital sex, birth control, and eating pork or shellfish, as well as the general rejection of antiquated sexist and racist ideas contained within the Bible. If the Reform movement is willing to accept or tolerate these formerly heretical ideas, Burgin argues, then certainly body modification, which warrants only one admonition in Leviticus, also can be accepted or tolerated.

Burgin's body modification may be regarded as the recuperation of a tattooing practice already performed on the body of the Jew. His voluntary tattoos in some sense are meant to expiate the suffering of the forcibly tattooed, the rage of those who had no choice about the needle and the ink. The process of acquiring tattoos as signs of Jewish ethnicity, however, seems not so much a question of mourning the past as one of grappling with the contemporary significance of Jewish identity.

Burgin further asserts that the admonition against cutting or marking the body was most likely directed at pagan practices and notes that there is nothing in the scriptures about not being buried in a Jewish cemetery because of one's tattoos. Italian survivor Primo Levi also reminds us that tattooing was forbidden by the law of Moses in order to distinguish Jews from other ancient peoples, who were considered barbarians. It was therefore particularly painful for Orthodox Jews in the concentration camps to be tattooed, because for them it represented an identification with barbarians. Levi describes the tattoo practice in Auschwitz: "From the beginning in 1942 in Auschwitz and the Lagers under its jurisdiction (in 1944 they were about forty) prisoner registration numbers were no longer only sewed to the clothes but tattooed on the left forearm . . . men were tattooed on the outside of the arm and women on the inside . . . . The operation was not very painful and lasted no more than a minute, but it was traumatic. Its symbolic meaning was clear to everyone: this is an indelible mark, you will never leave here; this is the mark with which slaves are branded and cattle sent to the slaughter, and that is what you have become. You no longer have a name; this is your new name. The violence of the tattoo was gratuitous, an end in itself, pure offense."[5] Levi points out that only non-Jewish German prisoners were exempt from these tattoos.

The tattoo was a necessary marker of difference, for the Jew was already indistinguishable from everyone else. For decades before the war, the dominant trend for most French and German Jews was to blend in with the majority culture. In an attempt to achieve even greater invisibility in the 1930s, more and more German Jews actually went uncircumcised, a remaining marker of difference. Sander Gilman argues that the increasing inability to distinguish the Jew helps explain "the need to construct another 'mark' of difference in the concentration camps of the 1930s." The tattoo was "an 'indelible' mark upon the body which uniformly signified difference."[6]

Those blue numbers, now fading, have come to mark those who bear them as history's witnesses. Discussing his own tattoo, Levi wrote: "At a distance of forty years, my tattoo has become a part of my body. I don't glory in it, but I am not ashamed of it either; I do not display and do not hide it. I show it unwillingly to those who ask out of pure curiosity; readily and with anger to those who say they are incredulous. Often young people ask me why I don't have it erased, and this surprises me: Why should I? There are not many of us in the world to bear this witness."[7] In an act of surrogate witnessing, some members of the postwar generation have gone so far as to have actual numbers tattooed on their bodies. While organizing an exhibition called "Tattooing Without Consent," at the Triangle Tattoo and Museum in Fort Bragg, California, artist "Chinchilla" came across the diary of a tattooer who had put the number 79496 on a baby girl born and killed in Birkenau in 1944. In an act of personal commemoration for an unknown child, Chinchilla had the same number tattooed on her arm on what would have been the baby's fifty-first birthday.[8]

The anxiety-charged work of Canadian artist John Scott, dealing with the consequences of industrialization and war, is suffused with an apocalyptic, post-Holocaust reckoning with the moral effects of the catastrophe. Scott had his thigh tattooed with three small roses and a seven-digit number—6339.042. The decimal point marked it as similar but different from the numbers of concentration camp inmates. This area of his skin was then surgically removed and displayed in a carefully fabricated metal and glass case. Entitled *Selbst* (1989), it was first shown at the Carmen Lamanna Gallery in Toronto in 1990, where it evoked a controversial reception among critics. Kenneth Baker, writing for *Artforum,* viewed it as a shallow attempt at direct identification, finding the work an unacceptable cultural misappropriation because "the parallel the title proposes between the artist's fate and that of death-camp victims is distastefully expedient."[9] Other critics perceived *Selbst* as a gesture of solidarity with the suffering of others.[10] Yet the issue here is both more complex and larger than that of either a presumptuous or empathic personal identification with suffering. Scott, a non-Jew, attempts to rattle the cultural boundaries between Self and Other. In a gesture of blood solidarity, Scott literally showcased the consequences of the behavior of ordinary people who became perpetrators of unspeakable acts. "When the allies opened the camps in 1945 and the rest of the world discovered what had happened there," Scott writes, "the trajectory of modernism, arcing from the enlightenment to that moment at the close of the war, ended. People saw that the notion of modernism had been unable to prevent the holocaust—had maybe even led to it. It changed forever our notion of what people were capable of and what culture was really about. As for *Selbst,* it was never a matter of *identification.* I was trying to reverse that process that the camps had redefined—a certain notion of our collective self image."[11] *Selbst* may be regarded as "an act of physical defiance against passivity."[12] Scott's deeply personal gesture stands against the silence, indifference, or resignation of the majority.

Confrontations with the Holocaust are more common, however, among Jews coming to terms with the meaning of Jewish difference. The revival of Jewish ethnic identity has found expression in a variety of mediums. Even fashion designer Jean Paul Gaultier got into the act with his Fall/Winter Collection of 1993 (fig. 51 a, b). Using the traditional black robes, wide-brimmed hats and *yarmulkes* of ultra-orthodox Judaism as his inspiration, Gaultier creates a chic new Jewish body, a Semitic look that anyone can wear, with sexy sidecurls and a stylish exoticism updated from that old-fashioned shtetl look and spiced up, for the more daring, with a hint of the dominatrix. This "Hasidic" collection by the "couturier-provocateur Gaultier," as Linda Nochlin dubbed him, figures the Jew as nothing if not excessive.[13] Gaultier, a Jew, played it to the hilt, sending out invitations to the show in Hebraic-looking script and serving Manischewitz wine at the opening. The show was also provocatively transgressive by cross-dressing women in traditional men's clothing. As Nochlin suggests, Gaultier's models in drag pointed to the traditional segregation of the sexes within Judaism, calling into question its fundamentalist authoritarian structure. It was this aspect which most offended the Orthodox Jews of Borough

Fig. 51 a, b. Jean Paul Gaultier, Fall/Winter "Hasidic" Collection, 1993. *Women's Wear Daily*, Fairchild Publications, Inc.

Park in New York, a center of Hasidic and Orthodox Judaism where French *Vogue* decided to photograph the collection. "The whole thing is very offensive," said Rabbi Morris Shmidman, the executive director of the Council of Jewish Organizations of Borough Park. "To take men's mode of clothing and make that into a modish thing for women is extremely inappropriate in this community."[14] Gaultier's transvestite gesture is one of parody, but also a daring confrontation with traditional Judaism. In the latter sense, it has something in common with the challenge to Orthodox bans on body modification practiced by young Jews today.

As part of the renewed ethnic consciousness movement, a new Jewish literary magazine emerged in 1996 called *Davka,* founded by four children of Holocaust survivors as a rallying point for a generation of disaffected, punked-out young Jews.[15] *Davka*'s editors perceived a Jewish cultural revolution and aimed the magazine at secular Jews searching for access to Judaism (*Davka* has since been transformed into the online magazine *Tattoo Jew—The Online Magazine for Jews with Attitude*). *Davka* included essays, interviews, poetry, and profiles by writers such as Allen Ginsberg, David Mamet, Kathy Acker, Jay Hoberman, and Tony Kushner. The journal responded to what it perceived as an explosion of Yiddish culture in the arts, a new iconography of Jewish painters, performance artists, writers and musicians who are celebrating Jewish culture with unprecedented enthusiasm. Within this contemporary approach, *Davka*'s mission to bring secular young Jews back into the religious fold is perfectly captured in the cover photograph of the first issue. A young woman with short, fuschia-colored hair, nose and lip pierces, and tattoos inspired by tribal designs is wrapped in the Jewish prayer shawl traditionally worn only by men (although now adopted by women in Reform Judaism). While crossing gender boundaries and defying the admonition against tattoos, this transgressive woman of the 1990s, who rejects mainstream values, nevertheless wraps herself in the traditional symbol of Jewish belief (fig.52).

Davka hopes to change the perception of Jewish tradition as old-fashioned, conservative, and unrelated to modern lives by relating Jew-

Fig. 52. Cover of *Davka: Jewish Cultural Revolution*, winter 1996. Cover concept: Alan Kaufman/photo: Marcus Hanschen/cover graphic design: Jill Bressler. ©1996 *Davka: Jewish Cultural Revolution*. Permission granted courtesy *Davka: Jewish Cultural Revolution* (now Tattoo Jew—www.tattoojew.com), Alan Kaufman, Editor-in-Chief, 1126 Bush Street, Apt. 605, San Francisco, CA 94109.

ish religious practice to the young, the hip, and the body-modified. At the same time, it attempts to restore a sense of secular Yiddish culture, because the contemporary sense of Jewish identity has become empty at its core, filled with whatever the surrounding culture has to offer. For many of those seeking to establish a sense of community, Jewish difference is reduced to the observance of ritual practice, and ritual practice is adopted by many without religious belief. Thus, many young Jews, who finally have the freedom to embrace Jewish identity, do so at a moment when definitions of Jewish identity have been lost due to the very process of assimilation and acceptance that has made this freedom possible.[16]

An episode that illustrates this identity confusion is the controversy among Reform Jews that was provoked by *Davka*'s cover. Rabbi Stephen Pearce, the leader of San Francisco's Reform synagogue who gave seed money to the magazine, who is listed on its advisory board, and who appears in a photo essay about hip Bay Area rabbis, was scandalized when he discovered that *Davka*'s tattooed cover model was not Jewish. If she had been, he said, she would have been "expressing her Judaism in some way."[17] Feeling betrayed, the rabbi resigned as a *Davka* board advisor after having bought subscriptions for his entire board of directors. No doubt the fact that Gaultier's models were non-Jewish would have been equally disturbing to him. But why should the rabbi have objected so strongly? Perhaps the fact that there is no absolute signifier for the Jew is at the core of his uneasiness. Indeed, anyone can pose as a Jew.

. . .

More than any young, body-modified Jew in America today, contemporary photographer Marina Vainshtein proclaims her identity concerns in ways both more explicit and more extreme through her permanent bodyart. By the age of twenty-three, Vainshtein had tattoos of graphic Holocaust imagery over most of her body. On her upper back, the central image represents a train transport carrying Jewish prisoners in striped uniforms toward waiting ovens (fig. 53).[18] Smoke billows above the train cars while a swastika, represented in negative space, wafts through the ashes that are spewed forth by a crematorium chimney. Across her shoulders, Hebrew letters carry the message, "Earth hide not my blood," from the Book of Job's passage, "O Earth, hide not my blood / And let my cry never cease." Atop the train car, figures, some blindfolded, hold each other or reach their arms hopelessly upward, one clutching a flag marked with a Star of David (fig. 54). Other figures are pressed together inside the cattle car, one shaven-headed person staring forlornly through the bars. Ribbons of barbed wire float upward from broken fence posts. Below the train and the brick-lined ovens, a tattoo represents the notorious inscription on a number of concentration camp gates, *Arbeit macht frei* (work is liberating), while the results of that absurdly false promise are presented as tombstones, engraved with Hebrew text, and a column of skeletons (fig. 55). To the right of the

Fig. 53. Marina Vainshtein, back tattoos, 1997. *Los Angeles Times* photo by Anacleto Rapping.

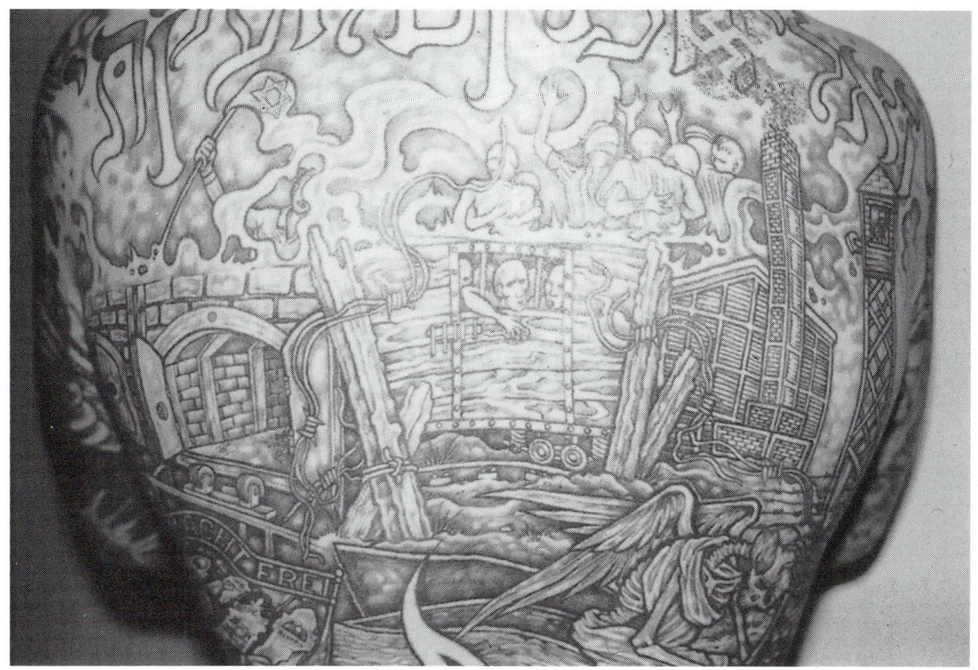

Fig. 54. Marina Vainshtein, back tattoos, 1997. Courtesy Marina Vainshtein.

Fig. 55. Marina Vainshtein, lower back tattoos, 1997. Courtesy Marina Vainshtein.

chimney is a guard tower with an armed guard who watches as an elderly man trying to escape dies on an electrified barbed wire fence. On the small of Vainshtein's back is an image of an elderly woman chained to a coffin of nails who is engulfed in the flames of a burning Star of David. Underneath are the words "Never forget" in Hebrew. Above the burning star is a tattoo of a skeleton, which Vainshtein identifies as an angel, sitting on an open casket. The skeleton holds the book of *Kaddish,* the Hebrew prayer for the dead (fig. 56).

Vainshtein was born in the Soviet Union. Her grandfather fought with the Red Army against the Nazis; her grandmother moved from town to town to escape anti-Jewish pogroms. Her family continued to be subjected to antisemitism under the Stalinist regimes until she and her parents were granted exit visas and moved from Ukraine to California in 1977, when Vainshtein was four years old. She grew up in Melrose, a neighborhood in Los Angeles inhabited primarily by Russian Hasidic Jews and, in the 1980s, by punks. Entering public school in eighth grade after spending her first seven years at a Jewish school, she experienced a kind of identity shock because there were so many different kinds of people. A secure sense of Jewish identity was suddenly destabilized by the realization that, except for saying she was Jewish, there was nothing which visibly distinguished Vainshtein as such. By the age of

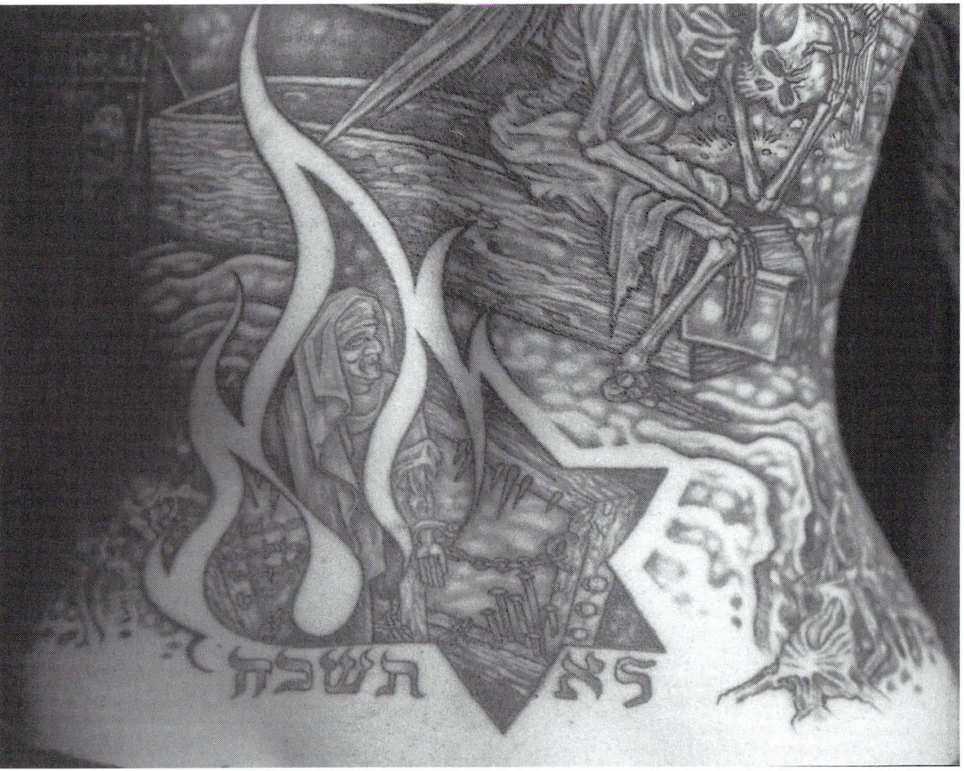

Fig. 56. Marina Vainshtein, lower back tattoos, 1997. Courtesy Marina Vainshtein.

fifteen, searching for a way to define her identity as other in a sea of pluralistic sameness, she started thinking about getting a tattoo and embracing the punk aesthetic. It was also while she was in high school that Vainshtein became obsessed with Holocaust literature, and was profoundly affected by meeting Nina Schulkind, a survivor of seven concentration camps, who spent a day with Vainshtein telling her story.[19] For Vainshtein, as for many Jews, being born even decades after the event does not prevent the Holocaust from playing a defining role in shaping their identity. It can be argued that the Holocaust stands behind any contemporary sense of Jewish identity, whether it is addressed obsessively, ambivalently, or not at all.

The reaction to Vainshtein's tattoos, made public by a full-page article in the *Los Angeles Times* when she was twenty-two, was mixed.[20] Some people congratulated her. Others, especially in her own Orthodox neighborhood, accused her of defiling the meaning of Jewish suffering by violating the Jewish law against body modification. In defending her tattoos, Vainshtein asks: "Why not have external scars to represent the internal scars?"[21] Like Burgin, Vainshtein reclaims the body of the tattooed Jew; in addition, the tattoos represent a form of explicit personal commemoration and a continuation of historical memory, the internal scars of a people made visible on the body of one of its young. To demonstrate her belief that the postwar generations must carry on the memory of the Holocaust, she places her own body between the past and future as a barrier to forgetting.

The growth of the Neo-Nazi and other white supremacist movements in the United States in recent years and the rapidity with which old hatreds have flared into new regimes of terror in Europe are chilling reminders that we may not allow ourselves to believe our forms of difference safe in our seemingly enlightened multicultural world. Faith in the possibility of successful assimilation has been a precarious position historically; in fact, it has never succeeded. Although assimilation for Jews would seem more successful at this moment in America than ever before, antisemitism is by no means dead, whether in the form of the ravings of the popular black demagogue Louis Farrakan, the program of the American militia movements, or the unchallenged rhetoric of Republican presidential candidate Patrick Buchanan in the 1996 New Hampshire primaries, or in more subtle forms, such as of the Southern Baptists' appointment in 1996 of a missionary to undertake the conversion of American Jews to Christianity.[22]

In another reaction to the *Los Angeles Times* article, a young Jewish man who grew up in an Orthodox family walked into a tattoo shop one day clutching the newspaper clipping about Vainshtein and requested his own first tattoo, a tribal (i.e., solid black) six-pointed Star of David. The tattoo artist, a friend of Vainshtein's who was moved by the young man's fervency, recounted the story to her. We don't know how the Orthodox family reacted, but it seems safe to say that for the young man, the contemporary reinvention of Jewish identity was a more powerful force than the prohibitions of the old European Jewish culture. Moreover, it connected him to contemporary youth culture across class and religious lines.

Fig. 57. Marina Vainshtein, arm tattoos, 1997. Courtesy Marina Vainshtein.

Not surprisingly, Vainshtein supports the revival of contemporary Jewish consciousness among many young Jews. Like Burgin, she defines herself as a Reform Jew and the most important principlc of Jewish faith for her is the concept of the *mitzvah.* A mitzvah is commonly understood as the doing of a good deed, but it is more than this. It means performing an act which fulfills a commandment or precept or the spirit of such a commandment or precept as defined in the body of Jewish scripture and scriptural commentary known collectively as the Torah. So one could argue that as a sign of an irreversible and *public* commitment to her Jewish identity, Vainshtein's tattoos ironically constitute the performance of a mitzvah, because, according to the Torah, it is a mitzvah to be seen in the world as a Jew.

Vainshtein's arm tattoos include a violin player, referring to the orchestra at Auschwitz composed of Jewish prisoners, surrounded by hanging corpses, a can of Zyklon B, the killing agent used in the gas chambers, and an anguished face (fig. 57). Screaming faces of prisoners being gassed are tattooed on her right breast (fig. 58). Other tattoos include a wrist bracelet of Hebrew text, "And now we are the last of many," between two rows of barbed wire from which flames arise; a black armband with a Star of David; a large eyeball pierced by needles, referring to the notorious medical experiments by Nazi doctor Joseph Mengele, in which attempts to change eye color through experimental injections left children blind. The large form of a skull fills the space on her stomach and chest (fig. 59). The eye sockets contain skeletons; the top of the skull depicts a bombing raid on the right and prosthetic body parts on the left (fig. 60). Gothic letters across the top of her chest declare "Never Again" in English. Below the skull is an image of a lampshade made of Jewish skin sewn together in patches. Next to it, a synagogue on fire refers to

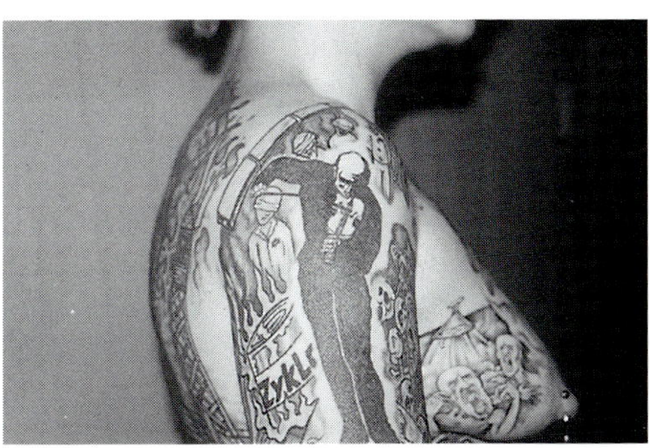

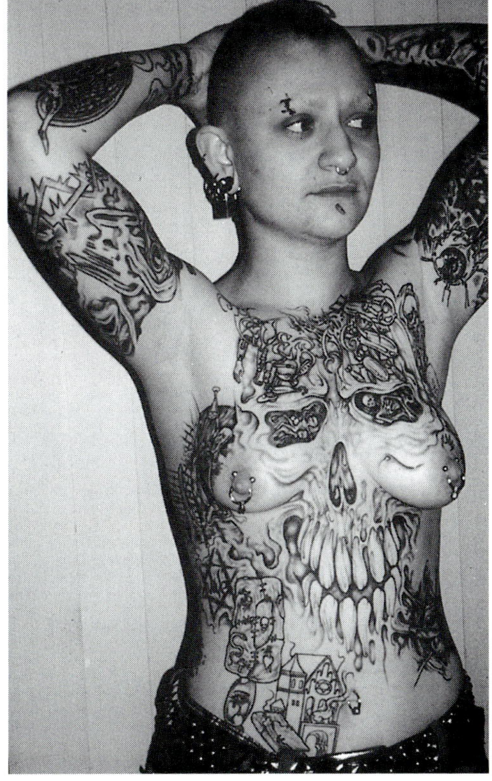

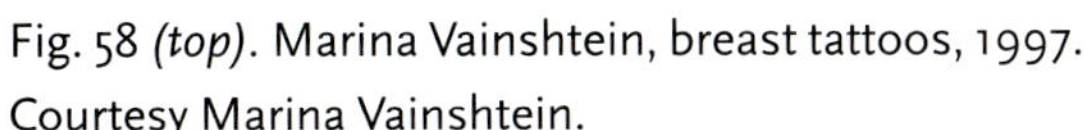

Fig. 58 *(top)*. Marina Vainshtein, breast tattoos, 1997. Courtesy Marina Vainshtein.
Fig. 59 *(bottom)*. Marina Vainshtein, chest tattoos, 1997. Courtesy Marina Vainshtein.

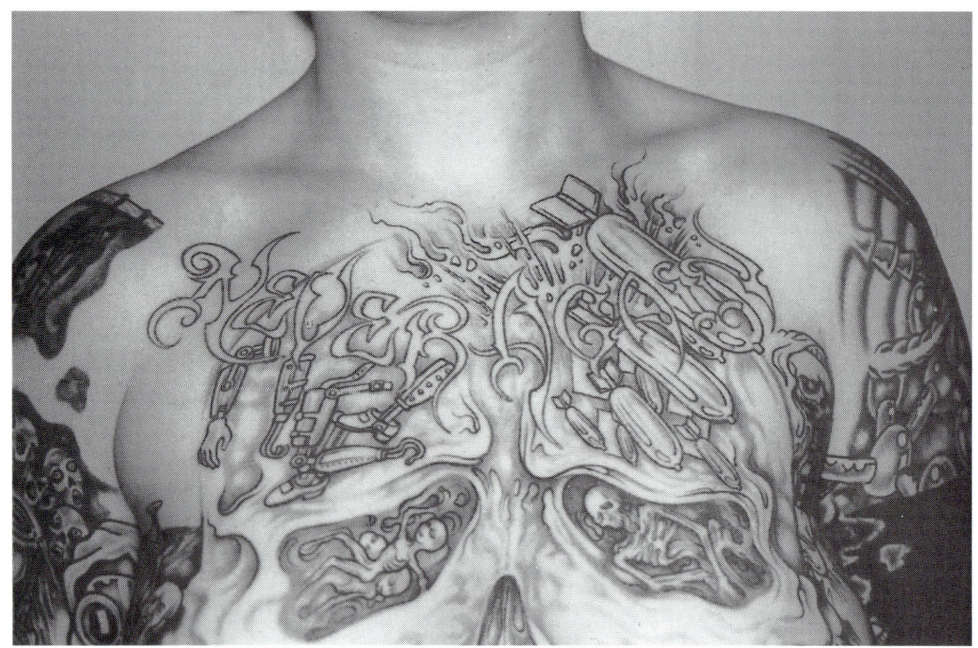

Fig. 60. Marina Vainshtein, chest tattoos, 1997. Courtesy Marina Vainshtein.

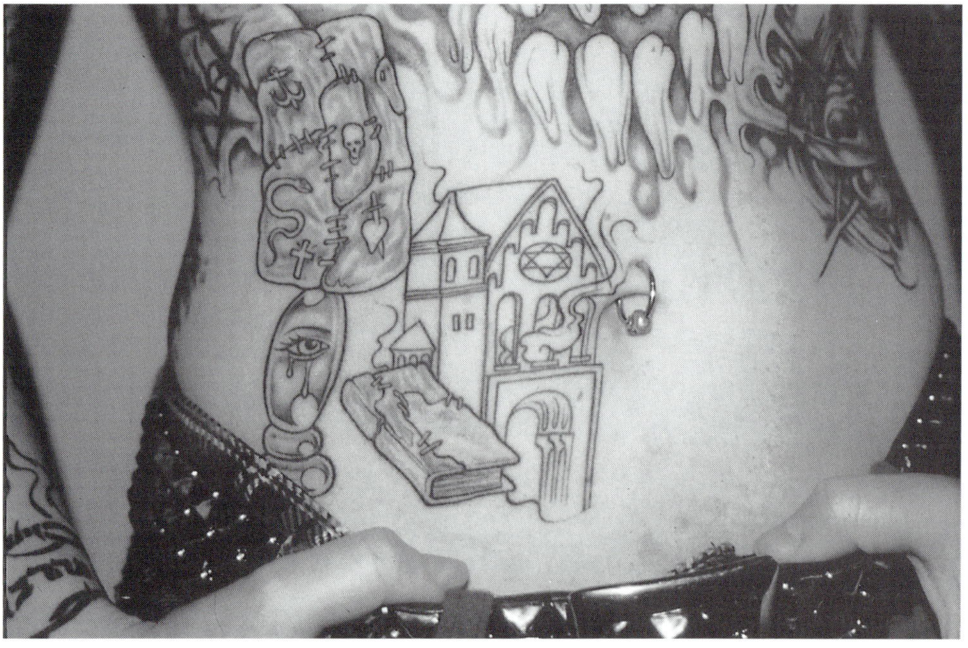

Fig. 61. Marina Vainshtein, stomach tattoos, 1997. Courtesy Marina Vainshtein.

Kristallnacht, the notorious Nazi pogrom of 1938 (fig. 61). On one leg, tattoos depict a train traveling through a European cityscape where people hide in ghettos; on the other leg, she has a plant of life with two fetuses, both branded with Stars of David on their foreheads. This is Vainshtein's only major color piece, and would seem to be the most optimistic image. For most survivors of the Holocaust, the very birth of a next generation was regarded as a kind of resurrection and ultimate defeat of Hitler's deadly vision. But we can also read the Stars of David branded on the foreheads of the fetuses as the mark of Cain; they are branded by and as the Other. Overall, Vainshtein has created a kind of body narrative which begins with Jewish ghettoization and deportation on her left leg and travels upward, showing the horrors of the concentration camps, the reign of terror, torture, and death that culminates in the ashes of the crematorium on her upper back.

For Marina Vainshtein and Joshua Burgin, their sense of Jewish identity is unequivocal. But for many American Jews, there is a contradiction between their sense of Jewish ethnicity and their rejection of the public visibility that that identity entails. In a discussion of Jews in America, anthropologist Karen Brodkin helps identify the roots of this reluctance. Brodkin asserts that race, gender, and class construction in America has been shaped by a public discourse founded on a core myth of the American nation as composed of only white men and women. Jews and other eastern and southern Europeans were assigned a nonwhite status, which rendered them "unfit to exercise the prerogatives of citizenship."[23] The performance of labor defined as menial or unskilled had a darkening effect, while the rise into middle-class status conferred a whitening effect. Thus, Jews and other European immigrants during the first half of the twentieth century, who formed the core of the industrial working class, found themselves in a nonwhite racial status, which was, de facto, a degraded status subject to institutional racism designed to keep them at the bottom of the economy in a vicious circle of containment.

Jews responded with what Brodkin calls "hegemonic Jewishness," based on identification with the community against mainstream antisemitism in the form of generalized Jewish socialism. This did not mean that all Jews were socialist or that this was the only way of identifying oneself as a Jew, but that "part of being Jewish was being familiar with a working-class and anticapitalist outlook on the world and understanding this outlook as being particularly Jewish."[24] Secular Yiddish culture, moreover, transcended differences between secular and religious Jews, progressive or conservative Jews and connected Jews to each other through a common Yiddish language. Not until after World War II did Jews in America traverse the spectrum from not quite white to whiteness, largely as a result of an upward mobility due to a lowering of educational and occupational barriers that opened up new fields to Jews and facilitated their migration into the middle class. African Americans, Latinos/Latinas, and others did not fare as well, being deliberately denied the advantages of institutional whiteness by being denied access in education, employment, and housing. The federal government, in fact, did its best to maintain institutional racism in regard to these groups while a postwar whitening of Jews and other eastern and southern Europeans took place in the period between 1940 and 1975.

The prewar opposition between Jewishness and whiteness that existed for an older generation of working-class American Jews, whose self-identification was consonant with and in part determined by their racial assignment and social segregation, thought of themselves first and foremost as Jewish. This binary reversed itself for later generations of assimilated middle-class Jews who thought of themselves primarily as part of the American mainstream, or white, and did not want to be associated with antisemitic stereotypes of the Jew which persisted after World War II (though becoming less socially acceptable) or even the implied subjectivity of difference associated with the concept of Jewishness.

The catalog for the 1996 exhibition *Too Jewish? Challenging Traditional Identities* at the Jewish Museum in New York focused on this ambivalence and pointed to the understanding that, until recently, almost any marker of Jewish ethnicity was regarded by many Jews as embarrassingly "too Jewish." The very conception that one could be too Jewish exposed the sense of continuing vulnerability that made the children of Jewish immigrants, and some immigrants themselves, anxious to assimilate. But new generations of Jews now strive to master the embarrassment of Jewishness, to redefine it and make it their own. As one critic commented on the reclamation of Jewish identity in the arts, particularly the revival of Yiddish music: "Generations removed from the immigrant Jews who hid their Jewish roots in exchange for acceptance in America, these artists, now securely American, pursue a heritage that more profoundly defines them, beyond their mere Americanness."[25]

The conflict for Jews, then, has been between a private and a public sense of Jewish identity which, in turn, came about because identity was seen as a question of race, an idea which itself has undergone major shifts in conceptualization since the nineteenth century. Early on, race was regarded as a category of social organization rooted in assumed differences that were often regarded as cultural, but eventually were seen as innately biological and psychological. The more recent emphasis on discourse and representation has transformed the treatment of race and ethnicity into socially constructed phenomena. In both North America and Europe, however, the far right has revived eugenic concepts of race, even as minorities have found a stronger voice. The continuing debate over the complexities of race, ethnicity, and hybridity, is itself complex. Suffice it to say that the concept of race has been used mainly for abusive ends, not the least of which are the legacy of slavery, colonial practices, hierarchical social structures and the slaughter of European Jews and Gypsies.[26] One important cultural response to the idea of race and the more general idea of racial homogeneity is to stress "the uniqueness of the individual over the uniformity of the group."[27] Thus, to be a public Jew, in the absence of so-called racial markers, ironically involves the reinscription of the category of Jew as a unified subject. It signals a cultural subordination of individuality, even as one seeks to assert it, by linking oneself with a generalized group. The courage of Vainshtein's stance, and those with tattooed Stars of David, is apparent in the sense that they openly and irreversibly associate themselves with a historically despised and persecuted group, rather than seeking the anonymity of invisibility in the dominant white mainstream.

The taint of race is still constructed on the body in a number of stereotypical ways; one of the best known is the Jewish Nose, which has spawned the medical invention of the Nose Job. As Sander Gilman notes, "suffering from a Jewish nose" became a powerful image in the 1930s, when being seen as a Jew meant being persecuted, and many Jews sought surgical solutions. (The nose job lost its efficacy as a means to invisibility, however, with the introduction of the yellow star.)[28] In the 1960s and early 1970s, tens of thousands of American teenage Jewish girls whose parents wanted their children to fit into the Protestant mainstream had their noses fixed through rhinoplasties. The effects of a surgical solution were immortalized by Andy Warhol as early as 1960 in his painting *Before and After,* which presents a female profile with a hooked nose followed by the same profile with its nose smoothed out (fig. 62).[29] While the nose job strives for assimilation, the Holocaust tattoo is implacably non-assimilationist. Yet the nose job and the Holocaust tattoo

Fig. 62. Andy Warhol, *Before and After*, lithograph, 1960. The Andy Warhol Foundation, Inc./Art Resource, NY ©2001 Andy Warhol Foundation for the Visual Arts/ARS, New York.

Fig. 63. Frédéric Brenner, *Jews with Hogs*, Miami Beach, 1994. Gelatin silver print. © Frédéric Brenner.

have something in common: each operates on the body of the Jew because of the effects of antisemitism. And each, in its own way, is a distortion. Although extreme, or precisely because of its extremity, Vainshtein's tattooed body, while establishing a unique late-twentieth-century form of Jewish identity, ironically reproduces central aspects of traditional Jewish identity: the Jew as outsider, the Jew as Other, the body of the Jew as deformed, the Jew as excessive and inassimilable. We can read her action as a backlash against a too successful assimilation into the dominant culture. Where there is no cultural specificity to distinguish the newly conscious Jew, the Holocaust tattoo itself becomes the mark of difference.

But it does not necessarily produce unity with other Jews, in general, but rather with those who also deliberately position themselves as outsiders, that is, in Vainshtein's case, with the community of those who practice body modification. Yet even in the world of the inked, Vainshtein's tattoos have incited an antisemitic response in the form of disdainful snickers by Hell's Angels at a 1995 tattoo convention (where the proud owners of tattoos go to strut their stuff and admire each other). The reaction of racist bikers produces the ironic spectacle of a widely distrusted segment of an outsider group (i.e., Hell's Angels) attempting to construct the tattooed Jew as more "outside" the inside than they are. The response of the Hell's Angels, however, might not impress another group of tattooed bikers captured in a photograph by French photographer Frédéric Brenner (fig. 63). Brenner documented a group of Jewish bikers perched astride their Harley-Davidsons as one of a series of unusual post-Holocaust forms of Jewish self-invention found even in this fringe enclave of American particularity. The tattooed Jews on bikes gathered in Miami Beach in 1994 and posed in front of a synagogue, in a picture Brenner entitled *Jews with Hogs.* The witty incongruity of the title parallels the peculiarly postmodern pairing of the Star of David poised between sacred tablets on the synagogue in the background with the Harley-Davidson logo on the T-shirt of the biker with a flowing white beard, like a latter-day Moses, in the foreground. The beard itself operates as a double signifier of modern cultural rebellion and the traditional, observant Jew.

This photograph is part of a larger series Brenner has produced over the past two decades on the subject of the Jewish diaspora. Brenner's project tracks the elusive Jew, trying to understand how Jews maintain a specific identity even as they immerse themselves in the culture of the nation in which they live, or, as Brenner puts it, "how much can one people become part of another and yet remain themselves?"[30] In his search for the diversity of the diaspora, Brenner has photographed groups such as the Jewish Lesbian Daughters of Holocaust Survivors; Jews who reenact a Civil War battle in period clothing; Passover celebrants at a maximum security women's correctional facility; and the staff of the Nice Jewish Boys Moving and Storage in Palm Beach, Florida, none of whom are Jewish.[31]

Marking herself as a public Jew with the imagery of the Holocaust, Vainshtein perhaps makes herself potentially vulnerable to the critique that her embrace of the "yellow star of ostracism" is an "appropriation" of an experience which is not her own, an act of "draping" herself with "the torture that others underwent."[32] This is how French writer Alain Finkielkraut, in *The Imaginary Jew,* criticized his own efforts as a radical youth who thought of himself as a persecuted Polish Jew in a period of revolutionary zeal. Finkielkraut confesses to a realization that he was only pretending, and argues that memory of the Holocaust must extend to memory of the Jewish community and culture based on the common language of Yiddish that the Holocaust destroyed. Because Jewish ethnicity itself was lost in that destruction, he contends, Jewishness today cannot properly link itself to its past and claim a mantle of continuity: "The Jew may be civilization's Other, but it is an otherness none can possess. To put it still more bluntly: the Holocaust has no heirs. No one can cloak himself in such an experience, incommunicable, if not the survivors. Among the people that constitute our generation, it is given to no one to say: I am the child of Auschwitz."[33] Finkielkraut sees himself as a proud, yet imaginary Jew, unable to claim any specific kind of cultural difference. He asserts that Jews no longer exist as they once did, that today's Jews are cut off from Jewish culture by the disaster in which it perished. For Finkielkraut, commemoration of the Holocaust still leaves in oblivion the face of the living culture that came before and has been lost forever. While courageously refusing "a tragic, heroic, self-righteous, and delusive identification on the part of children of Jewish survivors of Nazism with the victims themselves," in the words of Jonathan Boyarin, Finkielkraut's disillusionment with the possibility of a continued "Jewish" identity, based on his own sense of "pretending," is too categorical. Boyarin observes that Finkielkraut has left no "space of the imaginary within which 'Jewish' is constituted." Thus, "having once dismantled the illusion of a total identification with his ancestors, he still imagines identity as an all-or-nothing affair . . . Finkielkraut imagines the world of the 'real Jews' to be an actual whole, irretrievably in the past. He has made himself an imaginary 'not-Jew.'"[34]

Marina Vainshtein, on the other hand, feels no sense of pretense in her identification with the Jewish genocide. She projects a truth that many historians, children of Holocaust survivors, psychiatrists and psychoanalysts have come to understand: *even those born later can be traumatized by the Holocaust.* Geoffrey Hartman, founder of the Fortunoff Video Archive for Holocaust Testimonies at Yale University, calls those experiencing this phenomenon "witnesses by adoption," referring to those who have been damaged by the transmittance of memory by those who survived.[35] I find the term "secondary witness" more adequate to encompass this phenomenon. As a secondary witness, Vainshtein's body must be read as her own testimonial to the event, a reenactment of memory at a secondary remove performed by a surrogate witness in whom trauma has also been induced, even as she attempts to reclaim the body of the Jew that was tortured, burned, and forcibly tattooed.

Assuming the risks of exposing herself as a target for those who hate outsiders, Vainshtein defies what Finkielkraut calls that "crushing imperative," the one always borne by outsiders that says: "Don't stand out."[36] In rejecting Jewish invisibility and assimilation, the body of the tattooed Jew more broadly constitutes a postmodernist rejection of an idealized bourgeois norm. It represents an abandonment of the liberal humanist ideal of the flattening out of all difference, a homogeneous universalism. This modernist aspiration used as its universal model the white, middle-class, heterosexual, and *gentile* male.

A distinction must be made here between the assertion of difference, or the politics of identity, on one hand, and identity politics on the other. The politics of identity may be defined as articulating problems of everyday life, as well as criticism and theory, in an interrogative and analytical way. Identity politics may be defined as an organized way of articulating group identities and differences as both aim and strategy. The main complaint against identity politics has been a fear that once articulated, such identities are either triumphant or fixed, generating a potentially destructive tribal mentality. Art Spiegelman, author of the comic book volumes, *Maus,* argues against just this sort of ethnic excess. Spiegelman is regarded by many newly militant Jews as the godfather of renewed Jewish consciousness. Yet Spiegelman warns against the nationalist divisiveness of identity politics: "This is the problem with an America that has gone crazy," Spiegelman says, "that's just gone into ethnic madness. I think what you're seeing is a response to the Balkanization of America, where Jews who felt themselves too embraced in America's assimilationist arms have now started to desperately backpedal. It seems to me that America has entered into an age of competing victimhoods, and that the left has become sapped by the rise of multiculturalism. The energy that used to go into trying to create a generally more just society has been rerouted into competing claims of ethnic rights."[37] Spiegelman, in effect, counterposes a more materialist political view of history to the politics of liberal pluralism. A more nuanced view, argued by Jonathan Boyarin, suggests that specific differences can be used as a productive field for exploring more general issues related to the politics of difference.[38]

Despite the loss of prewar Yiddish culture, the language of Yiddish not only survives among certain ultra-orthodox communities, but is undergoing something of a revival, from the Broadway play *Mamaloshen* (Mother Tongue) starring Mandy Patinkin, to a segment of the Jewish gay and lesbian community. Yiddish is also the predominant language of Jewish klezmer groups such as the Klezmatics, who not only use it on their CDs but also teach it at their annual five-day Yiddish music, language, and culture extravaganza known as Klez/Camp.

Marina Vainshtein is also an open lesbian. In addition to her tattoos, she has twenty-five body pierces and a nine-inch red Mohawk. Perhaps precisely because Yiddish culture in Europe *was* destroyed, a culture which included its own forms of misogyny and homophobia, today's newly conscious postmodernist Jews can be anything they want—gay, feminist, pierced, and tattooed—and no one can tell them they don't belong. But, we might ask: What is the relationship between Vainshtein's pierces and her Holocaust tattoos? Marianna Torgovnik has argued that African initiation rituals are closest in spirit to contemporary Western piercing rituals because they physically mark the passage into adulthood with a badge of identity that is lacking in American culture.[39] The rituals that are available for Jews, such as the bar mitzvah or bat mitzvah for girls, only approximate initiation without achieving it, she suggests, because there is no visible marker left behind.[40] In the marriage of "mineral and flesh," by contrast, the piercing ritual is seen as "affirmation of the bodily self" through the acquisition of a permanent, recognizable mark of identity and as a rite of passage that symbolically confronts mortality.[41] We can extend the logic of piercing as a coming of age ritual to certain other forms of body modification, including tattooing and branding, as exemplified by the bodyart of Joshua Burgin and Marina Vainshtein.

When I asked Vainshtein about embracing two forms of body modification at the same time—the pierces and punk aesthetic as well as the Holocaust tattoos—she insisted that they had nothing to do with each other, despite the fact that they both were contemplated and adopted at the same time in her adolescence and both obviously have something to do with finding forms of self-expression that establish her sense of identity. She asserts her enjoyment of her twenty-five body pierces as adornment only and for the sensual pleasure they give her.[42] Her sense of their separateness from her tattoos points to the ironic tensions produced by the multiple ways in which we define ourselves. We are, indeed, always negotiating among various and even contradictory senses of self, other, and group.

Vainshtein is right to suggest that Jewish ethnicity per se has little or nothing to do with punk culture. American punk may be read as a "middle-class expression of alienation from and disgust with the mainstream values of society."[43] The punk ethos is anarchistic and nihilistic, focusing on apocalyptic themes of destruction and death, as well as the development of new styles of music, art, writing and body adornment. The most popular hairstyle associated with the punk aesthetic, the Mohawk, evokes stereotyped notions of the primitive, or youth on the warpath, an assertion of identity that challenges dominant notions of feminine beauty just as tattooing challenges dominant notions of the sanctity of the body. Punks create the impression that they are "sacrificing their bodies out of postmodern despair," that is, out of the conviction that our civilization has no future.[44]

But this brings us back to Vainshtein's imagery of the Holocaust and the use of her body as a medium. Her unique form of bodyart precisely expresses alienation from and disgust with mainstream values and is profoundly concerned with apocalyptic themes of destruction and death. For the postwar generations that were raised with filmic and photographic images of emaciated bodies bulldozed into open pits, it is only a short step to cynicism about the future of civilization and disgust with Western notions of beauty and the sanctity of the body. The experience of the camps, vicariously embraced, has subverted notions of the sanctified body. What unites the punk ethos and aesthetic that Vainshtein has adopted with the content of her bodyart is not the issue of Jewish ethnicity per se but the shattered idealism of the post-Holocaust era. The latter half of the twentieth century was the era of disillusionment with Enlightenment values of rationality, progress, the goodness of humanity, and the benefits of technology. This is the era of proliferating genocides. And yet, by converting the tattooed numbers, which mutely allude to the Holocaust experience, into a full-blown exposition of what those numbers mean, Vainshtein effects a symbolic reversal of Halachic law. Through her devotion, the desecrated body becomes the body beautiful.

Among historians and writers there has been a debate for some years over whether the Holocaust can be compellingly described or represented at all without being aestheticized or in some way ethically compromised. Writers such as Elie Wiesel, who has produced a number of his own books, have called for silence as the only response that will not trivialize the enormity of the event or produce what historian Saul Friedländer has called "Holocaust kitsch."[45] What about the aestheticization of the Holocaust in the easily recognizable icons of emaciated bodies, barbed wire, and ovens on Vainshtein's body? Is this a trivialization of the Holocaust into kitsch imagery? Vainshtein's tattoos succeed in evoking both horror and admiration: horror for the defamiliarization of the body with representations of death and suffering, but admiration for the level of commitment she demonstrates, for the extremity of her stance. The peculiar medium of the body for such painful imagery might remind us of Kafka's story, *In the Penal Colony,* in which history as inscription on the body also finds a literal treatment. In Kafka's penal colony a torture machine writes the prisoner's sentence on the body by piercing the flesh with needles. The condemned man then deciphers his sentence with his wounds. This is not to suggest that Kafka predicted the mass murder of the Holocaust; on the contrary, Kafka's story takes place on the level of internal, individual consciousness. Marina Vainshtein's body inscription is also a singular, albeit self-inflicted, act; she, however, knows who the enemy is and what the punishment was. The fact that Vainshtein marks this knowledge *on her skin* is what freights the familiar imagery with its sorrowful power. We are further reminded that it was the tattooed skin of hundreds of murdered prisoners that was selected to be tanned into lampshades and pocket-knife sheaths for the German SS, which Vainshtein herself has pictured on her chest.[46] The chilling resonance of this dimension to Vainshtein's body modifications allows us to read the imagery of catastrophe on the skin of her body as not only representing the subject of the Holocaust, but reproducing the abject subject at its center. For what is astonishing about Vainshtein's tattoos is perhaps not so much the imagery itself, but the willingness to imprint an experience of pain never actually felt on the feeling body, to physically inscribe herself into a history for which she was born too late.

The assimilating Jew wants to be recognized for his or her accomplishments without being noticed as a Jew, that is, visible as a universal citizen but unmarked by ethnicity. The assimilating Jew wishes, perhaps, to remain a Jew only on the inside, or among friends. Those who oppose assimilation denounce it as a trap; yet now that, on the whole, assimilation is no longer forced upon Jews, it is ironic how much like everyone else the Jew has already become—speaking the same language, wearing the same clothes, engaging in the same cultural practices. As a tattooed Jew with Holocaust scenes, Hebrew script and Stars of David, on the other hand, Vainshtein not only rejects assimilation but also its implied forgetfulness of Jewish history. The marked body says: "I am a remembering Jew, a public Jew, an unashamed Jew." At the same time, this is a form of memory in which the Jew as always-already dead or victimized is imprinted on the living body; it is not only a representation but, in a sense, a continuous performance of memory and difference. As such, the tattoos are not meant to convey information and knowledge about the Holocaust so much as to perform the unspeakable, to present the unpresentable. For the admonition to remember the Holocaust acquires a new meaning with the passage of time. With the dying out of the survivors, new ways of bridging the gap between then and now must be invented. What we cannot remember, we must imagine through representation, and our response is less immediately to the event than to the medium that has conveyed it to us.[47] It is precisely the medium of skin and the permanence of the action that gives the iconographic content of Vainshtein's tattoos its undeniable emotional charge, and thereby gives her project its power. Perhaps it is a way of reminding us that "ultimately, the world we live in is the same world that produced (and keeps producing) genocide."[48] While we can walk out of a film like *Schindler's List* or turn off the television, Vainshtein removes herself from a privileged position of spectatorship by using her own body as a medium for the message.

Above all, I would suggest that the Holocaust tattoos are meant to have what the Greeks called *apotropaic* value, to form a shield that repels enemies and wards off evil just as the fierce head of Medusa was meant do. Vainshtein inscribes herself with the memory of a horrific slaughter as a form of protection against its repetition. Armoring her body against the otherness without, against a history of fear, incarceration, mutilation, and murder, the tattoos are meant to resist the very events they represent. Marina Vainshtein, and Joshua Burgin, in different ways, claim the mark of the barbarian in order to subdue the terror of barbarism.

CONCLUSION

■

Tombeau II for Paul Celan (1920–1970)

to enter Hades do not go near the smokestacks
stammer far apart trauma's other name
saving yourself the cost of missing tongue
where every appearance of forgiving is washed
clean, cast to the winds, an amulet
strapped to the left arm

memory's glove has brought you here
to this cul-de-sac most likely to collapse
at the faultline irreproachable prayers
narrow your eyes, invert letters
all is well for the deaf and dumb
death sends her regards

CHRIS TYSH
from *Continuity Girl,* 2000

■

AT THE AGE OF NINE, watching *Judgement at Nuremberg* with my parents at the local drive-in theater, my understanding of the Holocaust was profoundly shaped by the archival footage taken by the Allies at the liberation of the camps embedded in that film. Lasting only a few seconds, the image of heaps of emaciated bodies bulldozed into pits seared itself into individual as well as public consciousness. This image, along with the kitchen narratives of my parents and their friends, and other forms of representation, such as Rudolf Vrba's account of Auschwitz in *I Cannot Forgive* (read at age ten), became the foundation for more images from other memoirs, testimonies, histories, photographs, films, and art about the Holocaust. But what does it mean when representations come to substitute for experience, when events themselves recede in time, and only the representations are left? Primo Levi answered this question, as suggested in the Introduction, with a clear-eyed but pessimistic recognition of the gap between "things as they were 'down there'" and "things as they are represented by the current imagination fed by approximative books, films, and myths. It slides fatally toward simplification and stereotype" of Holocaust experience. This leads to an increasing inability to perceive the extremity of the experience of others as these experiences become more distant from our own in "time, space, or quality."[1] Representations, then, become fictions that aspire to approximate the truth, either in a moralizing, sacralizing, or redemptive fashion, or, as we have dealt with here, more self-consciously, in anti-redemptive fashion, as traumatic realism, including an awareness of the difficulties of recuperation, the subjectivity of the maker and viewer, and the cultural and political conditions in which these representations emerge and publicly circulate.

What begins for many as a search for memory, a search that serves as an excavation for the roots of identity, in the end both reveals and withholds the continuity of identity. Shimon Attie describes "a longing for a past we've been robbed of by all those deaths. It's like looking for a lost city."[2] Like the pits into which the emaciated bodies were bulldozed, the chasm cannot be spanned; the enormity cannot be grasped, and what was lost cannot be regained, restored, or replaced—but knowing this does not impede the attempt to do so. Contemporary artists, often through mimetic performance, guide us through the difficulties of the salvage operation and reveal ways in which the use of documentary and the archive, in the end, distorts and even, at times, impoverishes our larger understanding of the vastness and complexity of the extremes of experience distant from our own, even as they enlarge our awareness and extend the archive. Documentary is subverted by its instrumentalization in representing the near impossibility of recovery, highlighting the politics of now with a certain irony for being marked by the absence of lessons learned. The art of secondary witnessing is thus based on a constant return to a past that is always beyond our grasp. Secondary witnessing ends in a kind of crisis, a greater sense of traumatic history's elusiveness, but also of its pervasiveness and its imminence, driving the compulsion toward reenactment or mimetic approximation. "We are on the edge of disaster without being able to situate it in the future," wrote Maurice Blanchot, "it is rather always already past, and yet we are on the edge or under the threat." For the secondary witness it is "a past which has never been, come back again."[3] Jonathan Boyarin observes, "the future has collapsed upon itself, and we are burdened more by what we come after than by what awaits us."[4] Walter Benjamin, who committed suicide to avoid falling into the hands of the Nazis, famously pictured history as catastrophe in a text that has continued to resonate in the postwar era:

> A Klee painting named "Angelus Novus" shows an angel looking as though he is about to move away from something he is fixedly contemplating. His eyes are staring, his mouth is open, his wings are spread. This is how one pictures the angel of history. His face is turned toward the past. Where we perceive a chain of events, he sees one single catastrophe which keeps piling wreckage upon wreckage and hurls it in front of his feet. The angel would like to stay, awaken the dead, and make whole what has been smashed. But a storm is blowing from Paradise; it has got caught in his wings with such violence that the angel can no longer close them. This storm irresistibly propels him into the future to which his back is turned, while the pile of debris before him grows skyward. This storm is what we call progress.[5]

Artist John Scott comments on the preoccupation with disaster: "The apocalypse is the perfect postmodern state. All history is present simultaneously."[6] Postmodernist disillusionment, presciently articulated by Benjamin, may be seen as a post-Holocaust response predicated on an inability to find redemptive meaning in the abyss and marked by the attention it has paid to the fragmentation and destabilization of identity.

Jon Stratton identifies a form of "Holocaust-Jewishness" in which the destruction of the Jews in the Holocaust and the recognition of how difference has been imposed on Jews becomes the prime motive for choosing to self-identify as Jewish. Stratton distinguishes between ethnicity and race as the difference between cultural versus biological distinctions and points out that post-Holocaust Jews have been "deracialized as a people in their own right and reracialized as an ethnic group within the 'white' race."[7] While ethnic groups within the white race can be assimilated into the national culture, groups racialized as black, as Karen Brodkin has also shown, are Othered and excluded. Stratton's most crucial argument, however, is that the construction of Jews as an ethnic group within the white race functions in an ambivalent way because the possibility of reracialization continues to exist, in America as elsewhere.[8] This, perhaps, is the imminent catastrophe always liminally present for Jews. Both ethnic and racial consciousness have been forcibly raised by continuing signs of ethnoracial hatred in America on the right-wing fringe: in the summer of 1999, for example, a number of shooting sprees against Jews, blacks, Filipinos, and Koreans were perpetrated by various individuals associated with white supremacist organizations in the United States who continue to assign African Americans, Jews, and Asians a nonwhite identity. For Jews, this represents a form of reracialization and suggests that Jewish identity stubbornly persists because it continues to be culturally constructed through continued identification by and as the Other.

Jewish identity is historically embodied, not only through racial genocide, but also through negative Christian stereotypes of Jews, still readily apparent in, for example, American evangelist Pat Robertson's 1999 prediction that the coming anti-Christ would be male and Jewish. While many entirely assimilated Jews reject a religiously based sense of identity, an active embrace of Jewish difference may still be founded on an unwillingness to forsake an identity for which ancestors were persecuted and murdered, both for religious and racial reasons, or to abandon a cultural legacy produced by those same ancestors. The art of secondary witnessing makes apparent the difficulties of constructing an ethnically specific identity, presenting identity as conditional, subjective, and performative. Within certain limits and especially if one is racialized as white, it is possible to choose the identity one wishes to perform, amid a postmodern consensus that identity is no longer transparent, given, unified, and universal.

Recognizing the dissipation and threatened disappearance of Jewish identity, Jonathan Boyarin attempts to project a third millennium of possibility for the Jewish collectivity. Boyarin uses Benjamin to gesture forward as well as backward: "I'm trying to *make the Angel turn around,* to demand that we think of thinking the future, albeit without 'progress' as our prop."[9] ("Most of us know, now," wrote poet Randall Jarrell, "that Rousseau was wrong: that man, when you knock his chains off, sets up the death camps.") Boyarin justifies his investment in Jewishness by way of the post-genocidal failure of all pretenses to a universal community. Thus, just as Jewish identity seems to be venturing toward obsolescence through integration and intermarriage, there is a renewed struggle to reinvent Jewish identity in the project of secondary witnessing. In addressing traumatic history and its effects on the instability of identity, the work of contemporary artists as secondary witnesses both asserts and resists the post-Holocaust metaphysical resignation and despair that has permeated postcatastrophic thinking. If there is a way that artists as secondary witnesses have assimilated the historical wound of the Holocaust, it is through the construction of memory as a site of opposition. They reject standard tropes of representation in favor of newer forms deemed more adequate for the construction of a new pictorial and conceptual language on the contemporary effects of the Holocaust. Conceptually, Holocaust imagery may function as a site of opposition to the loss of historical specificity, to the sentimentalization or pathos of victimhood, and to the closure and immutability of meaning. The photographs of the former residents projected onto the now renovated and gentrified buildings of the old Jewish quarter in Berlin or the train station in Dresden resist the aura of distant, exotic otherness of the prewar Jews, the rationalizations for the past, and contemporary racist policies. The photographs of the unmarked or well-tended pastoral camps and death march sites throughout Europe resist the sacralization of the Holocaust, the mythologizing of the death camps, and the loss of historical accountability. The virtual use of the former Gestapo headquarters in Vienna and the project of a global Internet collaboration resist the loss of community and connectivity, the passivity of despair, and acquiescence to abusive power. The testimonies of secondary witnesses, and the inscribed and tattooed body, resist the tropes of antisemitism and stereotyping, the suppression or homogenization of difference, and the fixity of identity.

Aaron Hass has observed that children of survivors often feel "the need to discover, to re-enact, or to live the parents' past" in an effort to repeat the suffering of the parents "so that their parents' humiliations, disgrace, and guilt can be converted into victory over the oppressors and the threat of genocide undone with a restitution of life and worth."[10] These are attempts, in effect, to change the past by providing a better outcome. The works of contemporary artists discussed in this study both produce and question such attempts to change the past and recuperate what has been lost. Even as the loss represented by the Holocaust is reenacted or performed, at the same time the present mediates and undermines the repetition, opening new possibilities for assertions of difference, identity, and agency. Historical awareness reveals the longed-for reclamations as always out of reach, yet, in a series of Janus-faced gestures, like Boyarin's attempt to "make the angel turn around," artists avow the longing for the continued existence of Jewish identity into the twenty-first century, and for a recognition of the universal significance of the Nazi genocide of the Jews, marked by the unprecedented extremity of its ideological, global, and totalizing character. As Primo Levi asserted, now that it has happened, it can happen again. Who will be the Jews next time? How should we resist?

EPILOGUE

PERSONAL NOTES ON SURVIVING THE PAST

■

"If to remember is to provide the disembodied 'wound' with a psychic residence, then to remember other people's memories is to be wounded by their wounds. More precisely, to let the traces of other people's struggles, passions, pasts, resonate within one's own past and present, and destabilize them."

KAJA SILVERMAN
from *The Threshold of the Visible World,* 1996

■

IN MY FAMILY, traumatic stories endlessly return but are not always the same. Subject to the difficulties of narrativizing trauma as well as to the delicate unspoken negotiations between the teller and the listener, the past is always vulnerable to the exigencies of the present. One of the memory effects that result from this form of transmission of Holocaust experience is the instability of meaning.

. . .

The Jewish survivors I knew, who did not call themselves survivors, nor refer to a historical event known as the Holocaust, came mostly from Poland, as did my parents, and settled in Vineland, New Jersey. Though coming from a variety of prewar occupations, a great many became chicken farmers until most were forced under by the much larger industrial farm operations in the Midwest. Growing up in this small eastern seaboard town, my sense of community was shaped by a world in which all the familiar grownups spoke Yiddish and hailed each other as compatriots from the old country.

I can't recall when I first learned about the genocide of the Jews. It seems I always knew. Our household was steeped with the memory of that other, faraway world, before. The first specific stories about the war that I remember were told by my cousin Jean. One summer afternoon, Jean and my mother leaned their heads together at a corner of the kitchen table as Jean talked about her odyssey through the concentration camps. I was four years old. Jean talked for what seemed a long time, but only one place name remains in my memory: Auschwitz. My mother and Jean wept, so deeply sunk into a universe of suffering, they were oblivious of me, sitting small and motionless, at the other end of the table.

Jean told of her arrival on the ramp at Auschwitz with her mother and the selection made by Mengele. She said the name with such awe and horror that it imprinted itself in my memory. After describing how Mengele sent people to life or death with a jerk of his thumb, she said, "He was so handsome that the women called him *Puppe.*" I was shocked. It means "doll." My mother called me her little Puppe.

Other images seized hold of my imagination that afternoon. Jean told of the desperate, starved prisoners in the camp. Crazed with thirst, they ran over with their tin cups to catch the stream of a urinating horse. They converged on a defecating horse, to pick out undigested kernels of corn. I tried to imagine this kind of hunger, but could not.

Years later, sitting next to Jean at my brother's wedding, I learned that she had been in eleven camps, including Budzyn, Bergen-Belsen, Majdanek, Auschwitz, Theresienstadt. More years passed before I began to ask her questions, and finally took her to Yale to have her testimony videotaped. But her later testimony was nothing like the stories I had heard that afternoon when I was four.

. . .

When I was five, my mother told me a story she would repeat many times over the years. She was on a train. Her younger sister Perle, her favorite sister, came to say goodbye and stayed aboard the train until the last moment, until, in fact, it was too late. When she tried to get off, a policeman would not let her. Perle's young husband and baby were waiting at home. She and my mother pleaded desperately with the policeman, to no avail. Finally, my mother got down on her hands and knees and kissed the policeman's boots. He relented and Perle got off the train. That was the last time my mother saw her.

I am sitting at the kitchen table with my mother, who is mourning the futility of her degrading gesture and, worse, blaming herself for Perle's death. She is not sure, even, how Perle died, along with her husband and baby, nor her parents, her two older sisters, their husbands and all their children. Some were shot and buried in mass graves at the edge of town; some were deported to Majdanek or other camps. In all, more than seventy members of her extended family, all of whom lived in the city of Hrubieszow, were killed.

Sometimes, when my mother is sewing, or reading, or drinking a glass of tea, and I am sitting nearby, she says, "Perle, would you . . ."

. . .

Why were you the only one who hid? I asked my mother this question over and over, never satisfied with the answer, unable to understand why the others didn't flee. *Why didn't your parents and sisters go too?* "They didn't know what was coming." "They didn't want to abandon their homes and businesses and lose everything." "They thought that only the men were in danger, that they would never touch women and children."

Why weren't you married? "I was engaged. He left with me and died of typhus on the way."

How old were your parents when you last saw them? "My mother was fifty-two. My father was about sixty. I always wondered if I would live past fifty-two." Through each generation, we measure our lives against those of our parents.

. . .

My mother walks with great difficulty now. "Ten times a day I almost fall. It must be my mother and father holding out their hands beneath me that keeps me from falling." These are the grandparents I always longed to meet.

My mother's own grandmother died at the beginning of the war. *What did she die of?* "A heart attack. When the Nazis fired the first shot, she fell away."

. . .

Even as a child I realized there were two kinds of survivors: those who talked about it and those who didn't. I heard my father's story from my mother. His parents died before the war. To help support his two brothers and sister, he went to work sewing sweatbands into hats when he was ten years old. Later he was in the Polish army, married and had a five-year-old daughter when the war came. As the Nazis approached, he heard a rumor of Jews being forced to wash the cars of Germans with toothbrushes and fled to the Soviet Union. (On her videotaped testimony Jean says, "Only the men left Hrubieszow. The women stayed behind." *Pause.* "I was left behind too.") They reasoned that only the men would be taken to labor camps. Indeed, when the Nazis entered Hrubieszow in 1942, they rounded up only the men. When the men were gone, they rounded up everyone else. My father's wife and child went into hiding and were betrayed by a Jew.

. . .

One Passover, at the Seder table, my father, in a rare moment, speaks about the war years in Siberia. I am ten. They worked hard, he tells us, and didn't get enough to eat. They slept head to foot like sardines in a can. In the summer, armies of red ants crawled up the walls. In the winter it snowed two stories high and they dug tunnels through the snow. And then my father says something unexpected. One day he found out that the Jew who had informed on his wife and child was in the camp. Silence falls. I cannot bear it.

What did you do?

My father looks at me, deadpan. "I killed him."

My mother jumps up from the table, protesting loudly that he did no such thing. He stares into his bowl of matzo ball soup. No one says anything for a time.

. . .

I have my father's passport photo, made shortly after his release from Siberia. His face is angular and haggard, tormented in a way I have seen only one other time. I was a junior in high school when I took a regional history examination in a contest sponsored by a veterans organization, perhaps the Veterans of Foreign Wars, I can't remember. The first prize was a free trip to New York and a day at the United Nations. One night I received a call from a girl who said her mother had graded the exams and wanted me to know that I had won. She also told me who had come in second—a girl in my class named Betsy. The next day at school we were called into the principal's office. A representative from the sponsoring organization was present. But something was wrong. The results were reversed. Betsy was now first and I was second. Betsy's parents were respectable Protestants who owned a McDonald's franchise. Mine were poor immigrant Jews who owned a chicken farm. It seemed to me that no one could look me in the eye. That evening I told my parents what had happened. My father grabbed his hair with both fists and stumbled blindly around the kitchen while my mother and I watched helplessly. It was much worse than being cheated out of first place in the history contest.

. . .

When I was five, my mother told me about the night she gave birth to my brother, in Berlin, just after the war. She was having a C-section. As her consciousness slipped away under the spell of ether, she heard the German nurse say to the German doctor, "You know, she's a Jew."

I am sitting at the kitchen table with my mother, picturing her lying on a bed with her eyes closed, the nurse standing by, speaking quietly. I feel a terrible dread overtake me. For years there will be nightmares of someone chasing my family. I am always the last, unable to keep up, about to be caught, before I awaken.

. . .

When I was five years old, one day my father and I drove down the street in his car. As we approached a house with pink plaster flamingoes in the front yard, I commented on how "goyish" they were, thinking my slur would amuse my father. To my astonishment, he stopped the car on the side of the road to looked at me full face. *"I don't ever want to hear you say that again."* I never did.

. . .

When my parents went back to Hrubieszow after the war, they found their Polish neighbors had expropriated their homes. My mother wanted to retrieve pictures of her family and her grandmother's jewels that she had buried in the basement. She was dissuaded by friends from going back when a returning Jew they knew was shot dead in the doorway of his former home.

. . .

My parents married, with ten refugee guests and a bottle of vodka to celebrate, and went to an American displaced persons camp in Berlin. One day they were handing out bags of groceries with extra rations for pregnant women. "Get in line," urged my father, "say you're pregnant." So she did. "When did you last have your period?" the nurse asked. "I don't know," my mother answered. I always thought when I heard this story that she was being disingenuous. Finally I realized that she was saying the truth. During the war, her weight had gone down to eighty-five pounds. Starvation had caused women to stop menstruating. (Many camp survivors, not knowing this, insisted that the Nazis put something in the soup to make them stop menstruating.) To my mother's surprise, a test showed she was indeed pregnant, and when she emerged with a bag of groceries, they rejoiced.

How did you feel when you found out you were pregnant? "We lived in one small room, a room as big as your bedroom at home, that we shared with three boys from another family. I was three months pregnant. We weren't so overjoyed. I was alone, afraid of poisoning by German doctors. That's what we thought, that they might poison us. We wanted Jewish doctors but there were no Jewish doctors. There was not enough food. We got food parcels, some sugar. Sugar was worth a million. Only pregnant women and children got sugar. We were happy about the extra food."

Bereft of her family, though married, my mother says, "I was alone."

. . .

While in hiding, my mother contracted typhus and lay in the hospital, emaciated and near death, with a high fever. In her delirium one night, she dreamed that her mother came to her, held out her hands, and said, "Here is the remedy." In the morning her fever was gone. The nurse declared it a miracle.

At other times she contracted malaria and dysentery, for which no drugs were available. She sent messages to Perle through others and Perle was able to send malaria medicine—but she never got it. Still, she recovered. "Yet so many fell ill and died around me!" *Like who?* "My nephew. He followed me and found me." *Who was his mother?* "Frida." *How old was he?* "Seventeen years old." This was Mottel. *Where was Frida?* "She was already dead!"

Mottel came down with malaria or typhus, she's not sure which, and she was unable to get him any medicine. They both stayed wherever they could, "*ungevorfen bei andere,*" unwelcome guests. My mother tried to save him, her favorite nephew, but couldn't. She says she has a picture of him, too. I know immediately which one it is: a young man with thick, dark wavy hair, full, sensuous lips, and intelligent eyes. "Don't speak of it," she says softly, not so much to me, but in a whispered incantation to herself. I realize that for fifty years she has not spoken of it.

The following week she calls me up: "Don't mention the boy in your writing. He only stayed with me for a day." She speaks in a rush of regret. Then she says, "It didn't happen."

. . .

Months later my mother says, "Sometimes I feel guilty. I think I should have stayed with my family and died with them. Your father would always say, 'What would you have accomplished by dying? This way you are the mother of two children.' But sometimes I feel guilty." *You did the best you could at the time. You shouldn't feel guilty about Mottel either.*

"No, I shouldn't have let him leave." *Leave where?* "He left to find a cousin in another town. He said he'd come back but he never came back. He got stuck." *I thought he got sick.* "Mottel? He was eighteen. He was very healthy." *Then who found you and got sick and died?* "No one. What are you talking about?" *How do you know Mottel didn't survive?* "He would have found me. I was all he had left." *Were his parents already taken?* "No, his mother was still on the other side."

. . .

What about the boy you were engaged to? "He was already dying of tuberculosis. He stayed behind in Hrubieszow."

. . .

Recently, I brought my five-year-old daughter to the doctor's office. Remarking on the resemblance between my daughter and me, the old Jewish doctor mused, "I don't know what the father looks like but now that I've seen the mother, you could never disavow this child." I feel a chill and think of the scene described by Tadeuz Borowski in *This Way for the Gas, Ladies and Gentlemen.* A young girl is sent to the gas on the ramp at Auschwitz and calls over and over for her mother, who is sent the other way. The mother disavows her.

. . .

In 1951 my parents sailed for America with a set of Rosenthal china, a china tea service, two sets of crystal wine glasses and decanters, crystal bowls, silver flatware, silver wine cups, and a silver candelabra. I grow up with these beautiful things, brought out and lovingly polished for the holidays. I imagine them carefully wrapped in a heavy trunk on the long ocean voyage. Now, realizing they were bought on the German black market, I inspect the china for clues. The bottom is marked "American zone." Made after the war. Relief.

. . .

My parents' friends: the Hertzes, the Alters, the Maisels, the Silversteins, the Bluesteins, the Steinwurtzels, the Golubs, the Spets, the Wilenskys, the two sets of Singers, the Levines, the Zeligmans, the Wasserstrums, the Distenfelds, and others. From these names, it seems to me I can recognize all Jewish names.

My parents' friends told stories in our kitchen: I remember a scrap of a story told by Genia Zeligman, about how the men were attracted to the women performing hard labor, because they were made beautiful by their flushed cheeks; Joseph Alter, while drinking tea in a glass with lemon and a sugar cube under his tongue, describing how he had lived under the kitchen floorboards of a Polish home for two years, never seeing daylight.

Joseph's wife, also a survivor, died when I was fifteen and he was devastated. One day he came to see my parents, but I was the only one home. He sat on the sofa next to me and tried to kiss me. I fled. A few weeks later, he tried to kiss me again. I never told my parents for fear they would not believe me, or else, that they would. I didn't know which was worse.

. . .

Recently, I ask my mother about my father's assertion that he killed the man who betrayed his wife and child. She gives the same vehement denial as decades ago. But I press her. Finally, she exclaims, "I don't know! I wasn't there! He didn't tell me about it!"

. . .

My cousin Jean has a younger sister living in Atlanta, who survived the war on "Aryan" papers in Warsaw. "She lived as a *shicksa,*" Jean says. *Why didn't your sister ever visit my family like you did?* "She was ashamed of where she came from. She was ashamed of her own mother when she would come to visit. She probably pretends she comes from European royalty."

I recall how embarrassed I was as a teenager when my mother spoke Yiddish in public. "Speak English!" I would hiss *sotto voce.* "Why, are you ashamed of me?" she would ask. I could not answer.

I finally meet Jean's sister, Eve, when she comes to visit my mother with her son to learn more about her father's side of the family. They haven't seen each for sixty-four years, since Eve left Hrubieszow. She is elegant, remarkably literate, and has written a number of reviews of Holocaust histories. Her sister always hated her, she tells me, was "always mad" about something.

. . .

I take Jean to have her testimony videotaped at the Fortunoff Video Archive for Holocaust Testimonies in New Haven. Before the taping begins Jean is eating a roll we had just bought across the street. "I can't eat any more of this," she says to the interviewer, who responds, "It's not too good?" "It's not fresh," says Jean. "I think it's from yesterday." My response to this, as I sit in the control room, is annoyance. "Typical," I think, "just like my mother." But the young archivist in the control room turns to me avidly: "Did you hear her remark about the bread? Survivors are always so sensitive to the freshness of bread." I had never thought of it this way.

. . .

In the Hrubieszow ghetto, Jean's first husband had been gone for some time. One night two men from Vilna arrived bearing his watch and a letter, scribbled as he was dying. They were witnesses to his death. She doesn't tell this story on the tape. I ask her about it during a break. "I don't want to tell them that," she says. This was the husband who had left her behind.

I learn that Jean had a child before the war and seven miscarriages after. The child was a four-year-old girl. Jean, her mother, and other friends all were living in one house in the ghetto and hid their children in the attic, trying to keep their existence secret. Every day the adults went to work in the ghetto, while the six children stayed in the attic. One day Jean's child said to her, "Mama, I wish I were a cat," because the cat could run about freely but not she. "This comment made them tear the flesh from their faces," says my mother. When the ghetto was liquidated, they came and took all the adults away, but the children remained in the attic. Jean didn't know until the end of the war what became of them. Then she learned that a Nazi officer took them all out and shot them.

After the war, Jean was called to Hanover to testify against a Nazi officer. When she stepped into the courtroom, she recognized him. "I suddenly felt that this was the man who had murdered my child!" She fainted and was carried out.

. . .

Before I leave, I ask Jean if she remembers telling my mother her story in our kitchen years ago, if she remembers Mengele at Auschwitz. "Mengele wasn't there," she says. "This was past Mengele's time." I know from the records of Auschwitz this is not so, but I do not wish to contradict her. Does she remember the story of the undigested corn kernels? "No," she says, "I don't remember that."

. . .

One day my mother is again recounting her prewar life. Again I ask, *Why didn't you marry?* "I had a boyfriend," she says, "but he was killed when a bomb fell."

. . .

Following her eighty-eighth birthday, my mother calls one day and in the course of conversation says she wants to tell me a secret. "I wanted to tell your father, too, but he died before I had a chance." I wait. "I might be a little older than you think," she finally announces. "In fact, I know I am." *By how much?* "Four years. I'm ninety-two." I am shocked. We both burst out laughing. I know that most of the immigrant Jews lied about their age because they thought they would be more employable. But it goes much deeper than this. "Don't tell anyone else," she says. *But why not? At your age, you should be proud of how old you are!* "No, I don't want anyone else to know. On my tombstone, put 1910, not 1906." She is still outwitting mortality.

NOTES

NOTES TO INTRODUCTION

1. Claude Lanzmann, "The Obscenity of Understanding: An Evening with Claude Lanzmann," *Trauma: Explorations in Memory,* ed. Cathy Caruth (Baltimore, Md.: John Hopkins University, 1995), 206.
2. Ernst van Alphen, "Playing the Holocaust," *Mirroring Evil: Nazi Imagery/Recent Art,* ed. Norman L. Kleeblatt (New York/New Brunswick, N. J.: The Jewish Museum/Rutgers University Press, 2002), 77.
3. Vera Frenkel, "A Kind of Listening: Notes from an Interdisciplinary Practice," *Thinking Across Culture: Interdisciplinary Practices in Canadian Art*, ed. Lynn Hughes and Marie-Josée Lafortune (Montreal: Concordia University/Optica Gallery, 2001).
4. Ernst van Alphen, "Playing the Holocaust," 77.
5. See James E. Young, *The Texture of Memory: Holocaust Memorials and Meaning* (New Haven, Conn.: Yale University Press, 1993), and *At Memory's Edge: After-Images of the Holocaust in Contemporary Art and Architecture* (New Haven, Conn.: Yale University Press, 2000).
6. Roger Simon, "Introduction. Between Hope and Despair: The Pedagogical Encounter of Historical Remembrance," *Between Hope and Despair: Pedagogy and the Remembrance of Historical Trauma,* ed. Roger Simon, Sharon Rosenberg, Claudia Eppert (New York: Rowman and Littlefield Publishers, Inc., 2000), 3–4.
7. Ibid., 5.
8. Ibid., 7.
9. Michael Rothberg, *Traumatic Realism: The Demands of Holocaust Representation* (Minneapolis: University of Minnesota, 2000), 3–4.
10. Ibid., 6.
11. Ibid., 9.
12. Quoted in Peter Novick, *The Holocaust in American Life* (Boston/New York: Houghton Mifflin Co., 1999), 201.
13. Stuart Hall, "Cultural Identity and Diaspora," *Identity: Community, Culture, Difference,* ed. Jonathan Rutherford (New York: New York University Press, 1990), 225.
14. Among other postwar artists who have dealt with imagery related to the Holocaust, but who are not discussed here, are Annette Lemieux, Brian DeLevie, Richard Posner, Michael Kenna, Ellen Rothenberg, Joan Silver, Karen Baldner, Richard Rappaport, Suzanne Hellmuth and Jock Sturges, and David Levinthal. On Hellmuth and Sturges, see Andrea Liss, *Trespassing Through Shadows: Memory, Photography and the Holocaust* (Minneapolis: University of Minnesota Press, 1998), 87–96; on Levinthal, see James Young, *Mein Kampf: Photographs by David Levinthal,* exh. cat. (Sante Fe, N.Mex.: Twin Peaks, 1996), and *At Memory's Edge.*

NOTES TO CHAPTER ONE

1. Omer Bartov, *Murder in Our Midst: The Holocaust, Industrial Killing, and Representation* (New York: Oxford University Press, 1996), 119.

2. For one of the best overall interpretations of the Holocaust, most balanced in its combined perspectives of perpetrator, victim and bystander and brilliantly insightful in its explanation of "redemptive anti-Semitism" as the guiding ideology of the Nazis, see Saul Friedländer, *Nazi Germany and the Jews.* Vol. 1 *The Years of Persecution, 1933–1939* (New York: HarperCollins, 1998).
3. Yehuda Bauer, *Rethinking the Holocaust* (New Haven, Conn.: Yale University Press, 2001), 47-53. Bauer provides a very thoughtful analysis of the primary historiography of the Holocaust as well as many of its main issues and categories.
4. Ibid., xi.
5. *Burnt Whole* included artists such as Ellen Rothenberg, Susan Silas, Anselm Kiefer, Christian Boltanski, Art Spiegelman, Olaf Metzel, Piotr Nathan, Yael Bedarshi, Astrid Klein, Guillermo Kuitca, Anna Bialobroda, Dagmar Demming, and Ronald Jones. Examples of other exhibitions, large and small, that have included North American artists, are *Witness and Legacy: Contemporary Art about the Holocaust,* a traveling exhibition that originated at the Minnesota Museum of American Art (1995); *After Auschwitz: Responses to the Holocaust in Contemporary Art* at the Royal Festival Hall in London and elsewhere (1995); *Between Spectacle and Silence: The Holocaust in Contemporary Photography* at the Photographic Resource Center in Boston (1995); *Impossible Evidence: Contemporary Artists View the Holocaust* at the Freedman Gallery at Albright College in Reading, Pa. (1994); *Mediated Memory* at the Starr Gallery of the Jewish Community Center in Newton, Mass.; *History, Memory and Representation: Responses to Genocide* at the List Gallery at Swarthmore College (1997).
6. Donald Kuspit, "Reducing the Holocaust to Artistic One-Liners," *Forward,* 3 February 1995.
7. Martha McWilliams, "Order Out of Chaos: 'Burnt Whole: Contemporary Artists Reflect on the Holocaust,'" *New Art Examiner* (April 1995): 12.
8. Primo Levi, *The Drowned and the Saved,* trans. Raymond Rosenthal (New York: Vintage International Books, 1989), 157–158.
9. The quote figures on the back cover of Aaron Hass, *In the Shadow of the Holocaust: The Second Generation* (1990. New York: Cambridge University Press, 1996).
10. Mindy Yan Miller, "Deluge/of Thirst/Lapped Her Tears," *The Embodied Viewer,* exh. cat. (Calgary: Glenbow Museum, 1991), 36.
11. See Helen Epstein, *Children of the Holocaust: Conversations with Sons and Daughters of Survivors* (New York: G. P. Putnam's Sons, 1979); Art Spiegelman, *Maus,* 2 vols. (New York: Pantheon Books, 1973, 1986).
12. Hass, *In the Shadow of the Holocaust,* 83–85.
13. Novick, *The Holocaust in American Life.* Novick argues that the guilt frameworks are retrospectively applied and did not exist during the war. Both the government and American Jews felt they had done all they could do or were essentially helpless to effect rescue, especially given the strong anti-immigration sentiment in both Congress and the general public. The postwar support for Israeli statehood was motivated by a number of political considerations, as well as concern for the plight of survivors, but there is no evidence that it was motivated by a guilty response. See pp. 47–59 and 69–84.
14. Ibid., 111.
15. Ibid., 122.
16. Ibid., 86.
17. Ibid., 87.

18. Jeffrey Shandler, *While America Watches: Televising the Holocaust* (New York: Oxford University Press, 1999).
19. Michael L. Morgan, "To Seize Memory: History and Identity in Post-Holocaust Jewish Thought," *Thinking about the Holocaust: After Half a Century,* ed. Alvin Rosenfeld (Bloomington/Indianapolis: Indiana University Press, 1997), 158.
20. Novick, *The Holocaust in American Life,* 151.
21. Ibid., 190.
22. Ibid., 173.
23. Annette Insdorf, *Indelible Shadows: Film and the Holocaust* (1983.Cambridge, Mass.: Harvard University Press, 1989), 6.
24. See Shandler, *While America Watches,* and Insdorf, *Indelible Shadows,* as well as Judith E. Doneson, *The Holocaust in American Film* (Philadelphia: The Jewish Publication Society, 1987); and Ilan Avisar, *Screening the Holocaust: Cinema's Images of the Unimaginable* (Bloomington: Indiana University Press, 1988).
25. Young, *The Texture of Memory,* 310; also see pp. 309–319.
26. Quoted in Novick, *The Holocaust in American Life,* 71.
27. Ibid., 79.
28. See Shandler, *While America Watches,* 207–209. Also see Geoffrey H. Hartman, ed., *Bitburg in Moral and Political Perspective* (Bloomington: Indiana University Press, 1986).
29. Hilene Flanzbaum, ed., "Introduction," *The Americanization of the Holocaust* (Baltimore, Md.: Johns Hopkins University Press, 1999), 6.
30. See Anson Rabinbach, "From Explosion to Erosion: Holocaust Memorialization in America since Bitburg," *Passing into History: Nazism and the Holocaust beyond Memory. In Honor of Saul Friedländer on His Sixty-Fifth Birthday. History and Memory: Studies in Representation of the Past,* ed. Gulie Ne'eman Arad, 9: 1–2 (fall 1997); also see Edward T. Linenthal, *Preserving Memory: The Struggle to Create America's Holocaust Museum* (New York: Viking, 1995).
31. Alvin Rosenfeld, "The Americanization of the Holocaust," *Thinking about the Holocaust: After Half a Century,* 123.
32. Ibid., 127.
33. Novick, *The Holocaust in American Life,* 15.
34. Flanzbaum, "Introduction," *The Americanization of the Holocaust,* 1–4. Also see Alvin H. Rosenfeld, "Popularization and Memory: The Case of Anne Frank," *Lessons and Legacies: The Meaning of the Holocaust in a Changing World,* ed. Peter Hayes (Evanston, Ill.: Northwestern University Press, 1991), 243-278, and Cynthia Ozick, "Who Owns Anne Frank?" in *Quarrel & Quandary: Essays by Cynthia Ozick* (New York: Alfred A. Knopf, 2000).
35. On *Schindler's List,* see Yosefa Loshitzky, ed., *Spielberg's Holocaust: Critical Perspectives on Schindler's List* (Bloomington: Indiana University Press, 1997); on the Goldhagen debate, see, in addition to Daniel Jonah Goldhagen, *Hitler's Willing Executioners: Ordinary Germans and the Holocaust* (New York: Alfred A. Knopf, 1996), Norman G. Finkelstein and Ruth Bettina Birn, *A Nation on Trial: The Goldhagen Thesis and Historical Truth* (New York: Henry Holt and Co, Inc., 1998), and Robert R. Shandler, ed., and Jeremiah Riemer, trans., *Unwilling Germans? The Goldhagen Debate* (Minneapolis: University of Minneapolis Press, 1998).
36. Council of Jewish Federation, *Highlights of the CJF 1990 National Jewish Population Survey,* 1991, cited in Novick, The Holocaust in American Life, 185.
37. Novick, *The Holocaust in American Life,* 202.

38. On the evolution of artistic representation, see the encyclopedic volume by Ziva Amishai-Maisels, *Depiction and Interpretation: The Influence of the Holocaust on the Visual Arts* (Newton, Mass.: Butterworth-Heinemann, 1992); on the political pressures against ethnic specificity in the early postwar period, also see Tony Kushner, *The Holocaust and the Liberal Imagination* (Cambridge, Mass.: Basil Blackwell Inc., 1994).
39. See Dora Apel's articles "Cultural Battlegrounds: Weimar Photographic Narratives of War," *New German Critique* 76 (winter 1999): 49–84, and "'Heroes' and 'Whores': The Politics of Gender in Weimar Antiwar Imagery," *The Art Bulletin*, Vol. LXXIX, No. 3 (September 1997): 366-384; also Kyo Maclear, *Beclouded Visions: Hiroshima-Nagasaki and the Art of Witness* (Albany: State University of New York Press, 1999); George H. Roeder, Jr., *The Censored War: American Visual Experience During World War Two* (New Haven, Conn.: Yale University Press, 1993); Cécile Whiting, *Antifascism in American Art* (New Haven, Conn.: Yale University Press, 1989).
40. James E. Young, "Germany's Memorial Question: Memory, Counter-Memory, and the End of the Monument," *The South Atlantic Quarterly* 96: 4 (fall 1997): 855.
41. Ibid., 856.
42. "Monuments: Holocaust Revulsionism," *New York Times Magazine*, 17 August 1997, 19.
43. Ibid.
44. Saul Friedländer, *Reflections of Nazism: An Essay on Kitsch and Death* (Bloomington: Indiana University Press, 1993), 30, 27. Another example of trivialization, commercialization, or kitsch representations of the Holocaust might be observed in St. Petersburg, Florida, where public relations efforts included a published list of "40 Fun Things to Do" in their city; No. 11 on the list is "Remember the Holocaust." This can be done by visiting the local Holocaust museum where visitors can purchase a scale-model replica of a Polish boxcar for $39.95, or, for a contribution of $5,000 to the museum, they can receive a genuine railway spike from Treblinka preserved in Lucite.
45. Young, "Germany's Memorial Question," 855.
46. Another example of a problematic evocation of the Holocaust is feminist artist Judy Chicago's *Holocaust Project*, a large multimedia installation produced in conjunction with the work of her husband, photographer Donald Woodman. *Holocaust Project* opened at the Spertus Institute of Jewish Studies in Chicago in the fall of 1993 and traveled to a number of other cities. In this work, Judy Chicago transforms the Holocaust into a non-specific and universalized "victim experience" that includes slavery, atomic warfare, animal vivisection, and the abuse and oppression of women. For critiques of this project, see Rosenfeld, "The Americanization of the Holocaust," 131–134, and Lawrence Langer, Chapter One, in *Preempting the Holocaust* (New Haven, Conn.: Yale University Press, 1998).
47. Jonathan Boyarin, *Thinking in Jewish* (Chicago: University of Chicago Press, 1996), 197.
48. Dominick LaCapra, *History and Memory After Auschwitz* (Ithaca, N.Y.: Cornell University Press, 1998), 155.
49. See Marianne Hirsch, *Family Frames: Photography, Narrative and Postmemory* (Cambridge, Mass.: Harvard University Press, 1997), and James E. Young, "The Holocaust as Vicarious Past: Art Spiegelman's *Maus* and the Afterimages of History," *Critical Inquiry* 24 (spring 1998): 666-699, and *At Memory's Edge.*
50. Young, "The Holocaust as Vicarious Past," 676.
51. M. J. Rosenberg, Letter to the Editor, *New York Times*, 25 July 1997.

52. Jonathan Mahler, "Jewish History is Not One Event," *New York Times,* Op-Ed, 23 July 1997.
53. John M. G. Plotz, Letter to the Editor, *New York Times,* 25 July 1997.
54. Friedländer, *Nazi Germany and the Jews.*
55. Bartov, "The Surfeit of Memory and the Uses of Forgetting," in *Murder in our Midst,* 117.
56. Quoted in Judith Miller, *One, by One, by One: Facing the Holocaust* (New York: Touchstone, 1990), 232.
57. Quoted in ibid., 231.
58. Ibid., 118–119.
59. Ibid., 135–136.
60. Finkelstein, for example, opposes efforts as monetary compensation for slave labor: "Small wonder that—as Haaretz reported—there is an 'increasingly pervasive sentiment' that 'Jewish organizations are using the Holocaust to extort money' (Yair Sheleg, "Profits of Doom," in *Haaretz,* 29 June 2001)." Norman Finkelstein, *H-Net Holocaust,* 11 July 2001. Available e-mail [Online]: mail to: listserv@h-net.msu.edu; Message: get h-holocaust [11 July 2001].
61. Novick, *The Holocaust in American Life,* 161.
62. Quoted in Michael Marrus, "The Use and Abuse of the Holocaust," *Lessons and Legacies,* 114.
63. Stephen Kinzer, "Israeli Leader Reaching Out on Bonn Visit," *New York Times,* 17 January 1996.
64. According to the last census taken in Poland before the Holocaust, in 1931, nearly 80 percent of those who declared Judaism as their religion claimed Yiddish as their mother tongue. About 12 percent claimed Polish, and 8 percent claimed Hebrew. Even this number of Hebrew speakers was inflated, because Zionists demanded that their adherents declare Hebrew as their mother tongue in protest against the Polish government's infringement on their rights and as a demonstration of national identity in terms of language. Thus, the actual number of Jews whose mother tongue was Hebrew was minute. See Chone Shmeruk, "Hebrew-Yiddish-Polish: A Trilingual Jewish Culture," *The Jews of Poland Between Two World Wars,* ed. Yisrael Gutman, Ezra Mendelsohn, Jehuda Reinharz, and Chone Shmeruk (Hanover: University Press of New England, 1989), 287–288.
65. Theodor Herzl, *The Jewish State,* London, 1972, quoted in Enzo Traverso, *The Jews and Germany: From the "Judeo-German Symbiosis" to the Memory of Auschwitz.* Trans. Daniel Weissbort (Lincoln: University of Nebraska Press, 1995), 93.
66. Robert Fisk, "Holocaust Study Stirs Passions on Harvard's Lawns," *Independent,* 13 April 1998. The views of organized American Jewry on Israel are far from unified, however. The inspiration of Zionist militarism as a defense against renewed fears of Jewish genocide among American Jewry during the 1967 war receded during Benjamin Netanyahu's regime and was replaced by a certain embarrassment at the regime's intransigence and bellicosity. U.S. government pressure forced Netanyahu to backpedal, setting off greater divisions within Israel. Organized American Jewry, as well as many within Israel, also experienced a decided disenchantment with the Orthodox monopoly on religious life in Israel, leading to calls by some American religious leaders for the cessation of financial donations to the Zionist state. Divisions became acute during the election of delegates in October 1997 to the World Zionist Congress, the 100-year-old parliament of Diaspora Jewry in which 73.7 percent of the

vote went to combined Reform and Conservative religious slates. The Likud slate that represented and controlled the Israeli Government won just 1.9 percent of the vote and the Labor slate, which represented the opposition party, won 3.4 percent. American Jews, once united in defense of Israel, are now painfully divided over religious issues that have come to the forefront since the 1993 peace accord between Israel and the Palestinian people.

67. Quoted in Fisk, "Holocaust Study Stirs Passions on Harvard's Lawns."
68. Ibid.
69. Steve Paulsson, *H-Net Holocaust,* 23 April 1998. Available e-mail [Online]: mail to: listserv@h-net.msu.edu; Message: get h-holocaust [23 April 1998].
70. Gabriel Schoenfeld, "Auschwitz and the Professors," *Commentary Magazine* 105:6 (June 1998). Available [Online]: http://www.commentarymagazine.com [6 June 1998].
71. Ibid.
72. Ibid.
73. Schoenfeld, "Auschwitz and the Professors."
74. Sid Bolkosky, "Gabriel Schoenfeld and Critics," *Commentary Magazine* 106:2 (August 1998). Available [Online]: http://www.commentarymagazine.com [25 April 1999].
75. Aharon Meytahl, *H-Net Holocaust,* 6 June 1998. Available e-mail [Online]: mail to listserv@h-net.msu.edu; Message: get h-holocaust [6 June 1998].
76. Joan Ringelheim, "Gabriel Schoenfeld and Critics," *Commentary Magazine* 106:2 (August 1998). Available [Online]: http://www.commentarymagazine.com [25 April 1999].
77. Ibid. See Ringelheim's article, "The Split Between Gender and the Holocaust," in Lenore J. Weitzman and Dalia Ofer, eds., *Women in the Holocaust* (New Haven, Conn.: Yale University Press, 1998). Also see Carol Rittner and John K. Roth, *Different Voices: Women and the Holocaust* (St. Paul: Paragon House Publishers, 1993). In the case of R. Ruth Linden, *Making Stories, Making Selves: Feminist Reflections on the Holocaust* (Columbus: Ohio University Press, 1993), the author, a sociologist, rather unsuccessfully searches for "a sociology of the Holocaust."
78. Lenore Weitzman," Gabriel Schoenfeld and Critics," *Commentary Magazine* 106:2 (August 1998). Available [Online]: http://www.commentarymagazine.com [25 April 1999].
79. "Gabriel Schoenfeld and Critics," *Commentary Magazine* 106:2 (August 1998). Available [Online]: http://www.commentarymagazine.com [25 April 1999].
80. LaCapra, *History and Memory after Auschwitz,* 100. See also pp. 95–138.
81. Ibid.
82. Quoted by Gabriel Schoenfeld, "Gabriel Schoenfeld and Critics," *Commentary Magazine* 106:2 (August 1998). Available [Online]: http://www.commentarymagazine.com [25 April 1999].
83. Steven T. Katz, "A Debate about Teaching the Holocaust; Mass Killings Define Modern Era and Must Not Be Played Down," Arts & Ideas, *New York Times,* 8 August 1998.
84. Ibid.
85. Ibid.
86. Ibid.
87. An "American Holocaust" has also taken shape in discourse on conquest of the New World and the history of Native Americans in books such as Ward Churchill, *A Little Matter of Genocide: Holocaust and Denial in the Americas, 1492 to the Present* (San Francisco: City Lights Books, 1998); David Stannard, *American Holocaust: Columbus*

and the Conquest of the New World (New York: Oxford University Press, 1992); and Russell Thornton, *American Indian Holocaust and Survival: A Population History Since 1492* (Norman: University of Oklahoma Press, 1990).

88. James E. Young, *Writing and Rewriting the Holocaust: Narrative and the Consequences of Interpretation* (Bloomington: University of Indiana Press, 1990), 85.
89. Quoted in the 1997 film *Blacks and Jews,* written and directed by Deborah Kaufman and Alan Snitow.
90. Ibid.
91. Ibid.
92. For a discussion of these issues, see Jack Salzman with Adina Back and Gretchen Sullivan Sorin, eds., *Bridges and Boundaries: African American and American Jews* (New York: George Braziller, Inc. in association with The Jewish Museum, 1992); for the ethnography and politics of being both Black and Jewish, see Katya Gibel Azoulay, *Black, Jewish, and Interracial: It's Not the Color of Your Skin, but the Race of Your Kin, and Other Myths of Identity* (Durham, N.C.: Duke University Press, 1997).
93. Michael André Bernstein, "The *Schindler's List* Effect," *The American Scholar* 63 (1994): 431–432.
94. Ibid., 431.
95. See, for example, Loshitzky, ed., *Spielberg's Holocaust; Critical Perspectives on Schindler's List.*
96. Bernstein, "The *Schindler's List* Effect," 432.
97. Fath Davis Ruffins, "Culture Wars Won and Lost, Part II: The National African-American Museum Project," *Radical History Review* 70 (1998): 85.
98. See Dora Apel, "Images of Black History: The Charles H. Wright Museum of African American History," *Dissent* 48:3 (summer 2001): 98–102.
99. Samuel G. Freedman, "Laying Claim to Sorrow Beyond Words," Arts & Ideas, *New York Times,* 13 December 1997. As regards the figure of "600 million," it bears no relation to reality. According to Peter Novick, the most recent scholarly estimates are that about twelve million African slaves were shipped to the Western Hemisphere, of whom perhaps two million died during the Middle Passage. See *The Holocaust in American Life,* 330 n.100.
100. Examples of such book titles are John Henrik Clarke, *Christopher Columbus and the African Holocaust: Slavery and the Rise of European Capitalism;* S. E. Anderson, *The Black Holocaust for Beginners (A Writers and Readers Documentary Comic Books; 52);* Gyasi A. Foluke, *The Real Holocaust: A Wholistic Analysis of the African-American Experience, 1441–1994;* Velma Maia Thomas, *Lest We Forget: The Passage from Africa to Slavery and Emancipation: A Three-Dimensional Interactive Book with Photographs and Documents from the Black Holocaust Exhibit.*
101. Shandler, *While America Watches,* xv.
102. Quoted in Bob Herbert, "The Hate Virus," Op-Ed, *New York Times,* 10 August 1998.
103. Quoted in Freedman, "Laying Claim to Sorrow Beyond Words."
104. Even in the case of the Jewish genocide the term Holocaust, as many historians have noted, is infelicitous. Arising from the Greek word *holokauston,* in turn translated from the Hebrew *churban*, meaning an offering or sacrifice to God that is entirely burnt, the term holocaust endows the Judeocide with a sense of moral purpose or martyrdom when, in reality, Jews had no choice in the matter and no moral purpose could possibly be served. Another common term is *Shoah,* a Hebrew word meaning "great destruction," which first appeared in Hebrew Bible accounts of the razing of the First and Second Temples in Jerusalem. By the late 1950s however, Holocaust came into

common usage among historians as a proper noun representing the Jewish genocide, connecting, as Young has noted, the contemporary disaster with a continuum of Jewish disasters in history.

105. Quoted in Freedman, "Laying Claim to Sorrow Beyond Words."
106. Novick, *The Holocaust in American Life,* 192.
107. Jonathan Boyarin and Daniel Boyarin, eds., *Jews and Other Differences: The New Jewish Cultural Studies* (Minneapolis: University of Minnesota Press, 1997), viii, vii, xi.
108. Ibid., xiii, xii.
109. Jonathan R. Smith, *Managing Editor, Mississippi Quarterly. H-Net Holocaust.* 25 November 1998. Available e-mail [Online]: mail to: listserv@h-net.msu.edu; Message: get h-holocaust [27 November 1998].
110. Vivian M. Patraka, "Situating History and Difference: The Performance of the Term Holocaust in Public Discourse," in *Jews and Other Differences,* 57–58.
111. Ibid., 54–55.
112. Ibid., 73.
113. Charles Pete Banner-Haley, "The Necessity of Remembrance: A Review of the Museum of African American History," *American Quarterly* 51: 2 (June 1999): 423–424.
114. Bauer, *Rethinking the Holocaust,* 9–10.
115. Quoted in Stacy Morford, "Abortion Protest Enrages Students," The Associated Press, 24 September 1998. Available e-mail [Online]: mail to keyword: AOL News [25 September 1998].
116. Laurie Goodstein, "Christians Gain Support in Fight on Persecution," *New York Times,* 9 November 1998.
117. István Deák, "Heroes and Victims," *New York Review of Books,* 31 May 2001. Available [Online]: http://www.nybooks.com/nyrev/WWWfeatdisplay.cgi?20010531051R

NOTES TO CHAPTER TWO

1. Boyarin, *Thinking in Jewish,* 112–113.
2. Ibid., 102, 114.
3. Shimon Attie, "The Writing on the Wall Project," in *The Writing on the Wall: Projections in Berlin's Jewish Quarter,* exh. cat. (Heidelberg: Edition Braus, 1994), 9.
4. James Young, "Sites Unseen: Shimon Attie's Acts of Remembrance, 1991-1996," *Sites Unseen: Shimon Attie European Projects,* exh. cat. (Burlington, Vt.: Verve Editions, 1998), 11.
5. Attie, "The Writing on the Wall Project," 10.
6. Ibid.
7. Heinrich von Treitschke, *Preussische Jahrbücher,* 1879, vol. 44, 572ff, quoted in John Weiss, *Ideology of Death: Why the Holocaust Happened in Germany* (Chicago: Elephant Paperbacks, 1996), 87.
8. Debórah Dwork and Robert Jan van Pelt, *Auschwitz: 1270 to the Present* (New York: W.W. Norton & Co. Inc., 1996), 52.
9. Ibid., 54.
10. Pierre Vidal-Naquet, *The Jews: History, Memory, and the Present,* trans. David Ames Curtis (New York: Columbia University Press, 1996), 64.
11. Following the First World War, a powerful wave of reaction and racism occurred in Germany fueled by the stab-in-the-back myth that blamed the Jews, among others, for

the German defeat. In 1919, Conservatives, the party of the elites, merged with völkists to declare unity in battle against the rule of the Jews. By 1920 there were about 300,000 antisemitic Free Corps irregulars, often from prewar völkisch groups, fighting against leftists and strikers. Among the clergy, officials of the Lutheran church were close to the Conservative party and denunciations of liberals, leftists, and Jews abounded in Weimar sermons. Among university students, most undergraduates supported the radical right and all national student organizations outlawed Jewish membership. See Weiss, *Ideology of Death.*

12. For details of the Scheunenviertel riot, I am indebted to David Clay Large, "'Out with the Ostjuden': The Scheunenviertel Riot in Berlin, November 1923," manuscript of paper delivered at the German Studies Association Twenty-First Annual Conference, Washington, D.C., 26 September 1997.
13. Quoted in ibid., 6.
14. Quoted in ibid., 8.
15. Ibid., 8-9.
16. Quoted in ibid., 9.
17. Quoted in ibid., 10. This advice seemed to bear fruit in 1924. Thus, days before the Reichstag elections in 1933, the board of the association again counseled, "In general, today more than ever we must follow the directive: wait calmly." See Friedländer, *Nazi Germany and the Jews,* 15.
18. Large, "'Out with the Ostjuden,'" 10.
19. Cf. Young, "Sites Unseen," 12.
20. Artist's statement in Monica Bohm-Duchen, *After Auschwitz: Responses to the Holocaust in Contemporary Art,* exh. cat. (Sunderland, U.K.: Northern Centre for Contemporary Art, 1995), 147.
21. Alain Finkielkraut, *The Imaginary Jew* (Lincoln: University of Nebraska Press, 1994), 42.
22. Quoted in Large, "'Out with the Ostjuden,'" 3–4.
23. Kenneth Baker, "Shimon Attie," *Artnews* (November 1994): 165.
24. Norman Kleeblatt, "Persistence of Memory," *Art in America* (June 2000): 98.
25. Sander L. Gilman, *Smart Jews: The Construction of the Image of Jewish Superior Intelligence* (Lincoln: University of Nebraska Press, 1997).
26. This led to the stereotype of the *schlemihl,* an ineffectual, bungling person who habitually fails or is easily victimized. The schlemihl was also known in Yiddish tradition for his pacifism and antimilitarism, in turn feeding the German myth of Jews as shirkers in the army. For a discussion of the schlemihl in the context of contemporary American culture, see Jon Stratton, *Coming Out Jewish: Constructing Ambivalent Identities* (New York: Routledge, 2000), 300-303.
27. Ferdinand Protzman, "An Artist Projects a Ghostly Past," *Forward,* 21 April 1995; Charles Hagen, "Mixed Images that Show the Mutability of Time," *New York Times,* 9 December 1994.
28. Young, "Sites Unseen," 11.
29. Shimon Attie, artist's lecture at University of Michigan, Ann Arbor, 28 January 1999.
30. See Friedländer, *Nazi Germany and the Jews,* esp. chapter 1.
31. Ernst van Alphen, *Caught by History: Holocaust Effects in Contemporary Art, Literature, and Theory* (Stanford, Calif.: Stanford University Press, 1997), esp. 1–37.
32. Ibid., 19.
33. Ibid., 21.
34. Ibid., 120–121. For an interesting discussion of Boltanski's representational strategies,

also see pages 149–175 and 193–222. Van Alphen argues that Boltanski's work does not "represent" the past but reenacts it. By manipulating pictures of Nazi victims until he has turned these subjects into objects, for example, Boltanski performs a central principle of the Nazi genocide, that of turning subjects into objects. In this sense, van Alphen argues, Boltanski produces an emphatic "Holocaust effect" rather than a "representation."

35. See John Czaplicka, "Commemorative Practice in Berlin," *New German Critique* 65 (spring/summer 1995): 155–187.
36. Allan Sekula, "Photography Between Labor and Capital," *Mining Photographs and Other Pictures 1938–1968: A Selection from the Negative Archives of Shedden Studio, Glace Bay, Cape Breton—Photographs by Leslie Shedden,* ed. Benjamin Buchloh and Robert Wilkie (Nova Scotia: Nova Scotia College of Art and Design, 1983), 202.
37. Attie's work can also be compared to that of Polish-born conceptual artist Krzysztof Wodiczko, who powerfully combines the past and the present by projecting contemporary images onto historic monuments. In one project, Wodiczko utilized the Soldiers and Sailors Civil War Memorial in Boston as a screen for images of Boston's homeless people. In another work, the façade of the Martin Luther Church in Kassel, Germany, served as a backdrop for a figure wearing a gas mask and a protective suit with his hands folded in prayer. In a 1998 project, Wodiczko chose the Bunker Hill Monument in Boston, which commemorates a battle in the Revolutionary War, to project the video-animated stories of bereaved Charlestown mothers whose children had been murdered and whose killings, through a rigid code of silence in an area known for its high murder rate, have remained largely unsolved. See *Krzysztof Wodiczko: Critical Vehicles; Writings, Projects, Interviews* (Cambridge, Mass.: MIT Press, 1999).
38. Shimon Attie, telephone conversation with author, 9 July 1998.
39. Sekula, "Photography Between Labor and Capital," 194.
40. Ibid., 199.
41. Jacques Derrida, *Archive Fever: A Freudian Impression,* trans. Eric Prenowitz (Chicago: University of Chicago Press, 1995), 29.
42. Quoted in Enzo Traverso, *The Jews and Germany: From the "Judeo-German Symbiosis" to the Memory of Auschwitz,* trans. by Daniel Weissbort (Lincoln: University of Nebraska Press, 1995), 155.
43. Attie, *The Writing on the Wall,* 12.
44. Thea Herold, "Die Zeit kommt ins Geschiebe," *Der Tagesspiegel,* 10 April 1992; Rüdiger Soldt, "Lichtbilder gegen das Vergessen," *Tages Zeitung,* 9 November 1993.
45. Shimon Attie, Email to author, 29 October 2001.
46. Young, "Sites Unseen," 12.
47. Lilli Vostry, "Nachdenken im Reisetrubel: Bilder deportierter Juden," *Dresdner Zeitung,* 11 October 1993.
48. Lutz Bittner, "Gegen Mauern des Vergessens: Die Ermordeten kehren wieder," *Sächsische Zeitung,* 29 October 1993.
49. Weiss, *Ideology of Death,* 90.
50. Ibid., 92.
51. Young, *Sites Unseen,* 14–15.
52. Traverso, *The Jews and Germany,* 54.
53. Young, *Sites Unseen,* 15.
54. For a discussion of nationalism and racism as relational constructs manifested in geographical codes in late-nineteenth-century Germany, see Russell A. Berman, *The Rise*

of the Modern German Novel: Crisis and Charisma (Cambridge, Mass.: Harvard University Press, 1986).

55. Nolte's article coincided with the publication of a volume of two essays by Andreas Hillgruber, *Two Kinds of Collapse: The Shattering of the German Reich and the End of European Jewry,* in which Hillgruber defended the Germans who fought on the Eastern front, asserting that they fought not only to preserve Germany's borders, but to preserve the near mystical destiny of the great power role of the Reich as a "Middle European" power. The ideology of *Mitteleuropa* sought to inscribe Germany onto the map of Europe as a privileged center between East and West that somehow maintained an equilibrium of forces. The betrayal of this destiny, as autonomous power broker between East and West, Hillgruber asserted, constituted Hitler's true crime. This geopolitical conception gave rise to the myth of Germany in World War I as a country in the middle encircled and threatened by foreign powers and compelled to assert itself against the hostile world outside. The recrudescence of nineteenth-century geographical codes in the late 1980s points to these geopolitical terms as signifiers which can be ever mobilized to serve the purposes of German nationalism.

    Social theorist Jürgen Habermas led the opposition to the conservative historians. See Jürgen Habermas, *The New Conservatism: Cultural Criticism and the Historians Debate,* ed. and trans. Shierry Weber Nicholsen (Cambridge, Mass.: MIT Press, 1989); Richard J. Evans, *In Hitler's Shadow: West German Historians and the Attempt to Escape from the Nazi Past* (New York: Pantheon Books, 1989), Charles S. Maier, *The Unmasterable Past: History, Holocaust, and German National Identity* (Cambridge, Mass.: Harvard University Press, 1988), and Peter Baldwin, ed., *Reworking the Past: Hitler, The Holocaust, and the Historian's Debate* (Boston: Beacon Press, 1990). For events leading up to the debate, centered on the controversy surrounding Ronald Reagan's visit to the cemetery in Bitburg, see Hartman, ed., *Bitburg.*

56. With the election of Gerhard Schröder in September 1998 to the German Chancellorship, and the formation of an alliance between the Social Democrats and the Greens, the governing parties have agreed to modernize the nation's eighty-five-year-old citizenship law. Declaring Germany a country of immigrants in recognition of the seven million foreign residents, including two million Turks, who make up nearly 10 percent of the population, the agreement would give automatic citizenship to German-born children of foreigners for the first time, if one of their parents has been living in Germany since age fourteen. Whereas Turks who became German citizens were forced to give up Turkish citizenship before, the agreement allows for dual citizenship, and shortens foreigners' eligibility for naturalization from fifteen years to eight years. Children of foreigners born in Germany would, however, have to choose one country or the other at the age of twenty-three, giving up their dual citizenship.

57. Traverso, *The Jews and Germany,* 161.

58. The political establishment was shocked when an extremist right-wing party, in April 1998, won 13 percent of the vote in Saxony-Anhalt, a state in eastern Germany. In the past decade, however, despite the debate over a Berlin Holocaust memorial, a number of state-sponsored Holocaust memorials, Jewish museums, research institutions and Jewish studies programs have appeared all over Germany, including Daniel Liebeskind's much acclaimed Jewish Museum, which opened in Berlin in 2001. On the debate over the Berlin memorial, see Jane Kramer, "The Politics of Memory," *New Yorker* 14 August 1995, 48–65; on Holocaust memorials in Germany, see Young, *The Texture of Memory* and idem., *At Memory's Edge.* On the wave of philosemitism, see Andrew Nagorski, "A Strange Affair," *Newsweek,* 15 June 1998, 36–37; for a socio-

logical account of Jews in Germany in the latter half of the twentieth century, see Lynn Rapaport, *Jews in Germany after the Holocaust: Memory, Identity, and German-Jewish Relations* (New York: Cambridge University Press, 1997).

59. Shimon Attie, telephone conversation with author, 9 July 1998.
60. Shimon Attie, Artist's Statement, in *Shimon Attie: Between Dreams and History,* October 22-November 14, 1998, brochure produced by Creative Time, 307 Seventh Avenue, Suite 1904, New York, N.Y. 10001.
61. *New York Times,* 30 July 1893, "East Side Street Vendors," reprinted in Karen Brodkin, *How Jews Became White Folks & What That Says About Race in America* (New Brunswick, N. J.: Rutgers University Press, 1997. Reprint, 2000), 29.
62. Ibid., 30.
63. Jonathan Rosen, "On Eldridge Street, Yesteryear's Shul," *New York Times,* 2 October 1998.

NOTES TO CHAPTER THREE

1. Among other places, *Body Missing* has been shown at the Setagaya Museum, Tokyo (1995), the Gesellschaft für Aktuelle Kunst, Bremen (1996-97), the Kungl Konsthogskolan, Stockholm (1997), the Centre of Contemporary Art, Warsaw (1997), the Elaine L. Jacob Gallery at Wayne State University, Detroit, Mich. (2000), the Goethe-Institut, Toronto (2000), and the Canadian Cultural Centre, Paris (2001). It has been proposed for the Freud Museum in Vienna.
2. Michael Century, C.I.T.I. (Centre d'Innovation en Technologies de l'Informa-tion), Available [Online]: http://www.uwo.ca/visarts/vol1num2/eva2.html [24 July 1998].
3. See Hector Feliciano, *The Lost Museum: The Nazi Conspiracy to Steal the World's Greatest Works of Art* (New York: HarperCollins Publishers, 1995), and Lynn H. Nicholas, *The Rape of Europa: The Fate of Europe's Treasures in the Third Reich and the Second World War* (New York: Vintage Books, 1995). Feliciano focuses on France, the most looted country in Western Europe; Nicholas surveys the cultural destruction of modernist art in Germany, as well as art looting in Austria, Poland, Holland, France, and the Soviet Union, and provides a comprehensive social history that encompasses both Jewish-owned and state-owned art, and postwar repatriation efforts.
4. "France Searches for War Loot," Broadcast transcript, *All Things Considered,* National Public Radio, 29 May 1997.
5. Ibid.
6. See Elizabeth Simpson, ed., *The Spoils of War* (New York: Harry N. Abrams, 1997), and Konstantin Akinsha and Grigorii Kozlov, *Beautiful Loot: The Soviet Plunder of Europe's Art Treasures* (New York: Harry N. Abrams, 1995).
7. Vera Frenkel, "Interview," with Dot Tuer, *Vera Frenkel: Raincoats, Suitcases, Palms,* exh. cat. (Toronto: Art Gallery of York University, 1993), 41.
8. *. . . from the Transit Bar* was subsequently shown at The Power Plant in Toronto, the Setagaya Museum of Contemporary Art in Tokyo, Ars Nova and Turku Art Museum in Finland, and the Centre of Contemporary Art in Warsaw. It also appeared together with *Body Missing* at the National Gallery of Canada in Ottawa, the Royal University College of Fine Arts in Stockholm, and the Lillehammer Art Museum in Norway.
9. Vera Frenkel with Dot Tuer and Clive Robertson, "The Story is Always Partial: A Conversation with Vera Frenkel," *Art Journal* 57 (Winter 1998), 12. The musical score was

arranged by the artist and Stan Zielinski and played on a Disklavier in a ninety-minute sequence. The narratives on the six video monitors run in eighty-minutes sequences.

10. Vera Frenkel, "Interview," with Dot Tuer, 55.
11. Ibid., 11.
12. Another artist who has dealt with the immigrant experience in powerful ways is Krzysztof Wodiczko. See *Krzysztof Wodiczko: Critical Vehicles; Writings, Projects, Interviews.*
13. Elizabeth Legge, "Analogs of Loss: Vera Frenkel's Body Missing, (http://www.yorku.ca/BodyMissing)," *Visual Culture and the Holocaust,* ed. Barbie Zelizer (New Brunswick: Rutgers University Press, 2001), 342.
14. Alan Riding, "Heirs Claim Art Lost to Nazis in Amsterdam: Another Collection Joins the Disputes Over Who Owns War's Cultural Booty," *New York Times,* 12 January 1998.
15. Felicia R. Lee, "Seattle Museum to Return Looted Work," *New York Times,* 16 June 1999.
16. "Principles with Respect to Nazi-Confiscated Art," *Washington Conference on Holocaust-Era Assets.* The principles were sent with a letter from Edward H. Able Jr. to all Directors of the American Association of Museums Art Museum Institutional Members, 7 December 1998. These principles parallel those developed earlier in the year by the Association of Art Museum Directors.
17. *Body Missing.* Available [Online]: http://www.yorku.ca/BodyMissing.
18. Sigrid Schade and Eva Schmidt, *Vera Frenkel: Body Missing,* exh. cat. (Bremen: Gesellschaft für Aktuelle Kunst, 1997), 20, 28, 30; also *Body Missing.* Available [Online]: http://www.yorku.ca/BodyMissing.
19. *Body Missing.* Available [Online]: http://www.yorku.ca/BodyMissing.
20. Legge, "Analogs of Loss," 344.
21. Frenkel, "The Story is Always Partial," 13.
22. In her project, *The Institute; or, What We Do for Love* (begun 1999), Frenkel carries her concern with power and its abuse in a new satirical direction. See Frenkel, "The Story is Always Partial."
23. Vera Frenkel, "The Body Missing Project," transcript of opening speech at the Schatz-Raub-Bildstürm Symposium at the Offenes Kulturhaus, Linz, 16 February 1996.
24. Vera Frenkel, email to author, 13 January 1999.
25. Maclear, *Beclouded Visions: Hiroshima-Nagasaki and the Art of Witness,* 58.
26. Gerald Bruns, quoted in Jonathan Boyarin, *Storm from Paradise: The Politics of Jewish Memory* (Minneapolis: University of Minnesota Press, 1992), 74.
27. Geoffrey Batchen, "The Art of Archiving," *Deep Storage: Collecting, Storage, and Archiving in Art* (New York: Prestel, 1998), 47.
28. Vera Frenkel, email to author, 13 January 1999.
29. Batchen, "The Art of Archiving," 46.

NOTES TO CHAPTER FOUR

1. Lawrence Langer, *Holocaust Testimonies: The Ruins of Memory* (New Haven, Conn.: Yale University Press, 1991). Langer in part bases this concept on the searing memoir by Charlotte Delbo. See Delbo's *Auschwitz and After,* trans. Rosette C. Lamont (New Haven, Conn.: Yale University Press, 1995), esp. "The Measure of Our Days." For a

critical discussion of Langer's book, see Rothberg, *Traumatic Realism: The Demands of Holocaust Representation,* 118–129. Rothberg argues that Langer overreaches his role, "legitim[ating] the nonvictim's role in the production of knowledge of the extreme that ought to be beyond the nonvictim's reach" (120) by refusing to recognize the possibility of any continuity between everyday experience and that of the camps.

2. Lori Hope Lefkovitz, "Inherited Holocaust Memory and the Ethics of Ventriloquism," *The Kenyon Review* XIX, no. 1 (1997): 38, 41.
3. Finkelstein and Birn, *A Nation on Trial,* 147.
4. LaCapra, *History and Memory After Auschwitz,* 35-138.
5. See *Written in Memory: Portraits of the Holocaust. Photographs by Jeffrey A. Wolin,* exh. cat. (San Francisco: Chronicle Books, 1997).
6. van Alphen, *Caught by History,* 47.
7. Quoted in Judith Miller, *One, by One, by One: Facing the Holocaust* (New York: Touchstone, 1990), 269.
8. Henry Greenspan, *On Listening to Holocaust Survivors: Recounting and Life History* (Westport, Conn.: Praeger, 1998), xx.
9. Langer, *Holocaust Testimonies,* 160–161.
10. Hirsch, *Family Frames,* 23.
11. Quoted in Shandler, *While America Watches,* 8.
12. Wolin, *Written in Memory,* 21.
13. Langer, *Holocaust Testimonies,* 59–60.
14. For an excellent essay on the effects of trauma on the Holocaust survivor, see Henry Krystal, "Trauma and Aging: A Thirty-Year Follow-Up," in Cathy Caruth, ed., *Trauma: Explorations in Memory* (Baltimore, Md.: Johns Hopkins University Press, 1995).
15. Pier Marton, email to author, 14 May 2001.
16. Ibid. Also see Feinstein, *Witness and Legacy,* 17.
17. Stratton, *Coming Out Jewish,* 12.
18. Lefkovitz, "Inherited Holocaust Memory," 40.
19. John Russell, "Views of Jewish Identity, Emotion and Healing in Museum Video Show," *New York Times,* 29 July 1988. This was a review of the exhibition *Time and Memory: Video Art and Identity* at the Jewish Museum in New York in July 1988.
20. Sander L. Gilman, *Difference and Pathology: Stereotypes of Sexuality, Race, and Madness* (Ithaca, N.Y.: Cornell University Press, 1985), 240, 242. Also see Gilman, *The Jew's Body* (New York: Routledge, 1991), and Smart Jews.
21. In the late 1980s, the videotape was shown at the Berlin Film Festival, the Museum of Modern Art, and the Jewish Museum in New York. In 1995, incorporated into the JEW installation, it became part of the traveling exhibition *Witness and Legacy: Contemporary Art about the Holocaust* co-curated by Stephen C. Feinstein and Paul Spencer, first shown at the Minnesota Museum of American Art.

NOTES TO CHAPTER FIVE

1. James Friedman, telephone conversation with author, 4 October 1998.
2. Jonathan Green, "James Friedman: Rephotographing the History of the World," *James Friedman: Color Photographs 1979–1983,* exh. cat. (Columbus: Ohio State University Gallery of Fine Art, 1983), [1].
3. Erich Hartmann, *In the Camps* (New York: W.W. Norton & Co., 1995).

4. Ibid., 102.
5. For ghetto pictures taken by Jewish photographers, see Roman Vishniac, *Polish Jews: A Pictorial Record* (1947. New York: Schocken Books, 1997); *With a Camera in the Ghetto: Mendel Grossman,* ed. Z. Szner and A. Sened (D.N. Western Galilee, Israel: Ghetto Fighters' House, 1970), which documents the underground activities in the Lodz ghetto; and *Hidden History of the Kovno Ghetto* (Boston, New York, Toronto, London: United States Holocaust Memorial Museum, 1997), in which Lithuanian Jews in Kovno, forced into a ghetto in 1941, attempted to document their own existence before they were destroyed. For ghetto pictures taken by German photographers, see *The Warsaw Ghetto in Photographs: 206 Views Made in 1941,* ed. Ulrich Keller (Mineola, N.Y.: Dover Publications, 1984), which reproduces photographs of the Warsaw ghetto taken in the spring of 1941 by Albert Cusian and Erhard Josef Knoblock; *The Stroop Report: The Jewish Quarter of Warsaw is No More!* ed. and trans. Sybil Milton (New York: Pantheon Books, 1979), which reproduces images of the destruction of the Warsaw ghetto sent by the Nazi commander Stroop to Hitler; *In the Warsaw Ghetto Summer, 1941: Photographs by Willy Georg with Excerpts from the Warsaw Ghetto Diaries,* Willi Georg (New York: Aperture Foundation Inc., 1993), which reproduces pictures taken by a German soldier sent by his commanding officer for a day into the Warsaw ghetto to take photographs.
6. Barbie Zelizer, *Remembering to Forget: Holocaust Memory Through the Camera's Eye* (Chicago: University of Chicago Press, 1998), 166.
7. Ibid., 181.
8. Susan Sontag, "In Plato's Cave," *On Photography* (New York: Farrar, Straus & Giroux, 1977), 20.
9. Jean Améry, *At the Mind's Limits: Contemplations by a Survivor on Auschwitz and Its Realities,* trans. Sidney Rosenfeld and Stella P. Rosenfeld (Bloomington: Indiana University Press, 1980), 32–33.
10. Ibid., 40.
11. See Carol Rittner and John K. Roth, eds., *Memory Offended: The Auschwitz Convent Controversy* (New York: Praeger, 1991).
12. Michael Steinlauf, *Bondage to the Dead: Poland and the Memory of the Holocaust* (Syracuse, N.Y.: Syracuse University Press, 1997), 95–96.
13. Ibid., 96.
14. Dwork and van Pelt, *Auschwitz: 1270 to the Present,* 366.
15. In October 1998, Pope John Paul II began the canonization process for Alojzije Cardinal Stepinac of Croatia, who was tried as a Nazi collaborator by the Tito government and is still viewed by Orthodox Serbs as the symbol of the Croatian Catholic Church's complicity with the Ustashe, the World War II fascist regime that killed tens or hundreds of thousands of Serbs, Jews and other minorities.
16. Steinlauf, *Bondage to the Dead,* 135.
17. Ibid., 141.
18. Ibid., 124.
19. James Friedman, telephone conversation with author, 4 October 1998.
20. Quoted in Steinlauf, *Bondage to the Dead,* 142–143.
21. Vincent Leo, "After the Fact," *Afterimage* 12:10 (May 1985): 18.
22. Simon Schama, *Landscape and Memory* (New York: Vintage Books, 1996), 26.
23. Leo, "After the Fact," 18.
24. A tenured professor in Friedman's department, Carl Clausen, was driven by conscience

to reveal to Friedman that he had been denied tenure because he was Jewish. Clausen testified at official Ohio State University faculty hearings that he had been told, "we have too many Jews on the tenured faculty already and the people coming up for tenure are Jews." Friedman was named, along with photography professors Thomas Andersen and Allan Sekula. Only Friedman is Jewish. When Clausen questioned the designation for Andersen and Sekula, the response, he says, was, "If a man's wife is a Jew, he is a Jew." Clausen asserted, "The most disturbing part is that the whole plan was described to me ahead of time. Now it's been implemented and they are all gone," referring to Sekula, Anderson, Friedman, and the former (non-Jewish) department chairman, Ron Green. Clausen says that he was told, "We have to get rid of Ron Green and his crowd," prompting the view of the older faculty members as forming an alliance that was variously opposed "to Marxist theory, to Jews, to change, to the thinking of East Coast and West Coast film people." Following his revelations, Clausen himself was forced to retire after twenty-four years in the department. Friedman filed a lawsuit in federal court charging the university with religious discrimination, which was settled out of court in 1984, the language of the settlement allowing no one to claim victory. See Larrilyn Edwards, "Professor's Lawsuit Charges Religious Bias at Ohio State, *Columbus Citizen-Journal,* 19 June 1984; Adrienne Bosworth, "A Department in Disarray at OSU," *Columbus Monthly,* July 1984; "Tenure Suit Settled," *The Ohio State Lantern,* 19 October 1984.

25. James Friedman, telephone conversation with author, 29 July 1998.
26. James Friedman, "Why Would Anyone in Their Right Mind Photograph 12 Nazi Concentration Camps?" in the session *The Holocaust and the Art of Secondary Witnessing,* chaired by Dora Apel, College Art Association Annual Conference, Chicago, 1 March 2001.
27. Christopher A. Yates, "James Friedman," *Dialogue,* March/April, 1998, 14.
28. Andreas Huyssen, "Of Mice and Mimesis: Reading Spiegelman with Adorno," *New German Critique* 81 (fall 2000), 72.
29. Ibid., 73.
30. Ibid., 81.
31. Andreas Huyssen, "Anselm Kiefer: The Terror of History, the Temptation of Myth," *October* 48 (spring 1989): 31.
32. G. Roger Denson, "Susan Silas' Pragmatic Gaze," *Susan Silas,* exh. cat. (New York: fiction/nonfiction, 1990), n.p. [4].
33. Quoted in Lisa Saltzman, *Anselm Kiefer and Art after Auschwitz* (New York: Cambridge University Press, 1999), 60.
34. Ibid., 60–61.
35. Silas received an MFA from the California Institute of the Arts. She has shown her work in solo exhibitions at various galleries in New York, San Francisco, Paris, and Ljublijana, Slovenia, and was included in the 1994 exhibition *Burnt Whole: Contemporary Artists Reflect on the Holocaust* organized by the Washington Project for the Arts in Washington, D.C.
36. Susan Silas, typescript of letter sent to *The Forward,* 5 February 1995.
37. Denson, "Susan Silas' Pragmatic Gaze," 4.
38. Susan Silas, letter to author, 17 June 1998.
39. Saltzman, *Anselm Kiefer and Art after Auschwitz,* 58.
40. "Testimonies of the last prisoners in the death camp Chelmno." Introduction by Shmuel Krakowski and Ilia Altman. Available [Online]: http://www.geocities.com/Paris/Rue/4017/index3.htm [10 September 1998].

41. This work was first shown at the Cooley Memorial Gallery in Portland, Oregon, in January 2002.
42. Anton Kaes, *From Hitler to Heimat: The Return of History as Film* (Cambridge, Mass.: Harvard University Press, 1989), 196, also quoting Botho Strauss.
43. Also "Jewish Gombin (Gabin, Poland, Jewish Geneology): Chelmno2." Available [Online]: http://weber.ucsd.edu/~lzamosc/gmoreinf.html;& gt: Chelmno and Operation Reinhard [31 August 1998]. Also see Arno Mayer, *Why Did the Heavens Not Darken?* (New York: Pantheon Books, 1988).
44. Quoted in "Jewish Gombin".
45. Levi, *The Drowned and the Saved,* 17.
46. Martin Gilbert, *Holocaust Journey: Travelling in Search of the Past* (New York: Columbia University Press, 1997), 376, 380.
47. Ibid., 216.
48. Ibid., 218.
49. Ibid., 250.
50. Ibid., 251–254.
51. Derrida, *Archive Fever,* 68.
52. Goldhagen, *Hitler's Willing Executioners,* 335–346.
53. Ibid., 348.
54. Ibid., 354.
55. The University Art Gallery, Staller Center for the Arts at SUNY Stony Brook mounted the exhibition from 9 November to 16 December 2000, produced by guest curators Nicholas Mirzoeff and Karen Levitov. Other artists in the exhibition included Ken Aptekar, Rachel Schreiber, Stephanie Snyder, and Albert J. Winn.
56. Jane Kramer, "The Politics of Memory," *New Yorker,* 14 August 1995, 48.
57. Ibid., 56.
58. Susan Silas, email to author, 17 June 1998. The work of Andy Goldsworthy, Hamish Fulton, and Richard Long provide such examples, albeit with very different objectives. Long, for instance, is known for his walks undertaken in his native England, as well as in Iceland, Lapland, Bolivia, Japan, Nepal, Central Africa, and the United States, which have included marking the landscape and documenting the walks with photographs and video.
59. Thomas Crow, *Modern Art in the Common Culture* (New Haven, Conn.: Yale University Press, 1996), 183.
60. Ibid., 216.
61. See Meyer Levin, *The Obsession* (New York: Simon and Schuster, 1974); Lawrence Graver, *An Obsession with Anne Frank: Meyer Levin & the "Diary"* (Berkeley: University of California Press, 1997); Ralph Melnick, *The Stolen Legacy of Anne Frank: Meyer Levin, Lillian Hellman, & the Staging of the Diary* (New Haven, Conn.: Yale University Press, 1997).
62. See Mikael Levin, *War Story,* exh. cat. (Munich: Gina Kehayoff Verlag, 1997).
63. Ibid., 130.
64. Quoted in ibid., 129–130.
65. Martin Gilbert, *Atlas of the Holocaust* (New York: William Morrow and Co., Inc., 1991), 223.
66. Christopher Phillips, "Mikael Levin at the International Center of Photography," *Art in America* 85 (May 1997):132.
67. Mikael Levin, email to author, 1 March 1999.
68. Ibid.

69. Mikael Levin, letter to author, 3 March 1999. See Mikael Levin, *The Burden of Identity: Portraits von Juden in Berlin 1998*, exh. cat. (Munich: Gina Kehayoff Verlag, 1998).
70. See Mikael Levin, *Common Places: Response Catalog* (2000). Newsprint publication with an essay by Christopher Phillips, "The Untidy Intimacy of Places," and essays by Jean-François Chevrier, Alain Demarquette, Béatrice Duprez, Catharina Gabrielsson, Hercules Papaioannou, Carole Parmat, Gatrude Sandquist, Kai Uwe Schierz, Ingo Schulze, Jacques Soulillou, and Alexandra Yerolympos; also available [Online]: http://www.mikaellevin.com/cplaces_text.htm [7 May 2001].
71. Susan Silas, email to author, 17 June 1998.
72. Paul Celan, "[Reply to an Questionnaire from the Flinker Bookstore, Paris, 1958]," in *Paul Celan: Collected Prose*, trans. Rosmarie Waldrop (New York: Sheep Meadow Press, 1986), 15.
73. Matthew Girson, email to author, 15 April 2001.
74. Stratton, *Coming Out Jewish*, 22.
75. Boyarin, *Thinking in Jewish*, 114.
76. Matthew Girson, email to author, 20 March 2001.
77. See Alain Finkielkraut, *The Imaginary Jew*, trans. Kevin O'Niell and David Suchoff (Lincoln: University of Nebraska Press, 1994), and Isaac Deutscher, *The Non-Jewish Jew and Other Essays* (New York: Hill and Wang, 1968).
78. Girson, email to author, 20 March 2001.
79. For an excellent discussion of Theodor Adorno's reflections in the wake of the genocide, see Rothberg, *Traumatic Realism*, chapter 1, "After Adorno: Culture in the Wake of Catastrophe."
80. From Celan's speech "The Meridian," delivered on the occasion of receiving the Georg Büchner Prize in Darmstadt on 22 October 1960, in *Paul Celan: Collected Prose*, 47.
81. For a discussion of countermonuments, see Young, *At Memory's Edge*.
82. For a discussion of Syberberg's film, see Kaes, *From Hitler to Heimat*.
83. From Celan's Meridian speech, 40, 47, and discussed by Pierre Joris in his introduction to Paul Celan, *Breathturn*, trans. Pierre Joris (Los Angeles: Sun and Moon Press, 1995), 18.
84. On Malevich see Briony Fer, David Batchelor, Paul Wood, eds., *Realism, Rationalism, Surrealism: Art between the Wars* (New Haven, Conn.: Yale University Press in association with The Open University, 1993), 264.

NOTES TO CHAPTER SIX

1. Quoted in Jordan Elgrably, "In Your Faith," *Los Angeles Times*, 13 May 1996.
2. Rachel Schreiber, email to author, 21 May 1996. Schreiber graduated from the California Institute of the Arts in 1995 and participated in the Whitney Independent Study Program in New York in 1995–96.
3. *This is Not Erotica* was shown in 1995 at the San Francisco Jewish Film Festival after winning an award in the experimental category of the Judah L. Magnus Museum video competition. It has been screened internationally at video festivals, museums, and galleries.
4. Rachel Schreiber, email to author, 21 May 1996.
5. Young, *The Texture of Memory*, 212. See the entire chapter on the ideology of Israeli memorialization.

6. Sidra DeKoven Ezrahi, quoted in *Mirroring Evil,* 103.
7. Kleeblatt, *Mirroring Evil,* 9.
8. Emily Apter, "Introduction," *Fetishism as a Cultural Discourse,* ed. Emily Apter and William Pietz (Ithaca, N.Y.: Cornell University Press, 1993), 5.
9. William Pietz, "The Problem of the Fetish," pt. 1, *Res* 9 (spring 1985): 12–13.
10. The relationship between the Holocaust and contemporary sexual practice deserves greater exploration, but has received little attention. See the essays in *Mirroring Evil,* which focus on the issues surrounding images of Nazis and identification with the perpetrator, and Susan Sontag's essay, "Fascinating Fascism," which is primarily about the filmmaker Leni Riefenstahl, but includes some comments on Nazi-fetish-based sexuality as a form of theater, in *A Susan Sontag Reader* (New York: Vintage Books, 1983), 305–328.
11. A very different allusion to the hair of women prisoners occurs in the installation *Dhimmi,* by artist Joan Silver, shown at Nexus Contemporary Art Center in Atlanta in 1994. Silver created twelve pairs of men's felt slippers resting in a row under a Plexiglas vitrine on salt blocks in the center of the darkened gallery. The slippers referred to boots worn by German U-boat crews during World War II that were made from the hair of women in Nazi labor camps. Silver notes that the sound-deadening, insulating qualities of this material finds a counterpart in the silence of the camp victims (artist's statement).
12. See *Women in the Holocaust,* ed. Ofer and Weitzman, 290–291, 336, 341–343.
13. Rebecca Scherr, "The Uses of Memory and the Abuses of Fiction: Sexuality in Holocaust Fiction and Memoir," *Other Voices: The (e) Journal of Cultural Criticism* 2:1 (February 2000): 2. Available [Online] at: http://dept.english.upenn.edu/~ov.
14. Ibid., 4.
15. Quoted in Levi, *The Drowned and the Saved,* 48.
16. Ibid., 48–49.
17. Langer, *Holocaust Testimonies,* 48. See chapter on "Anguished Memory."
18. Van Alphen, *Caught by History,* 47.

NOTES TO CHAPTER SEVEN

1. Joshua Burgin. "Judaism and Body Modification." [WWW Body Modification Ezine]. Available [Online]: http://www.BME.FreeQ.com/new/bmenews.html [23 January 1996].
2. The debate over who is a "proper" Jew has been particularly heated in Israel, both in regard to immigration laws that are still being determined on the basis of ethnic criteria, and even more notoriously, regarding the rule of Orthodox versus Conservative and Reform synagogues, affecting who may perform marriages, conversions, and the like. This debate has had strong repercussions in the organized Jewish community in the United States.
3. Burgin, "Judaism and Body Modification."
4. Reform Judaism is now the largest organized religious movement among American Jews, with a constituency of 1.5 million.
5. Levi, *The Drowned and the Saved,* 118–119. Many women in Auschwitz/Birkenau were also tattooed on the outside of their arms. It has also been reported that some prisoners in Buchenwald were tattooed on their stomachs, and photographs at

the U.S. Holocaust Memorial Museum show prisoners at one of the Gusen subcamps of Mauthausen with numbers tattooed on their chests.

6. Gilman, *The Jew's Body,* 219. For a discussion of American assimilation from the perspective of a non-assimilationist, see Barry Rubin, *Assimilation and Its Discontents* (New York: Times Books, 1995).
7. Levi, *The Drowned and the Saved,* 119–120.
8. Margot Mifflin, *Bodies of Subversion: A Secret History of Women and Tattoo* (New York: Juno Books, 1997), 115.
9. Kenneth Baker, *Artforum* (May 1990), quoted in Gary Michael Dault, "Painspotting: The Art of John Scott," *John Scott: Engines of Anxiety,* exh. cat. (Montreal: Gallery of the Saidye Bronfman Centre for the Arts, 1997), 13.
10. Melony Ward, *C Magazine* 25, spring 1990, cited in ibid.
11. Quoted in ibid., 14.
12. David Liss, "Engines of Anxiety," in *Engines of Anxiety,* 5.
13. Linda Nochlin, "The Couturier and the Hasid," *Too Jewish? Challenging Traditional Identities,* ed. Norman L. Kleeblatt, exh. cat. (New York/New Brunswick, N. J.: The Jewish Museum and Rutgers University Press, 1996), xviii.
14. Quoted in ibid., xix.
15. *Davka* is Yiddish for "doing something in spite of being warned not to," or more loosely, "up yours." See the inaugural issue, winter 1996.
16. See Rubin, *Assimilation and Its Discontents*. From Rubin's perspective, "Jewishness," which remains undefined, must be linked to religious practice, and further, to Zionist support for the state of Israel.
17. Quoted in E. J. Kessler, "An Upstart with an Underground Edge," *Forward,* 9 February 1996. In other interviews Rabbi Pearce said that the cover was not in "good taste" and was not the appropriate image to be associated with the largest congregation in the Bay Area. See Katherine Seligman, "Risky New Jewish Magazine Off to Lively Start," *San Francisco Examiner,* 25 February 1996, and Joseph Berkofsky, "Alternative Magazine Pushes Boundaries of Jewish Law, Taste," *Jewish Bulletin of Northern California,* 26 January 1996.
18. The content of Vainshtein's body art is based on documentary photographs and drawings she found in books of artworks by Holocaust survivors. Her backpiece was produced by tattoo artist Bob Vessells; her other tattoos were created by Jaime Schene, Louis Favela, Jason Schroeder, Mark Paramore, and Henry Martinez.
19. Marina Vainshtein, telephone conversation with author, 29 July 1996.
20. Jordon Elgrably, "In Your Faith," *Los Angeles Times,* 13 May 1996.
21. Marina Vainshtein, telephone conversation with author, 29 July 1996.
22. See Leonard Garment, "Christian Soldiers," *New York Times,* 27 June 1996, and Jeffrey Goldberg, "Some of Their Best Friends are Jews," *New York Times,* 16 March 1997. At a 1996 conference in New Orleans with 14,000 delegates, the Southern Baptist Convention adopted a resolution calling for a major campaign to convert American Jews to Christianity, and appointed a missionary to take charge of the conversion operations. Garment points out that this resolution is the latest in a centuries-long line of conversion efforts among Christians, as old as Christianity itself, in which Judaism is viewed as obsolete, unnecessary, and a challenge to the idea of the inevitability of Christianity as the natural culmination of Jewish history. Hence, only the Jews stand in special need of spiritual improvement. For a discussion of Christian antisemitism,

also see Steven T. Katz, "Ideology, State Power, and Mass Murder/Genocide," *Lessons and Legacies,* and Weiss, *Ideology of Death.*

23. Karen Brodkin, *How Jews Became White Folks and What That Says about Race in America* (New Brunswick, N.J.: Rutgers University Press, 2000), 24.
24. Ibid., 105.
25. Barry Singer, "In Yiddish Music, A Return to Roots of Torment and Joy," *New York Times,* 16 August 1998.
26. For a discussion of the evolution of concepts of race and hybridity, see Robert J. C. Young, *Colonial Desire: Hybridity in Theory, Culture and Race* (New York: Routledge, 1995).
27. See Gilman, *The Jew's Body,* 170–171.
28. Ibid., 184–185.
29. More recently the Jewish nose has been addressed in works such as *Jewish Noses* (1993–1995) by Dennis Kardon, an ongoing project that makes sculptural likenesses of noses belonging to Jews in the art world, and Deborah Kass's 1992 *Four Barbras (the Jewish Jackie Series),* which borrows the format of Andy Warhol's celebrity portraits to present the repeated stereotypical profile of Barbra Streisand. Both works were shown in the *Too Jewish? Challenging Traditional Identities* exhibition at The Jewish Museum in New York, 10 March to 14 July 1996.
30. Frédéric Brenner, quoted by Charles Hirshberg in "Portraits of a People," Life Special, *Life,* September 1996.
31. See Robin Cembalest, "Documenting the Diaspora with a Cast of Hundreds: Frédéric Brenner's Unconventional Portrait of American Jewry," *Forward,* Arts & Letters, 13 September 1996.
32. Finkielkraut, *The Imaginary Jew,* 32.
33. Ibid., 34.
34. Boyarin, *Thinking in Jewish,* 165–166.
35. See Geoffrey H. Hartman, *The Longest Shadow: In the Aftermath of the Holocaust* (Bloomington: Indiana University Press, 1996).
36. Finkielkraut, *The Imaginary Jew,* 126.
37. Quoted in Elgrably, "In Your Faith."
38. Boyarin, *Thinking in Jewish,* 5.
39. Marianna Torgovnick, "Skin and Bolts," *Artforum International* (December 1992): 64–65.
40. Ibid.
41. Ibid.
42. Marina Vainshtein, telephone conversation with author, 29 July 1996.
43. Daniel Wojcik, *Punk and Neo-Tribal Body Art* (Jackson: University of Mississippi Press, 1995), 8–9.
44. Ibid., 11.
45. See Elie Wiesel, "Art and the Holocaust: Trivializing Memory," *New York Times,* 11 June 1989, and, Friedländer, *Reflections of Nazism: An Essay on Kitsch and Death.* Also see Saul Friedländer, ed., *Probing the Limits of Repre-sentation* (New Haven, Conn.: Yale University Press, 1992), and Peter Hayes, ed., *Lessons and Legacies.*
46. Ilse Koch, wife of the commandant of Buchenwald, was apparently responsible for selecting the living prisoners whose skin she wanted, after they were killed, for her own collection and for making lampshades of tattooed skin and other objects to be forwarded to the main administrative office of the SS in Oranienburg. The SS also

requested shrunken heads, presumably to be used as desk ornaments. Koch was made SS-*Aufseherin* (overseer) at Buchenwald when her husband Karl Otto Koch was appointed SS-*Standartenführer* in August 1937, and became notorious for her extreme cruelty to prisoners. In 1945 her husband was executed, but Ilse Koch was acquitted. She was arrested by the Americans on 30 June 1945, tried in 1947, and sentenced to life imprisonment. In 1949 she was pardoned, re-arrested, and in January 1951 again sentenced to life imprisonment. In September 1967, she committed suicide in her prison cell in Augsburg. See Israel Gutman, ed., *Encyclopedia of the Holocaust* (New York: MacMillan, 1995), 809; and Arnold Krammer, review of David A. Hackett, *The Buchenwald Report* (1995), in *German Studies Review* 3 (October 1996): 593–94.

47. See Philip Gourevitch, "What They Saw at the Holocaust Museum," *New York Times Magazine*, 12 February 1995, 44–45.
48. Bartov, *Murder in Our Midst*, 53.

NOTES TO CONCLUSION

1. Levi, *The Drowned and the Saved*, 157–158.
2. Shimon Attie, quoted in Amanda Hopkinson, "Through the Past Darkly," *British Journal of Photography* 6976 (June 1994): 26.
3. Maurice Blanchot, *The Writing of the Disaster*, trans. Ann Smock (Lincoln: University of Nebraska Press [1980],1995), 1, 28, 17.
4. Boyarin, *Thinking in Jewish*, 143.
5. Walter Benjamin, "Thesis on the Philosophy of History," *Illuminations*, trans. Harry Zohn, ed. Hannah Arendt (New York: Schocken Books, 1985), 257–58.
6. Quoted in Julia Duin, "Four Horsemen Ditch Steeds for Exhibit's Trans Am," *Washington Post*, 1 January 1997.
7. Stratton, *Coming Out Jewish*, 276.
8. See Stratton, *Coming Out Jewish*; also Brodkin, *How Jews Became White Folks and What That Says About Race in America*.
9. Boyarin, *Thinking in Jewish*, 180.
10. Hass, *In the Shadow of the Holocaust*, 28.

REFERENCES

Akinsha, Konstantin and Grigorii Kozlov. *Beautiful Loot: The Soviet Plunder of Europe's Art Treasures.* New York: Random House, 1995.

Alphen, Ernst van. *Caught by History: Holocaust Effects in Contemporary Art, Literature, and Theory.* Stanford, Calif.: Stanford University Press, 1997.

American Jewish Congress. *In Everlasting Remembrance: Guide to Memorials and Monuments.* New York: American Jewish Congress, 1969.

Améry, Jean. *At the Mind's Limits: Contemplations by a Survivor on Auschwitz and Its Realities.* Trans. Sidney Rosenfeld and Stella P. Rosenfeld. Bloomington: Indiana University Press, 1980.

Amishai-Maisels, Ziva. *Depiction and Interpretation: The Influence of the Holocaust on the Visual Arts.* Newton, Mass.: Butterworth-Heinemann, 1992.

Apel, Dora. "The Tattooed Jew." *Visual Culture and the Holocaust.* Ed. Barbie Zelizer. New Brunswick, N.J.: Rutgers University Press, 2001.

_____. "Images of Black History: The Charles H. Wright Museum of African-American History." *Dissent* 48:3 (summer 2001): 98–102.

_____. "Cultural Battlegrounds: Weimar Photographic Narratives of War." *New German Critique* 76 (winter 1999): 49–84.

_____. "'Heroes' and 'Whores': The Politics of Gender in Weimar Antiwar Imagery." *The Art Bulletin* 79:3 (September 1997): 366–384.

Apter, Emily, and William Pietz, eds. *Fetishism as Cultural Discourse.* Ithaca, N.Y.: Cornell University Press, 1993.

Arad, Gulie Ne'eman, ed. *Passing into History: Nazism and the Holocaust beyond Memory. In Honor of Saul Friedländer on His Sixty-Fifth Birthday.* Special Issue of *History & Memory: Studies in Representation of the Past* 9:2 (Fall 1997).

Avisar, Ilan. *Screening the Holocaust: Cinema's Images of the Unimaginable.* Bloomington: Indiana University Press, 1988.

Azoulay, Katya Gibel. *Black, Jewish, and Interracial: It's Not the Color of Your Skin, but the Race of Your Kin, and Other Myths of Identity.* Durham, N.C.: Duke University Press, 1997.

Baigell, Matthew. *Jewish American Artists and the Holocaust.* New Brunswick, N.J.: Rutgers University Press, 1997.

_____. "Segal's Holocaust Memorial." *Art in America* 71 (summer 1983): 134–136

Baker, Kenneth. "Shimon Attie." *Artnews* (November 1994): 165.

Baldwin, Peter, ed. *Reworking the Past: Hitler, The Holocaust, and the Historians' Debate.* Boston: Beacon Press, 1990.

Banner-Haley, Charles Pete. "The Necessity of Remembrance: A Review of the Museum of African American History." *American Quarterly* 51:2 (June 1999): 420–425.

Bartov, Omer. *Murder in Our Midst: The Holocaust, Industrial Killing, and Representation.* New York: Oxford University Press, 1996.

Batchen, Geoffrey. "The Art of Archiving." *Deep Storage: Collecting, Storage, and Archiving in Art.* Exh. Cat. New York: Prestel, 1998.

Bauer, Yehuda. *Rethinking the Holocaust.* New Haven, Conn.: Yale University Press, 2001.

Benjamin, Walter. "Thesis on the Philosophy of History." *Illuminations.* Trans. Harry Zohn. Ed. Hannah Arendt. New York: Schocken Books, 1985.

Berenbaum, Michael. *The World Must Know: The History of the Holocaust as Told in the United States Holocaust Memorial Museum.* Boston, New York, Toronto, London: Little, Brown and Company, 1993.

Berman, Russell. *The Rise of the Modern German Novel: Crisis and Charisma.* Cambridge, Mass.: Harvard University Press. 1986.

Bernstein, Michael Andrée. "The *Schindler's List* Effect." *The American Scholar* 63 (summer 1994):429–432.

Blanchot, Maurice. *The Writing of the Disaster.* 1980. Trans. Ann Smock. Lincoln: University of Nebraska Press, 1995.

Bohm-Duchen, Monica, ed. *After Auschwitz: Responses to the Holocaust in Contemporary Art.* Exh. Cat. Sunderland, England: Northern Centre for Contemporary Art, 1995.

Borowski, Tadeusz. *This Way for the Gas, Ladies and Gentlemen.* Trans. by Barbara Vedder. 1959. New York: Penguin Books, 1967.

Boyarin, Jonathan. *Storm from Paradise: The Politics of Jewish Memory.* Minneapolis: University of Minnesota Press, 1992.

_____. *Thinking in Jewish.* Chicago: The University of Chicago Press, 1996.

Boyarin, Jonathan, and Daniel Boyarin, eds. *Jews and Other Differences: The New Jewish Cultural Studies.* Minneapolis: University of Minnesota Press, 1997.

Brenner, David. *Marketing Identities: The Invention of Jewish Ethnicity.* Detroit, Mich.: Wayne State University Press, 1998.

Brodkin, Karen. *How Jews Became White Folks and What That Says About Race in America.* 1997. New Brunswick, N.J.: Rutgers University Press, 2000.

Caruth, Cathy, ed. *Trauma: Explorations in Memory.* Baltimore, Md.: The Johns Hopkins University Press, 1995.

Celan, Paul. *Breathturn.* Trans. Pierre Joris. Los Angeles: Sun & Moon Press, 1995.

_____. *Paul Celan: Collected Prose.* Trans. Rosmarie Waldrop. New York: Sheep Meadow Press, 1986.

Christian Boltanski: Lessons of Darkness. Exh. Cat. Chicago: Museum of Contemporary Art, 1986.

Conkelton, Sheryl. Review of *New Photography* at Moma. *Moma Magazine* (fall/winter 1994): 30.

Crow, Thomas. *Modern Art in the Common Culture.* New Haven, Conn.: Yale University Press, 1996.

Czaplicka, John. "Commemorative Practice in Berlin." *New German Critique* 65 (spring/summer 1995): 155–187.

Deák, István. "Heroes and Victims." *New York Review of Books.* 31 May 2001. Available [Online]: http://www.nybooks.com/nyrev/WWWfeatdisplay.cgi?20010531051R.

Delbo, Charlotte. *Auschwitz and After.* Trans. by Rosette C. Lamont. New Haven, Conn.: Yale University Press, 1995.

DeMello, Margot. "The Carnivalesque Body: Women and Tattoos." *Pierced Hearts and True Love: A Century of Drawings for Tattoos.* Exh. Cat. New York: The Drawing Center and Hardy Marks Publications, Honolulu, 1995.

Denson, Roger. "Susan Silas' Pragmatic Gaze." *Susan Silas.* Exh. Cat. New York: fiction/nonfiction, 1990.

Derrida, Jacques. *Archive Fever: A Freudian Impression.* Trans. Eric Prenowitz. Chicago: University of Chicago Press, 1995.

Dinnerstein, Leonard. *Antisemitism in America.* New York: Oxford University Press, 1994.

Doneson, Judith E. *The Holocaust in American Film.* Philadelphia: The Jewish Publication Society, 1987.

Dwork, Debórah and Robert Jan van Pelt. *Auschwitz: 1270 to the Present.* New York: W. W. Norton & Co. Inc., 1996.

Epstein, Helen. *Children of the Holocaust.* New York: G. P. Putnam's Sons, 1979.

Evans, Richard J. *In Hitler's Shadow: West German Historians and the Attempt to Escape from the Nazi Past.* New York: Pantheon Books, 1989.

Feig, Konnilyn. *Hitler's Death Camps: The Sanity of Madness.* New York: Holmes & Meier, 1981.

Feinstein, Stephen C. *Witness and Legacy: Contemporary Art About the Holocaust.* Minneapolis: Minnesota Museum of American Art, 1995.

Feliciano, Hector. *The Lost Museum: The Nazi Conspiracy to Steal the World's Greatest Works of Art.* New York: HarperCollins Publishers, Inc., 1995.

Fénelon, Fania, with Marcelle Routier. *Playing for Time.* Trans. Judith Landry. New York: Atheneum Publishers, 1977.

Fer, Briony, David Batchelor, Paul Wood, eds. *Realism, Rationalism, Surrealism: Art between the Wars.* New Haven, Conn.: Yale University Press in association with The Open University, 1993.

Finkelstein, Norman G., and Ruth Bettina Birn. *A Nation on Trial: The Goldhagen Thesis and Historical Truth.* New York: Henry Holt and Co., Inc., 1998.

Finkielkraut, Alain. *The Imaginary Jew.* Trans. Kevin O'Neill and David Suchoff. 1980. Lincoln: University of Nebraska Press, 1994.

Flanzbaum, Hilene, ed. *The Americanization of the Holocaust.* Baltimore, Md.: Johns Hopkins University Press, 1999.

Frenkel, Vera, with Dot Tuer and Clive Robertson. "The Story is Always Partial: A Conversation with Vera Frenkel." *Art Journal* 57:4 (winter 1998): 2–15.

Friedländer, Saul, ed. *Probing the Limits of Representation.* New Haven, Conn.: Yale University Press, 1992.

_____. "The Shoah between Memory and History." *The Jewish Quarterly* 53 (winter 1990).

_____. *Reflections on Nazism: An Essay on Kitsch and Death.* Trans. Thomas Weyr. 1984. Bloomington: Indiana University Press, 1993.

_____. *Nazi Germany and the Jews.* Vol. 1. *The Years of Persecution, 1933–1939.* New York: HarperPerennial, 1998.

_____. *When Memory Comes.* Trans. Helen R. Lane. New York: The Noonday Press, 1991.

Georg, Willi. *In the Warsaw Ghetto Summer, 1941: Photographs by Willy Georg with Excerpts from the Warsaw Ghetto Diaries.* New York: Aperture Foundation Inc., 1993.

Geras, Norman. *The Contract of Mutual Indifference: Political Philosophy after the Holocaust.* New York: Verso, 1998.

Gilbert, Martin. *Atlas of the Holocaust.* New York: William Morrow and Co., Inc., 1988.

_____. *Holocaust Journey: Travelling in Search of the Past.* New York: Columbia University Press, 1997.

Gilman, Sander L. *The Jew's Body.* New York: Routledge, 1991.

_____. *Difference and Pathology: Stereotypes of Sexuality, Race, and Madness.* Ithaca, N.Y.: Cornell University Press, 1985.

_____. *Smart Jews: The Construction of the Image of Jewish Superior Intelligence.* Lincoln: University of Nebraska Press, 1997.

Goldhagen, Daniel Jonah. *Hitler's Willing Executioners: Ordinary Germans and the Holocaust.* New York: Alfred A. Knopf, 1996.

Gourevitch, Philip. "What They Saw at the Holocaust Museum." *New York Times Magazine* (12 February 1995): 44–45.

Graver, Lawrence. *An Obsession with Anne Frank: Meyer Levin and the "Diary."* Berkeley: University of California Press, 1997.

Green, Jonathan. "James Friedman: Rephotographing the History of the World." *James Friedman: Color Photographs 1979–1982.* Exh. Cat. Columbus: The Ohio State University Gallery of Fine Art, 1983.

Greenspan, Henry. *On Listening to Holocaust Survivors: Recounting and Life History.* Westport, Conn.: Praeger, 1998.

Gumpert, Lynn. *Christian Boltanski.* Paris: Flammarion, 1994.

Gutman, Israel, ed. *Encyclopedia of the Holocaust.* New York: Macmillan, 1995.

Habermas, Jürgen. *The New Conservatism; Cultural Criticism and the Historians Debate,* ed. and trans. Shierry Weber Nicholsen. New York: Cambridge University Press, 1989.

Hackett, David A., trans. and ed. *The Buchenwald Report.* Boulder, Colo.: Westview Press, 1995.

Hagen, Charles. "James Friedman." *Artforum* (May 1985): 103–104.

Hall, Stuart. "Cultural Identity and Diaspora." *Identity: Community, Culture, Difference.* Ed. Jonathan Rutherford. New York: New York University Press, 1990.

Hancock, Ian. "Roma: Genocide of, in the Holocaust." *Encyclopedia of Genocide,* Israel W. Charny, ed. 1997. Available [Online]:http://www.geocities.com/Paris/5121/genocide.htm.

Hansen, Miriam Bratu. "*Schindler's List* is Not *Shoah:* The Second Commandment, Popular Modernism, and Public Memory." *Critical Inquiry* 22:2 (1996): 292–312.

Hartmann, Erich. *In the Camps.* Exh. Cat. New York: W.W. Norton & Company, 1995.

Hartman, Geoffrey H., ed. *Bitburg in Moral and Political Perspective.* Bloomington: Indiana University Press, 1986.

_____., ed. *Holocaust Remembrance: The Shapes of Memory.* Cambridge, Mass.: Blackwell Publishers, 1994.

_____. *The Longest Shadow: In the Aftermath of the Holocaust.* Bloomington: Indiana University Press, 1996.

Hass, Aaron. *In the Shadow of the Holocaust: The Second Generation.* 1990. New York: Cambridge University Press, 1996.

Hayes, Peter, ed. *Lessons and Legacies: The Meaning of the Holocaust in a Changing World.* Evanston, Ill.: Northwestern University Press, 1991.

Hidden History of the Kovno Ghetto. Boston, New York, Toronto, London: United States Holocaust Memorial Museum, 1997.

Hirsch, Marianne. *Family Frames: Photography, Narrative, and Postmemory.* Cambridge, Mass.: Harvard University Press, 1997.

Hopkinson, Amanda. "Through the Past Darkly." *British Journal of Photography* 6976 (1 June 1994): 26.

Hornstein, Shelley. "Fugitive Places." *Art Journal* 59:1 (spring 2000): 45–53.

Huyssen, Andreas. *After the Great Divide: Modernism, Mass Culture, Postmodernism.* Bloomington: Indiana University Press, 1986.

_____. "Of Mice and Mimesis: Reading Spiegelman with Adorno." *New German Critique* 81 (fall 2000): 65–82.

_____. "Anselm Kiefer: The Terror of History, the Temptation of Myth." *October* 48 (spring 1989): 85–101.

Insdorf, Annette. *Indelible Shadows: Film and the Holocaust.* 1983. Cambridge, Mass.: Harvard University Press, 1989.

Jabès, Edmond. *The Book of Questions.* Vol. 1. Trans. Rosmarie Waldrop. Hanover, N.H.: Wesleyan University Press, 1972.

"Jewish Gombin (Gabin, Poland, Jewish Genealogy): Chelmo2." Available [Online]: http://weber.ucsd.edu/~lzamosc/gmoreinf.html; & gt: Chelmo and Operation Reinhard.

John Scott: Engines of Anxiety. Exh. Cat. Montreal: Gallery of the Saidye Bronfmann Centre for the Arts, 1997.

Kaes, Anton. *From Hitler to Heimat: The Return of History as Film.* Cambridge, Mass.: Harvard University Press, 1989.

Ka-Tzetnik 135633. *Shivitti: A Vision.* San Francisco: Harper & Row, 1989.

Keller, Ulrich, ed. *The Warsaw Ghetto in Photographs: 206 Views Made in 1941.* Mineola, N.Y.: Dover Publications, 1984.

Kleeblatt, Norman L., ed. *Too Jewish? Challenging Traditional Identities.* Exh. Cat. New York/New Brunswick, N.J.: The Jewish Museum and Rutgers University Press, 1996

_____. "Persistence of Memory." *Art in America* 88:6 (June 2000): 96–103.

_____. , ed. *Mirroring Evil: Nazi Images/Recent Art.* Exh. Cat. New York/New Brunswick: The Jewish Museum and Rutgers University Press, 2002.

Kramer, Jane. "The Politics of Memory." *New Yorker* (14 August 1995): 48–65.

Krammer, Arnold. Review of David A. Hackett, ed., *The Buchenwald Report* (Boulder, Colorado: Colorado University Press, 1995). *German Studies Review* 3 (October 1996): 593–594

Kushner, Tony. *The Holocaust and the Liberal Imagination.* Cambridge: Basil Blackwell Inc., 1994.

LaCapra, Dominick. *Representing the Holocaust: History, Theory, Trauma.* Ithaca, N.Y.: Cornell University Press, 1994.

_____. *History and Memory after Auschwitz.* Ithaca, N.Y.: Cornell University Press, 1998.

Ladd, Brian. *The Ghosts of Berlin: Confronting German History in the Urban Landscape.* Chicago: The University of Chicago Press, 1997.

Langer, Lawrence L. *Holocaust Testimonies: The Ruins of Memory.* New Haven, Conn.: Yale University Press, 1991.

_____. *Admitting the Holocaust.* New York: Oxford University Press, 1995.

_____. *Preempting the Holocaust.* New Haven, Conn.: Yale University Press, 1998.

Lanzmann, Claude. *Shoah: An Oral History of the Holocaust.* New York: Pantheon Books, 1985.

Large, David Clay. "'Out with the Ostjuden': The Scheunenviertel Riot in Berlin, November 1923," manuscript of paper delivered at the German Studies Association Twenty-First Annual Conference, Washington, D.C., 26 September 1997.

Lefkovitz, Lori Hope. "Inherited Holocaust Memory and the Ethics of Ventriloquism," *The Kenyon Review* 19:1 (winter 1997): 34–43.

Legge, Elizabeth. "Analogs of Loss: Vera Frenkel's *Body Missing(http://www.yorku.ca/BodyMissing).*" *Visual Culture and the Holocaust.* Ed. Barbie Zelizer. New Brunswick, N.J.: Rutgers University Press, 2001.

Leo, Vincent. "After the Fact." *Afterimage* 12:10 (May 1985): 17–18.

Levi, Primo. *Survival at Auschwitz: The Nazi Assault on Humanity.* Trans. Stuart Woolf. New York: Collier Books, 1995.

_____. *The Drowned and the Saved.* Trans. Raymond Rosenthal. New York: Vintage International Books, 1989.

Levin, Meyer. *The Obsession.* New York: Simon and Schuster, 1974.
Levin, Mikael. *War Story.* Text by Meyer Levin. Munich: Gina Keyahoff Verlag, 1997.
_____. *The Burden of Identity: Portraits von Juden in Berlin 1998.* Exh. Cat. Munich: Gina Kehayoff Verlag, 1998.
_____. *Common Places: Cultural Identity in the Urban Environment.* Institut Français de Thessalonique; Änglen, Katrineholms Konsthall; Centre Régional de la Photographie; Gererie am Fishmarkt—Kunsthalle Erfurt, 1998. With an essay by Christopher Phillips, "The Untidy Intimacy of Places."
Linden, R. Ruth. *Making Stories, Making Selves: Feminist Reflection on the Holocaust.* Columbus: Ohio University Press, 1993.
Linenthal, Edward T. *Preserving Memory: The Struggle to Create America's Holocaust Museum.* New York: Viking, 1995.
Lipstadt, Deborah. *Denying the Holocaust: The Growing Assault on Truth and Memory.* New York: Penguin Books, 1993.
Liss, Andrea. *Trespassing Through Shadows: Memory, Photography and the Holocaust.* Minneapolis: University of Minnesota Press, 1998.
Loshitzky, Yosefa, ed. *Spielberg's Holocaust: Critical Perspectives on Schindler's List.* Bloomington: University of Indiana Press, 1997.
Maclear, Kyo. *Beclouded Visions: Hiroshima-Nagasaki and the Art of Witness.* Albany: State University of New York Press, 1999.
Maier, Charles S. *The Unmasterable Past: History, Holocaust, and German National Identity* Cambridge, Mass.: Harvard University Press, 1988.
Marrus, Michael. "The Use and Abuse of the Holocaust." *Lessons and Legacies: The Meaning of the Holocaust in a Changing World.* Ed. Peter Hayes. Evanston, Ill.: Northwestern University Press, 1991.
Mayer, Arno. *Why Did the Heavens Not Darken? The "Final Solution" in History.* New York: Pantheon Books, 1988.
McWilliams, Martha. "Order Out of Chaos: 'Burnt Whole: Contemporary Artists Reflect on the Holocaust'." *New Art Examiner* 22:8 (April 1995): 12–17.
Melnick, Ralph. *The Stolen Legacy of Anne Frank: Meyer Levin, Lillian Hellman, and the Staging of the Diary.* New Haven, Conn.: Yale University Press, 1997.
Mifflin, Margot. *Bodies of Subversion: A Secret History of Women and Tattoo.* New York: Juno Books, 1997.
Mikael Levin. The Burden of Identity: Portraits von Juden in Berlin 1998. Exh. Cat. Munich: Gina Keyahoff, 1998.
Miller, Judith. *One, by One, by One: Facing the Holocaust.* New York: Touchstone, 1990.
Miller, Mindy Yan. "Deluge/of Thirst/Lapped Her Tears." *The Embodied Viewer.* Exh. Cat. Calgary: Glenbow Museum, 1991.
Milton, Sybil, and Janet Blatter. *Art of the Holocaust.* New York: Routledge, 1981.
Milton, Sybil, ed. and trans. *The Stroop Report: The Jewish Quarter of Warsaw Is No More!* New York: Pantheon Books, 1979.
Morgan, Michael L. "To Seize Memory: History and Identity in Post-Holocaust Jewish Thought." *Thinking about the Holocaust: After Half a Century,* Alvin Rosenfeld, ed. Bloomington/Indianapolis: Indiana University Press, 1997.
Nagorski, Andrew. "A Strange Affair." *Newsweek* (15 June 1998): 36–37.
Nicholas, Lynn H. *The Rape of Europa: The Fate of Europe's Treasures in the Third Reich and the Second World War.* New York: Vintage Books, 1994.
Nochlin, Linda, and Tamar Garb, eds. *The Jew in the Text: Modernity and the Construction of Identity.* London: Thames and Hudson, 1995.

Novick, Peter. *The Holocaust in American Life*. Boston/New York: Houghton Mifflin Co, 1999.

Ofer, Dalia, and Lenore J. Weitzman, eds. *Women in the Holocaust*. New Haven, Conn.: Yale University Press, 1998.

Ozick, Cynthia. "Who Owns Anne Frank?" *Quarrel & Quandary: Essays by Cynthia Ozick*. New York: Alfred A. Knopf, 2000.

Parfrey, Adam. *Apocalypse Culture*. Introduction by J.G. Ballard. Portland: Feral House, 1990.

Phillips, Christopher. "Mikael Levin at the International Center of Photography." *Art in America* 85 (May 1997): 132.

Rabinbach, Anson. "German Historians Debate the Nazi Past: A Dress Rehearsal for a New German Nationalism?" *Dissent* (spring 1988): 192–200.

_____. "From Explosion to Erosion: Holocaust Memorialization in America since Bitburg." *Passing into History: Nazism and the Holocaust beyond Memory. In Honor of Saul Friedländer on His Sixty-Fifth Birthday. History and Memory: Studies in Representation of the Past*. Gulie Ne'eman Arad, ed., 9:1–2 (fall 1997).

Rapaport, Lynn. *Jews in Germany after the Holocaust: Memory, Identity, and Jewish-German Relations*. New York: Cambridge University Press, 1997.

Reznikoff, Charles. *Holocaust*. Santa Barbara, Cal.: Black Sparrow Press, 1975.

Rittner, Carol Ann, and John K. Roth, eds. *Different Voices: Women and the Holocaust*. Saint Paul: Paragon House Publishers, 1993.

_____. *Memory Offended: The Auschwitz Convent Controversy*. New York: Praeger, 1991.

Roeder, George H. Jr. *The Censored War: American Visual Experience during World War Two*. New Haven, Conn.: Yale University Press, 1993.

Rosenfeld, Alvin H., ed. *Thinking about the Holocaust: After Half a Century*. Bloomington/ Indianapolis: Indiana University Press, 1997.

_____. "Popularization and Memory: The Case of Anne Frank." *Lessons and Legacies: The Meaning of the Holocaust in a Changing World*. Ed. Peter Hayes. Evanston, Ill.: Northwestern University Press, 1991.

Rothberg, Michael. *Traumatic Realism: The Demands of Holocaust Representation*. Minneapolis: University of Minnesota Press, 2000.

Rubin, Barry. *Assimilation and Its Discontents*. New York: Times Books, 1995.

Ruffins, Fath Davis. "Culture Wars Won and Lost, Part II: The National African-American Museum Project," *Radical History Review* 70 (1998): 78–101.

Salzman, Jack, with Adina Back and Gretchen Sullivan Sorin, eds. *Bridges and Boundaries: African American and American Jews*. New York: George Braziller, Inc. in association with The Jewish Museum, 1992.

Saltzman, Lisa. *Anselm Kiefer and Art After Auschwitz*. New York: Cambridge University Press, 1999.

Schaffner, Ingrid, and Matthias Winzen, eds. *Deep Storage: Collecting, Storing, and Archiving in Art*. Exh. Cat. New York/Munich: P.S.1 Contemporary Art Center and Prestel-Verlag, 1998.

Schama, Simon. *Landscape and Memory*. New York: Vintage Books, 1996.

Scherr, Rebecca. "The Uses of Memory and the Abuses of Fiction: Sexuality in Holocaust Fiction and Memoir." *Other Voices: The (e) Journal of Cultural Criticism* 2:1 (February 2000). Available [Online] at: http://dept.english.upenn.edu/~ov.

Schoenfeld, Gabriel. "Auschwitz and the Professors." *Commentary* 105:6 (June 1998). Available [Online]: http://www.commentarymagazine.com.

"Gabriel Shoenfeld and Critics." *Commentary* 106:2 (August 1998). Available [Online]: http://www.commentarymagazine.com.

Sekula, Allan. "Photography Between Labor and Capital." *Mining Photographs and Other Pictures 1938-1968: A Selection from the Negative Archives of Shedden Studio, Glace Bay, Cape Breton—Photographs by Leslie Shedden.* Ed. Benjamin Buchloh and Robert Wilkie. Nova Scotia: Nova Scotia College of Art and Design, 1983.

Shandler, Jeffrey. *While America Watches: Televising the Holocaust.* New York: Oxford University Press, 1999.

Shandler, Robert R., ed. *Unwilling Germans? The Goldhagen Debate.* Trans. Jeremiah Riemer. Minneapolis: University of Minneapolis Press, 1998.

Shmeruk, Chone. "Hebrew-Yiddish-Polish: A Trilingual Jewish Culture," *The Jews of Poland Between Two World Wars,* Yisrael Gutman, Ezra Mendelsohn, Jehuda Reinharz, and Chone Shmeruk, eds. Hanover, N.H.: University Press of New England, 1989.

Simon, Roger I., Sharon Rosenberg, and Claudia Eppert, eds. *Between Hope and Despair: Pedagogy and the Remembrance of Historical Trauma.* New York: Rowman & Littlefield Publishers, Inc., 2000

Simpson, Elizabeth, ed. *The Spoils of War. World War II and Its Aftermath: The Loss, Reappearance, and Recovery of Cultural Property.* New York: Harry N. Abrams, 1997.

Sites Unseen: Shimon Attie European Projects. Exh. Cat. Intro. by James Young. Burlington, Ver.: Verve Editions, 1998.

Sontag, Susan. "Fascinating Fascism." *A Susan Sontag Reader.* New York: Vintage Books, 1983.

Spiegelman, Art. *Maus: A Survivor's Tale,* vol. I. 1973; *Maus: And Here My Troubles Began,* vol. II. New York: Pantheon Books, 1986.

Steinlauf, Michael C. *Bondage to the Dead: Poland and the Memory of the Holocaust.* Syracuse, N.Y.: Syracuse University Press, 1997.

Stratton, Jon. *Coming Out Jewish: Constructing Ambivalent Identities.* New York: Routledge, 2000.

Szner, Zvi, and Alexander Sened, eds. *With a Camera in the Ghetto: Mendel Grossman.* D.N. Western Galilee, Israel: Ghetto Fighters' House, 1970.

Tagg, John. *The Burden of Representation: Essays on Photographies and Histories.* Amherst: University of Massachusetts Press, 1988.

"Testimonies of the last prisoners in the death camp Chelmno." Introduction by Shmuel Krakowski and Ilia Altman. Available [Online]: http://www.geocities.com/Paris/Rue/4017/index3.htm.

The Writing on the Wall: Projections in Berlin's Jewish Quarter; Shimon Attie Photographs and Installations. Exh. Cat. Essays by Michael André Bernstein, Erwin Leiser, and Shimon Attie. Heidelberg: Edition Braus, 1994.

Thornton, Russell. *American Indian Holocaust and Survival: A Population History Since 1492.* Norman: University of Oklahoma Press, 1990.

Torgovnick, Marianna. "Skin and Bolts." *Artforum International* (December 1992): 64–65.

Traverso, Enzo. *The Jews and Germany: From the "Judeo-German Symbiosis" to the Memory of Auschwitz.* Trans. Daniel Weissbort. Lincoln: University of Nebraska Press, 1995.

Tysh, Chris. *Continuity Girl.* New York: United Artists Books, 2000.

Vera Frenkel: Body Missing. Exh. Cat. Bremen: Gesellschaft für Aktuelle Kunst, 1996.

Vera Frenkel: The Bar Report. Exh. Cat. Toronto: Art Gallery of York University, 1993.

Vera Frenkel . . . from the Transit Bar; Body Missing; www.yorku.ca/BodyMissing. Exh. Cat. Stockholm: Riksutställningar, 1997.

Vera Frenkel: . . . from the Transit Bar. Exh. Cat. Toronto: The Power Plant, the National Gallery of Canada, 1994.

Vera Frenkel: Raincoats, Suitcases, Palms. Exh. Cat. North York: Art Gallery of York University, 1993.

Vera Frenkel: The Videotapes. Exh. Cat. Toronto: National Gallery of Canada, 1985.

Vidal-Naquet, Pierre. *Assassins of Memory: Essays on the Denial of the Holocaust.* Trans. Jeffrey Mehlman. New York: Columbia University Press, 1992.

_____. *The Jews: History, Memory, and the Present.* Trans. and ed. David Ames Curtis. New York: Columbia University Press, 1996.

Vishniac, Roman. *Polish Jews: A Pictorial Record.* 1947. New York: Schocken Books, 1987.

Weiss, John. *Ideology of Death: Why the Holocaust Happened in Germany*. Chicago: Elephant Paperbacks, 1996.

Whiting, Cécile. *Antifascism in American Art.* New Haven, Conn.: Yale University Press, 1989.

Wodiczko, Krzysztof. *Critical Vehicles: Writings, Projects, Interviews.* Cambridge, Mass.: The MIT Press, 1999.

Wojcik, Daniel. *Punk and Neo-Tribal Body Art.* Jackson: University of Mississippi Press, 1995.

Written in Memory: Portraits of the Holocaust. Photographs by Jeffrey A. Wolin. Exh. Cat. San Francisco: Chronicle Books, 1997.

Yates, Christopher A. "James Friedman." *Dialogue* (March/April 1998): 14.

Young, James E., ed. *Holocaust Memorials in History: The Art of Memory.* Munich/New York: Prestel-Verlag and The Jewish Museum, 1997.

_____. *At Memory's Edge: After-Images of the Holocaust in Contemporary Art and Architecture.* New Haven, Conn.: Yale University Press, 2000.

_____. "The Holocaust as Vicarious Past: Art Spiegelmans's *Maus* and the Afterimages of History." *Critical Inquiry* 24 (spring 1998): 666–699.

_____. "Germany's Memorial Question: Memory, Counter-Memory, and the End of the Monument." *The South Atlantic Quarterly* 96:4 (fall 1997): 853–880.

_____. *Mein Kampf: Photographs by David Levinthal.* Exh. Cat. Sante Fe: Twin Peaks, 1996.

_____. *The Texture of Memory: Holocaust Memorials and Meaning.* New Haven, Conn.: Yale University Press, 1993.

_____. "The Counter-Monument: Memory against Itself in Germany Today." *Critical Inquiry* 18 (1992): 267–296.

_____. *Writing and Rewriting the Holocaust: Narrative and the Consequences of Interpretation.* Bloomington: University of Indiana Press, 1988.

Young, Robert J. C. *Colonial Desire: Hybridity in Theory, Culture and Race.* New York: Routledge, 1995.

Zelizer, Barbie. *Remembering to Forget: Holocaust Memory through the Camera's Eye.* Chicago: University of Chicago Press, 1998.

_____, ed. *Visual Culture and the Holocaust.* New Brunswick, N.J.: Rutgers University Press, 2001.

Zipes, Jack, trans. *The Operated Jew: Two Tales of Anti-Semitism.* New York: Routledge, 1991.

INDEX

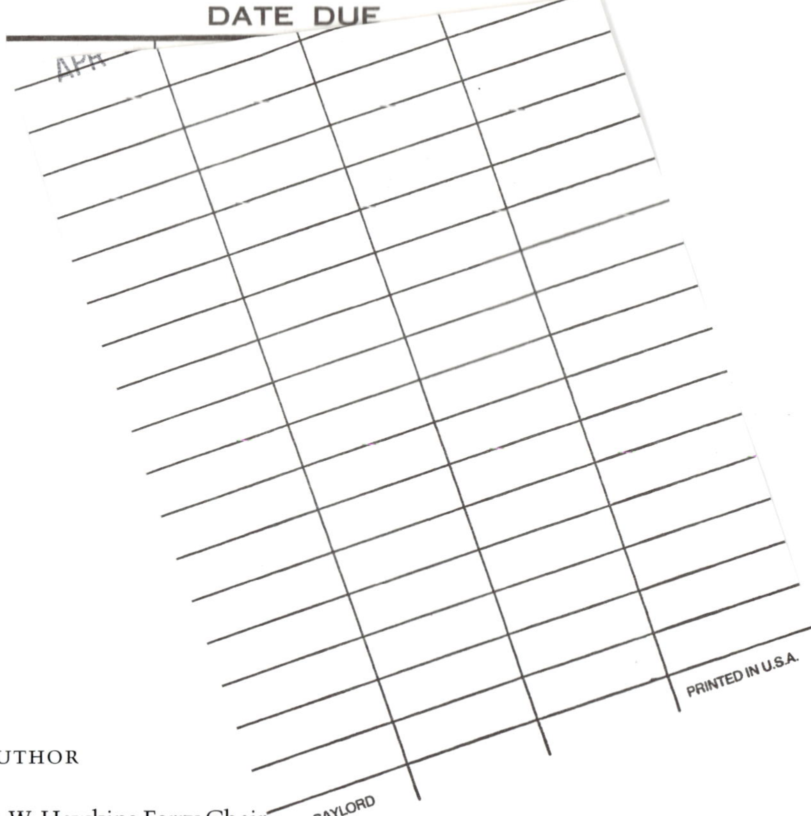

ABOUT THE AUTHOR

Dora Apel is the W. Hawkins Ferry Chair Modern and Contemporary Art History i the Art and Art History Department at Wayne State University. She has written on topics such as the politics of gender and imagery of war during the Weimar Republic for *The Art Bulletin* and *New German Critique*, Diego Rivera and the left for *Left History*, as well as articles and reviews for *New Art Examiner* and *Dissent*. She has also served as editor for Cranbrook Art Museum exhibition catalogs, including *Three Decades of Contemporary Art: The Dr. John and Rose M. Shuey Collection*, *Iñigo Manglano-Ovalle*, and *Weird Science*.